In the Way of Women

Also by Cynthia Cockburn

Two-Track Training: Sex Inequalities and the Youth Training Scheme

Machinery of Dominance: Women, Men and Technical Know-how

Brothers: Male Dominance and Technological Change

The Local State: Management of Cities and People

In the Way of Women

Men's Resistance to Sex Equality

in Organizations

Cynthia Cockburn

MACMILLAN

First published 1991

Published by
MACMILLAN EDUCATION LTD
Houndmills, Basingstoke, Hampshire RG21 2XS
and London
Companies and representatives
throughout the world

Edited and typeset by Povey/Edmondson
Okehampton and Rochdale, England

Printed in Hong Kong

ISBN 0–333–54912–0 (hardcover)
ISBN 0–333–54913–9 (paperback)

A catalogue entry for this book is
available from the British Library

Contents

Introduction

It is often said that we are living today in a 'post-feminist' age. People who say this usually mean one of two things: that the new wave women's movement of the 1970s and 1980s has achieved its goals, or that it has fizzled out, leaving little changed. In reality, neither of these things has happened. Women's activism continues and the touting of 'post-feminism' says less about the women's liberation movement than about a counter-movement in which men have attempted to reassert control of women. Thus it is often men who say 'Women are liberated now', or 'You see: women were never meant to be equal.'

It is not by chance that 'women's liberation' has shrunk to 'women's lib', a term implying an embarrassing foolishness. Nor was it inevitable that 'feminism' would become a word with connotations of extremism, alienating to many women. The meanings of these words have been actively produced over recent years in a counter-discourse in the media and everyday life, mainly by men who, quite rightly, saw their interests threatened by feminist ideas. We shall see evidence in this book that feminism has been anathematized by men, in an attempt to put a stop to its appeal to women. The process has been effective. Many women who in their ideas and practices are demonstrably feminist feel obliged to hedge their views with, 'I'm not a feminist but . . .'

Taking words and twisting their meanings is only one of the ways men have fought back against the women's liberation movement. Tougher tactics have been deployed as well. Many quite ordinary men simply do not vote for feminists, or do not appoint them to jobs for which they are qualified. Other men, perhaps with fewer material or emotional resources at their command, use violence.

1

Insubordinate wives are battered. Who knows how often a woman has suffered abuse at a man's hands because she was 'getting ideas'. On 10 December 1989 in the Polytechnic of Montreal fourteen women engineering students were shot dead by a man who said he 'hated feminists'. Systematic analysis of men's responses to feminism is long overdue.

This book attempts a very small part of that wider project. One kind of response by men to feminism has occurred within organizations. In the 1980s many feminists increasingly moved into institutions (political parties, trade unions, associations, employing organizations) taking their struggle with them. This has not been unique to Britain. In many countries we have seen feminists entering the state, either by standing for election or by becoming bureaucrats (in Australia they even have a name for them: femocrats). Women have sought involvement in equality commissions, *institutos de la mujer*, *bureaux des femmes*. Some feminists have deplored this as signalling an institutionalization of the movement. Others, however, point out that by such 'entrism' women have for the first time approached the places of power and begun to challenge powerful men and the way they operate.

One of the forms taken by women's struggle inside organizations is engagement in strategies for 'equality of opportunity', or 'equal opps' as it is tagged. Feminists have tried to give 'equal opps' real teeth by pressing for positive action measures in organizations to counteract women's disadvantage. The research on which this book is based was a study carried out in four large organizations noted for their formal commitment to positive action for sex equality. I wanted to know how individual men and man-led organizations might be interpreting, implementing, fostering or impeding, the equal opportunities strategies backed by women.

The project was quickly (and necessarily) rendered more complex by the fact that equal opportunities in most large organisations is not action on sex only, but also on race. Besides, it often incorporates policies of non-discrimination against homosexuals and people with disabilities. The various kinds of disadvantage signalled by such equality projects are compounded by a form of inequality that many would say was more fundamental than the rest: that of class. Class is often defined precisely by the positioning of individuals in organizations. In Marxist thought the ruling class is comprised of those who own the enterprise or manage the production of goods or services, while the working class is comprised of those below them whose labour power the organization is designed to exploit. Throughout this book we shall be aware of the interaction of class with other identities. On to the hierarchies of class are mapped gender, race and other rankings, so that disadvantage is compounded. A worker in a low-paid job at the base of an organization is more likely to be a woman, more likely to be black. A working class black woman experiences a triple oppression.

The research treatment of equality in this book, however, is not in this respect even-handed. It is mainly about *women*'s inequality and oppression. The analysis and the theories I draw on are mainly feminist. But always women are considered not as a unitary category but having identities formed in gender processes that vary according to whether they are black or white, whether they are lesbian or heterosexual and whether or not they experience disabilities.

Research approach

Four organizational case studies were involved in the research, each taking four months to complete. One was a large private-sector firm operating in the retail trade, with a chain of warehouses and shops. I call it 'High Street Retail'. This case study exemplified equal opportunity policy in a business environment, where public image, while important, must take second place to labour market strategies that have profit as a main aim. It happened that trade union organization was weak in this firm. Two other case studies showed unionism in more active mode. One was of a government department that I call 'the Service'. It afforded insights into a conventional state bureaucracy, with a formal structure and a white collar culture which, though changing, was still heavily influenced by the past. The third case study was of an local elected body I call simply 'the Council' or the 'Local Authority'. This gave me a base line for thorough-going efforts on the equality front, since it was led in the middle-eighties by a left Labour majority and became one of those inner-city authorities that won a reputation, and notoriety, for innovatory strategies against various forms of discrimination. Here, as in the Service, women and black people were particularly active in and through their trade unions. The fourth case study was of a national Trade Union with many low-paid women members. This and the Local Authority of course differed from the first two organizations in involving representation. The Union was a membership organization structured by elected branch, regional and national committees and councils. It was, however, also in its own way an employer. These four rather different organizations were selected not for purposes of formal comparison but to provide a panel of varying experiences to which similar questions might be addressed.

This was qualitative research. That is to say its legitimacy does not spring from numbers, either of organizations studied or of people interviewed. Rather it gains what authority it has from the depth of insight made available. Qualitative research is able to approach questions that are not answerable by quantitative research. It is better for seeing relationships, processes and contradictions. The methods, merits and difficulties of qualitative research have by now been widely discussed (see for instance, Taylor and Bogdan 1984, Silverman 1985, Marshall and Rossman 1989, Hammersley 1989). The three techniques employed here were observation, documentary investigation and, most importantly, in-depth interviewing supplemented by informal conversation and small-group discussion. As in most research, this study begins from existing theories that might explain the relationships, processes and contradictions observed and ends by amplifying or amending them a little, hopefully adding to a general understanding.

In each of the four organizations studied I spent a couple of months in and around its offices, reading files and interviewing. In total, over the two years of the project, I interviewed more than 200 people. Whom I chose for interview calls for some explanation. My aims were several. First I wanted to be sure to include the key personnel involved with equal opportunity policy. This necessarily pointed to some or all of top management, senior personnel managers and specialist 'equality' staff – women's officers, race equality officers. Beyond this I wanted to extend the interviewing to a sample of employees 'down the line' but to make sure I was not directed by friendly personnel managers only to employees they, for their own reasons, thought I should see. My practice therefore was to obtain a computer print-out or more humble manual list of the relevant 'population' and make a random selection myself, stratifying the sample by grade and using an alphabetic device to arrive at individuals. I did not select for age because this inform-ation was not consistently available. However, as it turned out, the sample had a reasonable age spread. The overall sample of interview subjects was two-thirds male, one-third female. Though the study was intended to be mainly one of male responses on the equality issue, it was important to obtain women's views of the organization, of the policies and of men's reactions. I included in each case study one or more interviews with women and men who were willing to be identified as lesbians or gays, and with women and men with disabilities.

I also ensured that around 15% of those interviewed were black – rather more than the percentage of these black groups in the various organizations' workforce or membership. Here and throughout the book I use the term black to cover people of West Indian, African, Indian, Pakistani and Bangladeshi origin. When employing organizations keep statistics of the ethnicity of their workforce it is usually these groups they monitor. They are generally understood to be most vulnerable to racism and exclusion in Britain. (The distinction between racism as an ideology and exclusion as practice is to be found in Miles 1989.) Since the concept of 'race' (as will be discussed in Chapter 6) has no scientific basis I use the word 'ethnicity' when wishing to refer to the cultural and community differences according to which many people identify themselves and are identified by others. 'Race' I use only in contexts where the existence of racism is explicitly or implicitly referenced, as 'racial discrimination' and 'race equality policies', and in situations where the term is officially employed, as in 'Commission for Racial Equality', 'race unit' or 'race relations officer'. (For further discussion of the concepts of ethnicity and race see Miles 1989 and Cohen 1988.)

During the process of analyzing the resulting material I found it helpful to interview a number of women and men outside the case study organizations, people who had experience of one or another of the aspects of equality work. In all, these interviews amounted to a further thirteen, of which some were with consultants or trainers in positive action for sex or race equality, some with specialists in disability rights.

The interviews were semi-structured. That is, I worked in each case study from a guiding schedule covering all the questions I wanted answered in the course of the case study as a whole; this was then used to guide the construction of category schedules, one for white men, one for black women, etc. Often individual schedules were prepared in the case of unique informants such as a top manager, a disabled woman and so on. I allowed these schedules to develop over time so as to be able to make the most productive use of insights and incidents thrown up by earlier interviews. In any case they operated only as a framework in which the interview might unfold. Always I used the rule of thumb: 'go with the material'. If an informant seemed to have a special contribution to make to the overall story I allowed time for this.

The interviews lasted an hour and fifteen minutes on average. Almost all were tape-recorded. In the first three case studies I transcribed all the tapes in full. In the last, suffering by this time from repetitive strain injury after thirty years of wrist-abuse, I was forced to develop an alternative technique of handwritten notes supplemented by partial transcripts. Transcripts, notes and supporting documentary evidence were photocopied, coded and sorted by theme, while the original interviews remained intact to enable each research subject's account to be studied 'in the round' and its logic, inconsistencies and contradictions traced. It was thus possible to lay out to view the main themes or issues in women's and men's encounters with 'equality policy' and the field of fact and feeling within each, particularly the tensions between and within different subjects' accounts.

Conceptual tools: 'patriarchy' and 'parity'

If the United Nations Decade of Women, 1975–85, did nothing else it demonstrated the reality of patriarchy. The opening years saw the assembling of detailed evidence of women's subordination around the world; the end of the decade confirmed just how hard it was to change anything. Patriarchy was real and it was durable. What feminism proposes is that we should understand female subordination as *systemic*. That is, it is not casual but structured, not local but extensive, not transitory but stable, with a tendency to self-reproduction.

What is patriarchy? At simplest we could define it as 'a system of social structures and practices in which men dominate, oppress and exploit women' (Walby 1990:20). Or we could emphasize the apparent persistence of men's domination of each other and call it 'a set of social relations which has a material base and in which there are hierarchical relations between men, and solidarity among them, which enable them to control women' (Hartmann 1979:232). The wide scope of the social relations subsumed in patriarchy needs emphasizing. Caroline Ramazanoglu calls patriarchy 'a concept used to attempt to grasp the mechanisms by which men in general manage to dominate women in general. It refers to ideas and practices ranging from the most intimate of sexual encounters to the most general economic and ideological factors' (Ramazanoglu 1989:34). Patriarchy has particular sway over reproductive, sexual and familial relations, but is not limited to these spheres. Patriarchal relations operate throughout society, including production. Everywhere they are in interaction with economic class relations and relations of racial domination. Likewise patriarchy is not the sole determinant of reproduction and sexual relations, since relations of class and race also in turn structure these.

Some feminists have criticized the use of the concept of patriarchy on the grounds that it appears fixed and unchanging: 'it is redolent of a universal and transhistorical oppression' (Barrett 1980:14; see also Rowbotham 1980). However, this is true only of certain uses of the concept. We need to use a different, over-arching term to enable us to introduce the notion of historical development. Gayle Rubin coined for this purpose the term 'sex/gender system' (Rubin 1975). So we can say that, just as capitalism is only one of successive modes of production, so patriarchy is only one of other possible sex/gender systems (Cockburn 1983). We can speculate, as women enjoy doing, as to whether there were woman-centred sex/gender systems in some tribal societies of the past (Coontz and Henderson 1986) and wonder, along with feminist utopian novelists, whether one day women will create their own worlds (Gearhart 1985) or whether together we will achieve a sex/gender system in which women and men are truly equal (Piercy 1979). Meanwhile, as we shall see, patriarchy itself changes historically – under the impulsion of changing modes of production (feudalism, capitalism, state 'socialism') and of other factors. We shall see that today father-right as such is giving way to a more generalized male sex-right, that might be better termed 'fratriarchy'. However, 'patriarchy' has come to be a popular shorthand term for systemic male dominance and for that reason I use it here.

There have been fierce debates as to whether patriarchy and capitalism are two interacting systems ('dual systems' theory) or a unity – patriarchal-capitalism, or capitalist-patriarchy (Eisenstein 1979, Acker 1989). It seems to me unnecessary to problematize this. Few feminists really deny the existence or the specificity of class relations, gender relations and relations of racial domination. From one empirical perspective one set of relations will be salient, from another a different set. Whether or not we are thinking of one complex system or several interacting systems depends more on what interpretation we give 'system' than what interpretation we give patriarchy and capitalism. In practice women continue to use the terms patriarchy, capitalism, sex, class and race, to describe our lives. We know it is the articulation of these sets of relations, the way they are lived and reproduced, we have to study and specify.

Due to its systemic nature, patriarchy is not something in which membership is optional. A woman cannot escape, even by climbing to elite status by marriage or career promotion, since she will modify her own subordination only at the expense of that of other women. Women as women can only be liberated from patriarchy through a struggle to change the system as system.

For men likewise membership in patriarchy is not optional. Men may strive to change their personal lives so as to be more equal with women with whom they are close. But being male they continue to be seen by others as members of the patriarchy, and they are bound to share, even if unwillingly, in the benefits it affords men. That is why men, if they are to do anything to end patriarchy, must organize with each other to work alongside women as supporters of feminist struggle. Though it is hard for men to see it, they have an interest in doing so. Because it is a hierarchical system, in which dominance relations among men are imposed with ferocity, patriarchy corrupts the man at the top and mutilates the one at the bottom, whether the boy at school, the army squaddie or the factory hand. Those who have seen the film *The Last Emperor* by Bertolucci will not easily forget the image of hundreds of eunuchs filing out of the palace, each carrying his amputated testes in a jar. Men in patriarchy castrate men, literally and symbolically, in the interests of phallocracy. The male power system of a distributive company or a civil service bureaucracy today may leave men intact, but they exact a masculist discipline of their own. Men in today's power structures, however, cannot say no alternative to the patriarchal model of society exists. Feminists have invented one. And men today have a choice: accept the patriarchal system or work collectively to contradict it. Be part of the problem or part of the solution.

A second theme running through this book is gender 'difference'. There has long been heated debate in the feminist movement as to whether women should be seen as essentially different from men or essentially similar. The 'difference' lobby proposes that women's physical sexual difference from men results in a different life pattern, a different psychology and different (and better) moral values (Mary Daly 1979, Dale Spender 1982, Carol Gilligan 1982 and Susan Griffin 1984 are often cited as instances). By contrast, the 'sameness' lobby argues that women and men are more or less a blank slate on which gender identity is inscribed in the process of a lifetime of learning experiences. (Cynthia Fuchs Epstein 1988 documents this position admirably). Anyone approaching the subject of equal opportunities for women is obliged to state a position on this, for reasons which will become very clear in the ensuing pages. I find most useful Carol Bacchi's formulation that a sameness/difference framework places unacceptable boundaries on the possibilities for change. She shows that feminism gets caught up in this dichotomy only when women feel trapped in a situation in which they have no choice, in a world they cannot change.

> Sameness/difference debates are . . . substantive debates about the shape of the social order. They become expressed as debates about women's sameness to or difference from *men* because of the general assumption that marketplace rules either suit men or are unchallengeable. This is a critical point. Debates *among feminists* along sameness/difference lines surface in contexts where there appear to be only two options, joining the system on its terms or staying out. The debates dissolve, or never even surface, when it is possible to expect humane living conditions for everyone (Bacchi 1990:259).

In this analysis of men's responses to positive action for sex equality I take the position that women need to keep the idea of sexual and gender 'difference' in play, but on their own terms. Women are the ones who must be able to say when 'difference' is relevant. Otherwise we are led either into seeking equality as being 'just like men', or into rejecting the equality movement altogether, abdicating from many excellent qualities and possibilities (rationality for instance, and scientific knowledge) because we are 'different from men'.

These matters will be discussed at length in the pages that follow. It is important to establish this position here, however, in order to make a further introductory point. I believe that a study of equality strategies in organizations calls for a feminist approach that does not reject out of hand as heretical any of the three significant tendencies in feminism (they are often called liberal feminism, socialist-feminism and radical feminism) but rather draws on insights from all three. Feminists of different persuasions of course will fight their corner. The movement towards equality in organizations however is the product, as we shall see, of all three strands within feminism. Though their co-existence produces tensions, their characteristic themes (for example economic exploitation on the one hand, sexual exploitation on the other) are in practice deeply intertwined and each critique of male-dominated society has some legitimacy and a valid purpose. As Caroline Ramazanoglu has argued, 'it is the connections we need to work on, rather than devaluing each other in efforts to decide whose version of feminism is the purest' (Ramazanoglu 1989:189).

I have chosen as a theoretical context in which to approach equality issues the work of certain contemporary feminists in what some of them call a *historical materialist feminist* tradition. Their work is historical in the sense of examining the changes and the continuities over time in the relationship between women and men. It is materialist in going beyond ideology or discourse to analyse the economic, social, political and bodily specificity of women's lives. It acknowledges the significance of the mode of production, and of relations of racial domination, as well as of the sex/gender system in structuring women's experience.

This historical materialist feminist tradition, together with an openness about definitions and validities in feminist practice, enable us to transcend the contradiction of equality. Men tell us 'women cannot claim to be equal if they are different from men. You have to choose.' We now have a reply. If we say so, as women, we can be both the same as you *and* different from you, at various times and in various ways. We can also be both the same and different from each other. What we are seeking is not in fact *equality*, but *equivalence*, not *sameness* for individual women and men, but *parity* for women as a sex, or for groups of women in their specificity.

Presenting the material

The findings of the research are not presented case study by case study but theme by theme. The four organizations make their appearance one at a time, and by Chapter 4 all are fully in play. But they are cited only as and when the theme under discussion draws them into view. As a consequence, some of the material from each case study is foregrounded, other aspects of that equality policy are presented in less detail. Thus strategies within the Trade Union and the Local Authority around the re-evaluation of the worth of low-paid women's work are given high profile. The Service provides material for a discussion of hierarchy. High Street Retail features particularly in Chapter 1, as an introductory example of an equality strategy in the private sector, and in Chapter 5 where the sexual culture of organizations is discussed.

Sequentially, the material develops as follows. Chapter 1 presents something of the history of equal opportunities activism in Britain and shows how the three tendencies or strands within the women's movement all contributed to the legislation of the 1970s on Equal Pay and Sex Discrimination, and in the 1980s, to its expression at organizational level. High Street Retail is introduced as an example of policy for positive action for sex equality. We begin to see 'equality opportunities' as a struggle between interests in the organization that are against or for such a policy, or wish to impose different interpretations.

There is thus in all organizations with an equality policy a short agenda for change and various versions of a longer agenda. Chapter 2 takes the first item on all such agendas: the unbiased and representative recruitment and promotion of women with the aim of breaking both horizontal sex segregation (by moving women into characteristically male occupations) and vertical sex segregation (by enabling women to climb the career ladder). The account here focuses on the latter, demonstrating the masculine nature of the hierarchy of a civil service bureaucracy and the ways in which women pressing forward into high-status jobs backed by sex and race equality policies meet with resistance from men. Both institutional and cultural means are used to impede women. This theme gives rise to a discussion of the hierarchical relations of patriarchy and their interaction with capitalist processes and class relations. It leads to questions concerning the limited agenda of equality for individual women, the longer agenda of transformational change in organizations.

An important factor in women's disadvantage in work and in public life more generally is their disproportionate responsibility for domestic work, including care of the young, old and ill. Chapter 3 looks at the nature of this disadvantage, the way it is exploited by employers and the contradictory effects of equality strategies designed to enable women better to combine paid and unpaid work. The absence of any serious policy to extend such 'privileges' to men, and men's unwillingness to make use of them when they exist, are identified as a significant form of resistance by men to women's progress in organizations.

Equality strategies often focus on promoting the career chances of individual women to the neglect of the low-paid, supposedly 'unskilled' women (among whom are a disproportionate number of black women) found in large numbers at the base of most organizations. Chapter 4 looks at the more class-aware equality activism around grade restructuring and 'equal value' in the Local Authority and the Trade Union, and the way this leads to a concern with profounder issues of democracy and power.

Sexuality is a vexed issue in most organizations. Sex is routinely exploited by employers (women are very often employed for their looks as much as their skills) but it is also feared as a source of indiscipline. Chapter 5 considers the 'sexual regime' of organizations and in particular the way sexual harassment is dealt with in the context of sex equality. The theme of women's 'difference' is explored further here. We see men's fear of separate activity or organization by women, and the ideological 'work' in which men engage to divide women from each other and tarnish the appeal of 'feminism'.

Chapter 6 picks up the theme of ethnicity and racism that has interwoven the foregoing account and shows the response of white people to positive action for race equality in the four organizations. The differences between the oppressions experienced by women as women, black people as black, homosexuals and people with disabilities are established. Yet a similar process can be seen to underlie the experiences of these groups: a process in which one group creates its own identity and secures its dominance by defining another as 'other' and inferior. Disadvantaged groups are inferiorized on account of their bodily difference and their cultures so that all are obliged to aspire to conformity with the white male heterosexual ablebodied norm. The dominant group sets *assimilation* as the price of acceptance. 'You can't be equal *and* different.' A counter strategy has to involve acknowledging and asserting our bodily and cultural specificity.

Finally the last chapter draws together the various themes of positive action for sex equality and recapitulates. There is the short agenda, that of the powerful male sponsors of 'equality'. But there is another agenda, much longer and more ambitious, that is the aspiration of feminist equality activists, whether these are formal equality officers or simply women expressing their demands within the organization. Male power is long-lived and systemic. Is it being reproduced or effectively contradicted? There is much talk today of men changing, of The New Man. Individual men, however, like women, are caught up in patriarchal power relations that are not easy to evade. In the 1990s more women are likely to find themselves with responsibility for promoting sex equality in organizations. Some conclusions are drawn from the experience of their forerunners of the 1980s, principles that, if they could but be lodged from the start within an equality process would make the difference between the short and long agenda, between a goal of equality and one of parity, between cosmetic treatment and a project of transformative change in organizations.

This then is a reading of social situations and relationships based on careful study of practices in four organizations and accounts of their intentions, experiences and feelings by women and men who work in them or are members of them. But it is only one reading, of many that are notionally possible. It is specific to my own subject position: as a white middle-class heterosexual woman operating in an academic mode, age fifty-five, mother of two adult daughters. A very different reading would have been produced by, for instance, a young Asian woman, a senior white male manager, a black male trade unionist – and so on. None of these standpoints can be seen today as producing 'the truth'. But all can perhaps be the basis for respectful negotiation on the question of what the world is like.

The black American writer bell hooks has warned it is not a simple task for women to write about men. Within patriarchal society, silence has been for women a gesture of submission but also of complicity. We have been the repositories of male secrets, and we have kept faith with them. Yet, she says, women have a deep longing to share feminist consciousness with men in their lives and work with them in transforming relationships. When women write about men, she says, such work alters the subject-object relationship that has been a sign of our oppression.

> Rather than focussing on men in a way that renders them objects, feminist scholarship on men by women is informed by a politic that resists domination, that is humanizing and liberatory. This feminist scholarship is informed by the longing for a subject-to-subject encounter, by the longing for a meeting place, a place for solidarity where women can speak to and/or about men in a feminist voice, where our words can be heard, where we can speak the truth that heals, that transforms – that makes feminist revolution (hooks 1989:132).

It is in this spirit that I tentatively put forward the ideas that follow as discussion material for use by the women and men who have to share organizations.

There are many institutions and people I would like to thank for their help in developing these ideas. First, I appreciate the financial support of the Economic and Social Research Council and the administrative support of the Department of Social Sciences, The City University, London, where I am a research fellow. Second, I valued very much the generous cooperation of the four organisations studied and the many women and men I met within them. I wish I could thank them by name, but the requirements of anonymity forbid it. I can and do, however, thank the following individuals for talking through ideas with me and for reading and commenting on successive drafts of the manuscript: Randhir Auluck, Keith Armstrong, Rheena Bhavnani, Angela Coyle, Kate French, Cynthia Griffin, Catherine Itzin, Christine Jackson, David McDonnell, Margaret Page, Di Parkin, Heather Rabbatts, Anne

Sedley, Brenda Smith, Drew Stevenson, Sylvia Walby, Anne Watts
and Jackie West. They are in no way responsible for any errors and
confusions that remain in the book, the blame for which is mine
alone. They will have contributed immeasurably to any relevance
the book may prove to have. My warm thanks too to Jo Campling,
as publishing editor of feminist titles, for her encouragement and
guidance.

1

Equal opportunities: 'rights' and wrongs

Many job advertisements today state 'we are an equal opportunities employer'. Behind such adverts are companies, local authorities and other kinds of organization that claim to have introduced policies against discrimination in employment. They may refer to sex or race discrimination, but usually it is both. This term 'equal opportunities' means something positive to some women looking for a job. But there are other women who are sceptical. They see 'equal opps' as a con.

This ambivalence is unsurprising, because the workplace equality movement is essentially contradictory. On the one hand sex equality is a demand women make on their own behalf: the right to paid work, to the chance of an occupation with fair pay, training and prospects, and to support with childcare. On the other hand it is a policy introduced into organizations by owners and managers 'on behalf of' women. Though some employers are genuinely concerned with justice, often it is transparently clear that it is organizational ends they have primarily in mind. They aim to improve recruitment and retention of women whose qualities they perceive themselves as needing. Or they just want a good public image.

However, if 'equal opportunities' initiatives did not exist we would have to invent them. Even those women who are bitterly disillusioned with the equality experience would no doubt begin anew the fight for fairness at work were it not already occurring. Not all women who experience discrimination, who are stuck in

women's-work ghettoes, will accept their subordination as inevitable. Women have a growing sense of their own worth.

The research I carried out inside organizations showed their
equality initiatives to involve a *struggle*. Different people have
different purposes for them. Different outcomes are possible in
different kinds of organization. I came to formulate this to myself
as negotiation over the 'length' of the equality policy agenda: what
would be included, what would be left off. In practice, as we shall
see, the gains for women are seldom much to write home about. But
the story is not finished yet, and sometimes women do challenge the
assumptions of organizational life in promising ways. We should
not expect men to relinquish their privileged position voluntarily.
Organizations, whether we are talking about banks and businesses,
armies, universities, hospitals or city councils, are significant
concentrations of power. Indeed organization is precisely and
uniquely the means by which power is effected. Men are not about
to let down the drawbridge on their castles.

Why, however, should we say that men have an interest, a
project, as a sex, in maintaining their control of and through organizations? Why should they strive so persistently to keep women in a
subordinate place within them? We have to look at what men as a
sex gain from the *status quo*.

The average man in Britain is paid for more than forty-three
hours of work per week. the average woman for less than thirty.
Yet women work as many or more weekly hours than men. The
difference is that much of women's work is done at home and is
unpaid. For the paid work, hour for hour, a woman earns less than
three-quarters of what a man earns. The average man thus has
considerably more income at his disposal than the average woman,
and more leisure time. It is a privilege enjoyed by most men that
food, clothing, cleaning and other contributions to comfort and the
quality of life are organized for them by women – their wives,
mothers or daughters. Men benefit too from having their dependents (children, aged relatives) looked after by women. Such
advantages accrue to men of all social classes and ethnic groups
in Britain, but those (mainly middle-class and mainly white) who
have wealth or a measure of power in organizations gain addition-
ally.

Men have a higher status at work and, through their work, in
social life. Thus men have more of the particularly remunerative

and prestigious technical and managerial skills and qualifications. Partly because their hands are not tied by domesticity, partly because (as we shall see) they have the power to keep women down, men are free to climb higher. Men can feel more important as a sex, their status amplified by having women working for them or beneath them. They get all the perks that come from being a valued employee: bigger and faster cars, foreign travel, less restrictive supervision. Being in control of organizations provides the leverage to give effect to one's ideas. It is more often a man than a woman who decides which market the firm will enter, where the council will locate the new technology park, whether or not the nuclear power plant will be built. Besides, an important role in an organization is often a springboard to public status, getting to be a personage in the community, a justice of the peace or a member of parliament.

These are just a few of the many benefits that have accrued to men from participating in a society-wide and ages-old male power system, within which the organizations we are talking about are functioning parts. The story of patriarchy, the story of our male dominant sex/gender system, has been told many times. Feminists have approached it from a number of different angles. To what extent history affords evidence of such a sustained system, what were its origins, how it has changed with changing modes of production, have been widely debated (Rubin 1975, Eisenstein 1979, Lerner 1986, Walby 1990). What this book will, I believe, make evident is that 'patriarchy' is not merely a colourful term used by feminists to rebuke men. It is not a thing of bygone days, nor a rhetorical flourish. It is an important dimension of the structuring of modern societies, whether capitalist or state socialist. It is a living reality, a system that quite observably shapes the lives and differentiates the chances of women and of men. The struggle for sex equality, however innocently it may present itself, is an attempt to contradict, to undo, patriarchy.

The movement for sex equality is not, however, one thing but many. Women have traced its history and categorised the themes or tendencies within it. The strands are in practice deeply entwined and the terminology is problematic. I will call them – rather loosely, allowing the following account to fill out the meanings – liberal or 'rights' feminism; socialist-feminism, which has been in part labour movement feminism; and radical feminism.

Women's rights: liberal feminism

The story of modern feminism could be said to begin with the American Revolution of 1776 and the French Revolution of 1789, which embodied aspirations for equality, liberty and fraternity, shaking the old feudal and monarchical order. However, while these social cataclysms and the period of change of which they were symptomatic, ultimately transformed relations between men of different classes, they left the unequal relation between women and men as sexes much as before. Mary Wollstonecraft, whose *Vindication of the Rights of Woman* was published in 1792, was stirred by what she and other women felt to be a bitter injustice. Fraternity clearly meant what it said: a brotherhood that excluded sisters. Liberty and equality, the new rights of 'man', were not intended for women.

Throughout the nineteenth century and into our own women have fought to obtain the personhood that the new order withheld from them – in marriage and divorce laws, property rights, the guardianship of children. It is this movement for 'rights', involving an appeal to the authority of the state, that is today often termed liberal feminism. In this 'liberal' tradition, in the nineteenth and early twentieth centuries, feminists claimed the right to train for the professions, they fought for the vote, for welfare rights and tax reforms. In 1919 they achieved the Sex Disqualification Removal Act that enabled them to hold public office. Campaigns such as those for a married woman's right to retain her paid work and for independent taxation have dented the authority of men in the family. Today women are even demanding the right of access to the priesthood, a historic redoubt of patriarchy. These are projects in the liberal feminist tradition.

In a society where law and processes of political representation formally govern social relations, equality of rights for women is a necessary step in advancing women's interests. It is not, however, sufficient in itself. One recent account of women's subordination is particularly helpful in understanding the complex relationship between women's liberation and human rights.

In *The Sexual Contract* (1988) Carole Pateman, a feminist political theorist, explores the change in social relations that occurred with the end of feudalism and the advent of capitalism in Western Europe. I will deploy her analysis rather fully here, since it will prove a useful tool for understanding much of the empirical material on positive action for sex equality that will follow.

Pateman looks in particular at the theories men used in the eighteenth century to explain the nature of the society they now lived in and the one they saw passing away. The theories of course were in turn influential in legitimating and even moulding the new social relations. Pateman gives particular attention to the notion of 'contract'. Contract, she explains, as used by liberal philosophers such as Rousseau and Locke, is a principle of social association, a means of creating stable, consensual social relationships (Pateman 1988:5).

The patriarchy of early societies, including classical times and the feudal era in Western Europe, is usually represented in liberal accounts as having been based first and foremost on the authority of the father over his sons. Political right sprang from the father's procreative power. The firstborn son inherited his father's status, subordinating younger brethren. Father-right was exemplified in the rule of lords and king. Pateman claims, by contrast, that patriarchy must be seen as being based fundamentally on the right of this father over a *woman*, without whom there could, she argues, have been no sons. The foundation stone of classical and feudal patriarchy, therefore, ignored by liberal theorists, was *conjugal right*. In the words of the Bible, 'God ordained Adam to rule over his wife and her desires were to be subject to his' (Genesis 3:16).

Rousseau, Locke and other political theorists heralded the end of feudalism as the end of a world ordered by formal patriarchal hierarchy. The seventeenth and eighteenth centuries seemed to them to be about the advent of a society of individuals, their rights and responsibilities enshrined not in status and force but in a *social contract* freely agreed and honoured. The sons had united to overthrow the father. Absolutism, monarchy and serfdom were dying in Europe. State monopolies and the guild system were ending. Free trade and a free market in labour, the capitalist mode of production and accumulation, were being born. This new civil order was represented in liberal theory as anti-patriarchal and post-patriarchal.

Again, however, Pateman insists that something is missing from this concept of 'social contract'. The new settlement did not in reality abolish patriarchy. It in fact affirmed it, though in a modernised form. For the contract was one between men only. And it was predicated on, as it were, a hidden *sexual contract*, unacknowledged by contract theory, assuring the 'brothers' of modern society equal access to women and rights over them, a share in the father's former privilege. The new order, just as the old, was to be based on *male sex-right*. A man was now constituted in law as a free and equal citizen, yet a wife was technically a non-being. English Common Law continued to enshrine total legal subjection of wife to husband.

The social contract of Western capitalist 'democracies', then, is by no means incompatible with patriarchy. Indeed it is the means through which the male dominance system has adapted to an otherwise much-changed world. Pateman calls it 'fraternal patriarchy'.

> The character of civil freedom cannot be understood without the missing half of the story that reveals how men's patriarchal right over women is established through contract. Civil freedom is not universal. Civil freedom is a masculine attribute and depends upon patriarchal right. The sons overturn paternal rule not merely to gain their liberty but to secure women for themselves . . . (Pateman 1988:2).

From the Declaration of the Rights of Man in 1789 to the Universal Declaration of Human Rights of 1948 and the Council of Europe's Convention on the Rights of Man in 1950, rights to equality have been conceived as those of 'the citizen', without specifying sex. That this has in effect meant men, not women, is evident in the fact, for instance, that many kinds of violence against women are not considered a violation of human rights under existing international law and enforced prostitution has never been accepted as falling within the scope of the United Nations conventions outlawing slavery (Apprill 1990).

Since there is no place for women *as women* in men's social contract, for women to seek 'equal rights' with men is to seek to be surrogate men. If women are to be fully present in their specificity as women, the social contract has to be rewritten. The hidden sexual contract on which it is founded has to be exposed and annulled. This implies a feminist struggle wider and deeper than a 'rights' movement.

Women's labour under capitalism: socialist-feminism

The 'contract' for civil equality of the individual, then, is real in so far as it underpins juridical and political thinking in Western European-style societies. Yet at other levels it is a fiction. Its relation to practice is indirect and negotiated. Capitalist production is a key instance. One aspect of the new contractual social arrangements that came into existence in the seventeenth and eighteenth centuries in Western Europe was the right of individuals to sell their labour and to buy that of others. Thus under capitalism, feudal bondage was replaced by the employment contract. The wage labourer was now represented as standing in a relation of a civil equality with his employer in the public realm. Yet, as Marxists and socialists have long argued, this central 'pact' of capitalist social relations itself involves a deception. The employer and the worker are in truth far from equal, since the former, having access to capital, owns and controls the means of production, while the worker, who possesses nothing but his labour power, must sell it on disadvantageous terms if he is to live.

If the employment contract, like the social contract of which it is a part, fails to distinguish individuals by gender, subsuming 'woman' into 'man', capitalist employers in reality distinguish acutely between the two sexes and for many purposes positively prefer a female paid workforce. What did Marxists and socialists have to say about women in the relations of production? Engels, and later Lenin, were of the opinion that women's emancipation from patriarchy would be achieved precisely by their entry into the productive labour force. Twentieth-century experience showed, however, that, though many more women now had an independent wage, their oppression as a sex continued. Its persistence was clearly 'not merely a hangover from a pre-industrial stage or from pre-capitalist society, nor of sexist attitudes and prejudices but . . . of fundamental economic, political and ideological importance to the capitalist mode of production' (Beechey 1987:56).

Feminist analysis therefore challenged and built upon Marxist theory. In the first place it was argued that women labouring in the home without pay, invisible to the economists, were in fact already 'in production', since they were subsidising the employer by maintaining free of charge, in a condition fit for work, those husbands and sons who would turn up at the factory gates each morning (Dalla Costa 1972, Political Economy of Women Group 1976). Besides, in a situation where the daughters and wives depended primarily on the male breadwinner's wage, women as a form of paid wage labour had a special value for capital. On the assumption that their wage was but a secondary income for the family, and given that male workers lent them no solidarity in demanding more, they could be paid less than the equivalent man. Though the existence of the family permitted the super-exploitation of all women, it was in particular married women's labour that was most advantageous to capital, 'since it is married women who do not, by virtue of the existence of the family, have to bear the total costs of production and reproduction out of their own wages' (Beechey 1987:63). Because women could be paid less than men, employers were able to use them to depress the value of labour power over all. The interaction between women's family status and their engagement in paid labour seemed to be an important mechanism in perpetuating both their low pay and their subordination to men (Coulson *et al.* 1975).

Here again Carole Pateman's analysis can provide a way of seeing the relationship between women's lack of 'rights' in society and their inequality in employment. She shows how this fraternal, contractual patriarchy that structures modern capitalism bears on women not only in the family but also in paid work. Women, says Pateman,

> have not been incorporated into the patriarchal structure of capitalist employment as 'workers'; they have been incorporated as women; and how can it be otherwise when women are not, and cannot be, men? The sexual contract is an integral part of civil society *and of the employment contract*; sexual domination structures the workplace as well as the conjugal home (Pateman 1988:142, my italics).

Pateman's line of reasoning here is useful to us in several ways. The rights of working men over 'their' women are normally, as we shall see in Chapter 2, honoured by the employer in their employment contract with their male employees. The terms of the fraternal contract govern the relations of the employer and his men, big men with little men. They also structure the relations of men as comrades in trade unions. We shall see that men are usually placed in positions senior to women. Direct comparison is avoided so that women, however talented, cannot put men in the shade. Relative to women, as Pateman puts it, 'the terms of the sexual contract ensure that all men, and not just craftsmen, form an aristocracy of labour' (Pateman 1988:139). Thus we see that while men are subordinated as workers they are not mere wage slaves. In their own sphere, that of sexual relations, they are masters.

The analysis also throws light on the relation of woman and employer. It makes clear for instance that women are seldom employed as undifferentiated labour power. While capitalism implies an identical employment contract for male and female worker, patriarchy in reality makes women's engagement in the organization different from that of men. When women are employed it is precisely because they are women: employers are never sex-blind. Everyday observation shows occupations to be sharply segregated into male jobs and female jobs. Sex segregation at work is not decreasing in Britain in modern times. Indeed as we shall see in Chapters 3 and 4, employers are increasing the use of part-timing, of temporary contracts and casual work, a process which tends further to distinguish men's from women's work. The lowest paid and least secure jobs continue to be gendered female. Such strategies for profit, accumulation and cost-efficiency are quite transparently predicated on the continuation of the sexual contract. Young women anticipate, older women live out, the social relations of housewife, owing duties to husband, children and home, undertaking paid work (for an income that is an economic necessity to the household) only in ways that can be made to fit. If the working man enters the workplace dressed in his masculine authority, the woman goes clad in her subordination. In production too she will be constituted as an inferior in patriarchal relations and her disadvantage here will reduce her status in the home.

The struggle for women's equality as workers in the paid workforce therefore has had to take the form of a double resistance. On the one hand women have had to struggle against the terms of engagement between employer and employed. Their struggle has been against the general tendency to exploitative pay and conditions of work. It has, in other words, had to be a *socialist* struggle, alongside working men, using similar resources of organized labour in the workplace and in society. On the other hand it has necessarily had to be a feminist struggle against the imposition of male sex-right by both employer and male colleagues.

And indeed a tendency of this nature runs consistently through the women's movement.

In the late nineteenth century, when Marxist and socialist thought were inspiring new forms of trade union and political party, women had to struggle with men to be admitted to membership. They had to compete with men for skilled work. They resisted exclusion from certain kinds of work imposed by the Factory Acts of the mid-nineteenth century – an exclusion welcomed by many male workers. Women's organizations at this time included the Women's Protective and Provident League, later the Women's Trade Union League, and the National Federation of Women Workers (Walby 1986:3). Activism in this tradition persisted throughout the present century and, as we shall see, did much to achieve the equal pay legislation of 1970.

The result then, has been shopfloor struggle for working women, now against the boss, now against the brothers. One way or another, a socialist-and-feminist movement for working women as a class has been as important a component of the women's movement as the campaigns for the rights of women as individuals before the law. The convergence of these two strands, liberal feminism and socialist-feminism, will be visible at many points in the ensuing account of contemporary equal opportunities initiatives.

Sexuality and difference: radical feminism

So too will a third. To limit women's struggle to the demand for inclusion in what is essentially men's social contract, or for engagement in work on identical terms with those of men, ignoring the reality of women's lives, is to seek to make women surrogate men in a world that is still a man's world. That is not only to deform the women who achieve such a goal – it is necessarily to exclude the majority of women from the project. Women's struggle therefore has needed to be more than on the one hand liberal and on the other socialist-feminism. It has also had to have the form of a movement in which the highly personal issues of procreation and sexuality, bodies and identity, are recognized as political. It has had to be a movement which can question even the benefits to women of participation in heterosexual sexuality and in which women can assert the values that seem to them to inhere in women's current lives. These are the insights most centrally located in what is now termed 'radical feminism'.

Such a tendency has never been entirely absent from the women's movement. It swept dramatically to the fore, however, in the late 1960s and early 1970s in the new wave of feminism which continues today and which we call 'the women's liberation movement'. This movement arose in the prosperous years of a long postwar economic boom, and was the creation of women who had already tasted new freedoms. Most women now had paid jobs. Their wages and salaries allowed them to purchase a proliferation of commodities and services. Many more were acquiring higher education, taking part in an expanding civil society, in sport and travel. They had the greater confidence in their bodies and in their sexuality that came from a more permissive culture and from the possession of 'the pill', which at least put contraception, new health hazards notwithstanding, under women's own control.

New wave feminism also arose in the context of a dissatisfaction both with a politics of 'women's rights' and with women's labour movement struggles. Women from both these traditions were radicalized and younger women brought new perceptions. The movement was, however, predominantly middle-class and predominantly white. It was provoked in particular by the experience of many university-educated women in the new left of the sixties. The participatory and prefigurative themes in the socialism of student, civil rights and anti-war movements offered women a political resource that the traditional left had not. Yet within these movements men continued to exploit, oppress and abuse women. Women's anger this time around was therefore addressed directly to men, including their own colleagues and comrades. It was understood that the way forward for women had to be autonomy and sisterhood (Coote and Campbell 1982).

The feminism of the 1970s was characterized by a profound ambivalence towards the notion of 'equality'. While the movement formulated demands in terms of an end to 'discrimination', for legal 'rights', and financial independence for women, and while it actively promoted equality legislation, there was scepticism about both the possibility and the desirability of equality with men. An alternative theme was emerging in these years, that of 'women's difference'. It was not of course entirely new; it echoed past discourses of women.

It took several forms, some women portraying gender difference as having a biological or natural basis, others representing it as historical and cultural. But one way or another the contemporary women's liberation movement brought into currency the idea that, as Carole Pateman puts it, 'women's equal standing must be accepted as an expression of the freedom of women *as women*, and not treated as an indication that women can be just like men' (Pateman 1988:231).

Difference, as we shall see in Chapters 5 and 6, is a contradictory and contentious matter for women. While the movement was strengthened by the perception that women's specificity should not be buried or lost in the struggle for equality, 'sameness-versus-difference' has been a source of conflict between feminists in the 1970s and 1980s. It has also cut across in complex ways the experience of black women. Black feminists increasingly protested that white feminism, in proclaiming all women as sisters and all different from men, ignored black women's experience of oppression by white women (as well as white men and black men) (Carby 1982). Black women wanted an acknowledgment of 'difference', but it was a different kind of difference. It was a specificity not only of sex but of ethnicity.

The value of radical feminism, however, was that, in identifying not only woman but womanhood as a source of strength, it clearly *embodied* women. One effect was to enable us to discuss the politics of bodies in the workplace – which we will see in Chapter 6 has relevance in issues of 'race', homosexuality and disability as well as of sex. This is important, because one of the ways in which women's employment can be seen to be gender-specific is that women's bodies are often involved in the deal between women workers and their employer. They are relevant to employers, not only in the way that men's bodies are used, for their labouring effectiveness, but for what they represent sexually and emotionally to men – to male managers, colleagues, clients, suppliers. Hiring a woman employee may not legally buy an employer or his managers the right of sexual intercourse with her. But, as we shall see in Chapter 5, a woman's sexuality, her smile, her dress, her femaleness, is often an implicit part of the bargain. Where it is not a positively desired attribute in the job, it is perceived as a management problem, for it is woman's sexuality, not man's, that is seen as a potential threat to organizational discipline.

Above all perhaps, radical feminism enabled women unhesitatingly to use the concept of 'patriarchy', to designate the continuing system of male supremacy in which we feel ourselves to live. Carole Pateman's analysis further enables us to employ the idea of systemic male power today while distinguishing classical or feudal patriarchy, based specifically on husband-and-father-right, from its modern replacement, fraternal patriarchy based more generally on male sex-right. We can see there a reflection of what we know from experience – that the *pater familias* may be dead or dying, but the gang of lads on the street, the men in the union branch, the male executive committee and board room, are inheriting his power.

This account has sketched the nature of three orientations within the women's movement and we can in fact see all three – liberal feminism, socialist-feminism and radical feminism – in the campaigns that led to the passing of the legislation on which 'equal opportunities in the workplace' are founded. I would argue that all three have been and remain equally needed. And further, that most feminists are a little bit of each.

Legislating for equality

In one sense the equal opportunity policies visible today in local councils, government offices, clearing banks and TV companies arise from a juridical move: they reflect quite precisely the provisions of particular laws passed in Britain in the 1970s.

The Equal Pay Act 1970, which came into effect in 1975, made it unlawful to discriminate between women and men in pay and other terms in their contracts of employment. It specified that women were entitled to the same pay as men if doing the same or broadly similar work, or if their job had been rated as equivalent to that of a man in a job evaluation study. A companion Act, the Sex Discrimination Act 1975, made it unlawful to treat women less favourably than men (or married people less favourably than single people) in education, training or employment, or in the provision of goods, facilities or services. It introduced a concept of indirect discrimination, which is deemed to occur when an employer applies a condition to both sexes of a kind such that the proportion of one sex who can comply with it is considerably smaller. An example might be when a police force specifies that all candidates for the post of police officer must be two metres tall.

The law had a bearing on recruitment. Employers were forbidden to advertize a job as for one sex or the other ('doorman', 'dinner lady'), to refuse an applicant a job on grounds of sex, or to discriminate in the arrangements made for deciding who should be offered a job, or in the terms of the job offer. Tribunals have ruled, for instance, that an employer shows 'an intention to discriminate' if questions are asked in a job interview of women (but not of men) about their domestic situation or childcare arrangements. Employers may, however, discriminate against one sex or the other in recruiting to jobs where they can show sex to be a 'genuine occupational qualification'. An example would be the job of resident worker in a hostel for girls. In principle the provisions that apply to non-discriminatory recruitment apply also to promotion, transfer, training and redundancy.

A Race Relations Act in similar form to the Sex Discrimination Act was passed one year later, strengthening earlier legislation of 1965 and 1968. The Act made it unlawful to discriminate directly or indirectly on 'racial' grounds in a variety of situations, including employment. For example an employer would now be discriminating if, in a catchment area with a high proportion of black residents, the existing workforce was almost all white and recruitment was found to be by 'word of mouth', that is by informal processes in which existing workers simply informed their friends and relatives about job vacancies. In recruitment interviews it is unlawful to ask questions that have a different impact on black people than they would have on white. One could not ask, for instance, 'How do you feel about working in an all-white team?'

The Equal Pay Act and the Sex Discrimination Act were the product of a sustained social movement in which it is possible to detect the contribution of all three of the tendencies within the women's movement mentioned above. The changes in the law reflected the concerns of a classic liberal, 'rights' feminism. Organizations such as the National Council for Civil Liberties and the Fawcett Society, one of the older women's organizations that had been active in the suffrage movement, were lobbying throughout the sixties and seventies.

Yet what had characterized the postwar movement was a greater activism of women in the workplace, in trade unions and in the

Labour Party. The Civil Service Women's Associations had joined with other women's organizations in 1944 to create an Equal Pay Campaigning Committee and by 1955 had pressed a Conservative Government to concede equal pay in the civil service. Urged by its Women's Advisory Committee the Trades Union Congress put equal pay top of a six-point charter of trade union aims for women in 1963. The following year women in the Labour Party won the leadership's commitment to observing what was by now the policy of the European Economic Community and the International Labour Office. In 1968 women sewing machinists at Fords began what would be many years of sustained industrial action to obtain equal pay with skilled men in the car industry. Demonstrations by trade union women and pressure by women within the Labour Party led Barbara Castle, Labour Minister of Employment, to introduce a Bill in the autumn of 1969. It became law in 1970.

In contrast to this long-drawn out campaign over equal pay, the Sex Discrimination Act was achieved in a much more rapid burst of activity. In 1968 Joyce Butler, a Labour MP, formed a parliamentary group on women's rights. Despite backing from some MPs of all parties and vocal support outside Parliament several attempts at private Bills failed. The pressure thus generated, however, obliged both Conservative and Labour Parties to produce their own draft legislation. It was Labour, a year after its return to power in 1974, that finally placed the Act on the statute book. Not only in passing supportive legislation but also, as we shall see, in introducing positive action for sex and race equality at local level, the state under Labour Party administration has been a significant factor.

This time, however, what made the difference was the engagement of the third tendency in feminism: autonomous women of the newly emerging women's liberation movement. By 1975 the upsurge of women active on issues ranging from discrimination in tax and benefit rules to nurseries, male violence and abortion, had helped to generate a live public awareness. A Women's Lobby of these new groups worked with active Labour MPs. April Carter has documented the way the combined energies of liberal, socialist and radical feminist women pressured the new legislation into being. Together they had created in the public 'a general feeling that the time had come for action in a self-evidently just cause' (Carter 1988:123).

Discrimination against women, discrimination for women

The legislation for sex equality in Britain has to be seen in the
context of similar moves in other countries in the last two decades.
Conventions and laws purporting to end sex inequalities tend to
diverge on one important issue. Some legislate for equality of
opportunity, *égalité des chances*. Others by contrast require equality
of outcomes, *égalité des faits*, a goal which inevitably entails
mandatory special treatment or positive discrimination. Equality
of opportunity involves ensuring that women have no doors closed
to them that are open to men. If, however, women's past history
and present circumstances prevent them from taking up the
opportunities offered or competing on equal terms in the use of
them, equality of results will never be achieved. Special actions are
needed discriminating in favour of women as a sex if women are to
make progress towards equality of outcomes. Paid maternity leave
and training programmes are examples.

The first clear international juridical instrument to embody this
perception was the United Nations Convention of 1979 on the
'elimination of all forms of discrimination against women'. Article 4
of this Convention stated clearly that temporary special measures in
any sphere – political, civil, economic, social or cultural – intended
to bring about actual equality between women and men, must not
be considered as unlawful sex discrimination. Indeed member states
were expected to institute and pursue such measures until such time
as the right of women to equality with men proclaimed by the
United Nations had been achieved (Vogel-Polsky 1989). This
convention introduced into the internal legal systems of signatory
states (of which the United Kingdom is one) a concept that was new
for most of them: *positive or affirmative action for women.*

In the context of Europe, the European Economic Community's
founding document, the Treaty of Rome of 1957, enshrined the
principle of sex equality. What is more, Article 119 established
women's right to pay equal with that of men doing work that could
be shown to be of *equal value*. More recently the Council of Europe,
which unites in Strasbourg the 23 states of Western Europe,
recognized the need in international and national law to distinguish
women as a sex rather than assuming their inclusion in the unitary
category of 'person'. A seminar organized under the auspices of the
Council of Europe in 1989 introduced a new concept, an alternative

58263

to 'equality', whether of opportunity or results. It was '*démocratie paritaire*', a democracy of *parity* or *equivalence*. The phrase acknowledges the sex-specificity of women and men. A true democracy would ensure the full representation of each sex as a sex (Apprill 1990).

Among countries whose legislation has adopted the principle of positive discrimination for women, or as it is sometimes called in French, '*mésures de rattrapage*', are Sweden, Norway and the United States. Sweden's Equal Opportunities Act of 1980 states that employers *must* realize its provisions through systematic positive action. In Norway an Equal Status Act of 1978 has led the way in Europe in requiring, among other things, appropriate 'quotas' of places for women on all committies or bodies to which members are elected or nominated by government agencies (Michel 1990).

In many ways the British legislation on both race and sex discrimination was influenced by developments in the USA. It was weaker, however, both in its attitude to discrimination and measures for implementation. In the States positive action for race equality was already featured in the civil rights legislation of 1964. Indeed, US race law offered considerably greater prospects of successful litigation and heavier penalties for transgressors than British law (Bindman 1981). Besides, presidential orders subsequently *required* positive action programmes for women. Equality measures in the USA are considerably strengthened by a law of 'contract compliance.' US federal public authorities may not contract business with enterprises that cannot demonstrate that they have programmes 'to accelerate changes in women's expectations, education and eventual employment destinations' (Meehan 1985:25).

Even within the United Kingdom there is now a precedent for mandatory positive action – in connection with employment for Catholics and Protestants in Northern Ireland. The Fair Employment (N.Ireland) Act 1989, while it falls short of the positive discrimination for sex equality countenanced in some countries is more extensive than that provided for in the case of sex equality in Britain. It places a legally enforceable obligation on employers to monitor and report to a Fair Employment Commission on both workforce composition and job applications; to review recruitment, training and promotion practices at least every three years; to take affirmative action if fair participation is not being secured by members of the two communities; and to 'target' achievements by setting both goals and timetables. Here too 'contract compliance' is in force. Public authorities are obliged to require firms with whom they contract for goods and services to be satisfactorily complying with this law (Department of Economic Development 1989).

By contrast, the British legislation on sex equality was weak in conception. Despite the head of steam behind reform, its opponents succeeded in limiting its scope. The Equal Pay Act 1970 provided only for equal pay for like work: women were obliged to compare themselves with men doing the same job. Given the extent of occupational sex-segregation in Britain, few women could find such comparators. In 1983 Britain was obliged finally to respond to an EEC directive to institute the principle of 'equal value'. Embodied in the Equal Pay (Amendment) Regulations 1984, this was an important step forward for women in Britain. Yet it has been difficult to enforce 'equal value' either through collective bargaining or through the courts. British tribunals have proved ungenerous in their interpretation of the law. Cases won are often overturned at a higher level on appeal. Women who have brought cases have reported a punishing experience. Those who have won have found the cash compensation mean (Leonard 1987). Besides, whereas in the USA the law allows a group of women to take and benefit from a 'class action' in the courts, the British law deals with women one by one.

The use women can make of the Sex Discrimination Act 1975 and the subsequent amendment of 1986, is seriously limited by its design. It is a law giving rights not to women, as a historically disadvantaged group, but to *both sexes*. Men have been enabled to bring successful actions against some equal opportunity measures for women, on the grounds that they discriminate against men. Where discrimination against women is proven, a tribunal has no power to order the guilty employer to reinstate the aggrieved woman or to take positive steps to ensure the avoidance of further abuse. Despite the fact that Britain signed the UN convention of 1979, ratifying even the controversial Article 4 calling for positive discrimination in favour of women, the British law forbids all discrimination except where expressly permitted. The extent of the permitted discrimination is extremely small, amounting to little more than providing sex-specific training for a particular occupation or workplace in which one sex can be shown to be under-represented. Even that provision applies to men as well as women. With the exception of elected bodies, the law does not permit the setting of 'quotas' of places for women. Local authorities that attempted to use a process of 'contract compliance' to effect change among local businesses soon found this loophole closed by government action. The Equal Opportunities Commission (EOC), set up under the Act to monitor the new laws and to promote sex equality, has fewer powers than comparable organizations and commissioners in the USA and some European countries, and in practice it has proved a poor watchdog, unwilling to undertake investigations or press charges.

In moments of despair women express the feeling that an Act so even-handed in its treatment of the dominant and the disadvantaged sex must have been designed to prevent rather than to achieve equality for women. In spite of the problems in the law and its implementation, however, feminists quite rightly defend it and seek to extend it and to strengthen the EOC. Rights, for all the intrinsic inadequacy of formal measures, are better than no rights.

The Race Relations legislation in Britain is a little less limiting on positive discrimination than the Sex Discrimination Act: it is permitted to provide persons of a particular ethnic group with special access to facilities or services to meet the special needs of that group in education, training or welfare. The Local Government Act 1966 had already provided for local authorities to fund provision to meet the needs of the 'new commonwealth' communities. Section 11 funding, as it is called, has been used by supportive (particularly Labour-led) local councils to pay the salaries of race equality officers and to set up race equality units. Overall, however, the race relations legislation too has proved a flimsy tool that activists have found frustrating in use. The Commission for Racial Equality (CRE), like the EOC, has had too few sanctions with which to enforce compliance (Gregory 1987).

After this sorry tale, it will not come as a surprise that women's inequalities in employment continued into the eighties. Women's pay, relative to that of men, rose from 63.1% in 1970 to 75.5% in 1977. This was due, however, less to the Equal Pay Act than to a period of incomes restraint imposed by a Labour government which curbed men's pay proportionately more than women's. At that point the gains for women ceased and little more has been achieved since (Department of Employment 1987). It appears that many employers, helped by the five years' grace afforded them between the passing and implementation of the Act, evaded the intention of the new law by introducing yet clearer distinctions between women's work and men's work so that the two could not be considered comparable (Snell *et al.* 1981). Partly as a result of such manoeuvres, sex-segregation in the British workforce, far from ending, in some respects increased in the late seventies and early eighties (Hakim 1981).

Some women, particularly better-educated and professional women, did benefit from the climate generated by the Acts in the context of a women's movement that encouraged greater assertiveness. But

> the great majority of women benefited much less from legislation and pressure for change. Although a very small number of women did break into manual jobs previously reserved to men, to become lorry drivers or garage mechanics, for example, the general trend was towards narrowing the job opportunities open to women. (Carter 1988:86)

Besides, the equality legislation had been very much the product of the era of welfare capitalism that ended definitively with the election of a Conservative government in 1979. 'As the economy moved into recession the principles of equality and participation sank to the bottom of the political agenda' (Gregory 1987:148). Female unemployment shot up between 1979 and 1981 and continued to climb steadily until 1986. Men were also suffering from high unemployment, of course, and this was an added reason for the male-led trade unions to back-pedal on sex equality. Besides, the policies of the Thatcher government in the 1980s included an onslaught on trade unionism, support for employers in holding down the wage and reducing job security, cuts in spending on public services in which many working-class women found their employment, and eventually a sweeping programme of privatization. 'Flexibility' of employment has been a strategy for the intensification of the exploitation of women's labour power. The percentage of women on temporary contracts is twice as high as that of men (Equal Opportunities Commission 1988). Meanwhile the number of women working part-time increased by 50% between 1971 and 1987. While part-timing serves the needs of many women who have domestic responsibilities, it often involves unsocial hours, no holiday pay and lower average hourly rates.

Meantime, with growing male unemployment, the importance of women's wages to family wellbeing was increasing. The Royal Commission on the Distribution of Income and Wealth in 1978 found that without the wife's earnings three times as many families would be below the poverty line (cited in Carter 1988:105). It was in the eighties, the 'equality era', that we began to hear, not only in Britain but in other European countries, the USA and indeed the world at large, of 'the feminization of poverty'. Such economic trends undermined any possibility that the new laws could bring about an overall improvement in the position of women in the workforce. Formal 'rights' for women will not on their own eradicate structural subordination and the suffering it generates.

Equal opportunities: the practice

With few exceptions, then, neither the race nor the sex discrimination legislation in Britain had *compelled* employers to take positive measures to combat inequality, and few employers had their hearts in change. The Equal Opportunities Commission and the Commission for Racial Equality published guides to the new laws, with interpretations of the positive discrimination they permitted and other forms of positive action encouraged. They urged employers to act (Commission for Racial Equality 1983, Equal Opportunities Commission 1985). But employers dragged their feet. By the end of the 1970s only a few had declared themselves to be 'equal opportunity employers' and most of those meant little more than that they were observing the letter of the law (Robarts 1981). By 1986 there was a handful of initiatives to cite: a few progressive local councils, inspired by the Greater London Council, led the way. A few private-sector employers were experimenting: Weekend Television and Thames TV, Austin Rover (Stamp and Robarts 1986).

Nor were the unions proving much help. Though the Trades Union Congress had been passing motions on equal pay since the end of the last century and though unions were recognized as having a key role to play in inducing employers to bring in positive action, the authors of the NCCL review found disappointingly slender evidence of unions' commitment to making the new policies work.

> We have yet to see the majority of trade unions mounting an effective challenge to the iniquities of job segregation and pay disparity among their membership. Recent years have seen extensive job losses and consequent fall in membership for many unions; and the protection of jobs and industries has inevitably taken precedence. For many trade unions this means protecting *men*'s jobs and thereby defending the 'family wage'. Challenging sex discrimination – and racism – is often, in this context, seen as irrelevant (Stamp and Robarts 1986:83).

From the middle-1980s, however, an 'equality' movement within organizations did begin to gather pace. The provision for positive discrimination in the law might be weak, yet there was plenty of positive action a willing employer could take to diminish inequalities of sex and race. The ensuing chapters will furnish examples of what was possible. But why should an employer voluntarily embark on positive action? First, perhaps, was the question of public image: managers and owners like their organizations to look progressive, socially responsible. Second, employers were hearing more and more about a 'demographic time-bomb' ticking away, primed to devastate the labour market in the 1990s. By the mid-1990s, due to a decline in the birthrate two decades earlier, 25% fewer young people would leave school each year and enter the job market (Confederation of British Industry 1988). Employers realized that they would be obliged to compete with each other for other unemployed or under-employed groups: ethnic minorities, women. A progressive policy for such groups might give them a competitive advantage. Third, women and black people themselves were fighting discrimination. Employers did not relish the idea of being dragged through the courts. Besides, would unrest be confined to legal action? Employers thought uneasily of the so-called 'urban riots' of the early eighties that the yellow press had persuaded them should be blamed on black unemployment.

In the remainder of this chapter I will present an introductory example of an equality policy and related positive action measures in one organization. It is a private firm that I shall call High Street Retail – one of Britain's larger distributive chains. Subsequent chapters will deal one by one with a sequence of issues involved in positive action for women and, drawing on the experience of High

Street Retail and the other case study organizations, will dissect in detail the policies and the responses to them. Here we will be content with a broad-brush picture of what is typically involved overall in equality work at organizational level.

In 1988 High Street Retail employed approaching 30 000 people, located in numerous shops, offices, warehouses and distribution centres up and down the country. Like most firms of its sector it is a flat pyramid with a mass of women at the bottom, a few men at the apex. In fact it is a living example of the contemporary uses made by business of that particular kind of labour power we have been discussing, the labour power that is constituted in the families of Britain, that of wives, mothers and daughters. For though the firm employs men too, in jobs traditionally seen as male work, their family status is not relevant to their job. Women's is.

Seventy-five per cent of the company's workforce is female, 87% is in manual and other routine work. As is the case throughout the retail sector, the occupations here are highly segregated by sex. In the manual areas men load and offload goods, drive vans, maintain conveyor systems and vehicles, manage stocks and stores. Women fill orders and pack them, key in data, take telephone orders, work as shopfloor assistants and at cash tills. In the less routine occupations too sex segregation occurs. In buying and merchandising, for instance, women normally handle certain kinds of goods (children's wear or lingerie), men handle others (shoes, hardware). There is a pronounced vertical segregation too of course. Though women are half of the white-collar employees, over 60% of them are in the two most junior grades. The pyramid with its female base is topped by a pinnacle of men. The company is governed by a board of directors among whom the members of one family are particularly influential shareholders.

High Street Retail had long been a paternalistic, even patriarchal, company with the head of family possessing great authority. Employees were said to be very 'loyal' and a 'family' ideology was emphasised. When recruiting, priority was often given to family members of existing employees. The caring ethos, however, combined with an authoritarian management style. The firm was rather rigid and rule-bound, 'system driven', with decision-making held tightly within the main board. In the early 1980s a profitability crisis had prompted a rethink. New strategies were devised and a managerial revolution set in process. A new chief executive, appointed in 1983, introduced fresh management blood, people who were more market-oriented, risk-taking and inventive, who gave less priority to traditional formulae and more to the 'bottom line': profit. Among the new strategies was a greater customer service orientation, 'putting people first'; a drive for publicity and image; and a stress on managerial 'excellence'.

In 'equal opportunities' (EO) initiatives High Street Retail was a trend-setter. The area in which its head office was located had seen an influx of ethnic minorities at several periods in its past. A sense of social responsibility had led the firm, as early as 1967, to take steps to increase the recruitment of black employees. As yet, however, only 4% of manual workers and 2.3% of supervisory/ managerial staff were of ethnic minority origin and very few indeed were to be found in the higher grades, despite the fact that many of High Street Retail's employment sites were in urban areas with ten, fifteen or twenty per cent black populations. Attention was extended to sex equality somewhat later. A company equal opportunities committee was created to respond to the Sex Discrimination Act 1975.

It is quite common to find equality initiatives backed by white men in senior positions in organizations. In High Street Retail the prime mover was the major shareholder, a member of the founding family. He was a powerful sponsor for 'equal opps', since he was personally (in his own definition) a pro-feminist and transparently committed, despite the odds, to working towards a non-sexist and non-racist society and firm. Through his initiatives from around 1982 the role of the EO committee, which was made up of senior personnel and line managers (predominantly men) was strengthened. In addition an EO unit was established around the existing black male race equality officer by the recruitment of two very well-qualified women, a white female EO manager and a black female EO training officer. All three had been community or women's movement activists. The unit's brief was to monitor the policies and practices on equal opportunities, to recommend changes where necessary, to provide training in equality matters and deal with queries and complaints brought by individuals. The unit was located in a strategically significant position, reporting directly to the chief executive's office.

Policy-making for equality now intensified. Initiatives were drafted by the equality staff in consultation with the major shareholder. The equal opportunities manager (white, female) was particularly influential in this phase. Proposals were discussed and agreed by the EO committee, which the major shareholder chaired. They were then referred on to the personnel executive committee. Though this had much the same membership it was chaired by the assistant chief executive. The majority male resistance to equality policies surfaced here and proposals often had to be defended against criticism. One or two committed women managers were important factors both in policy formulation and implementation, though other women managers kept their distance.

In this way a code of practice had been devised and circulated to employees. It embodied a commitment by the company to 'use to the full the talents and resources of all our employees'. It promised to ensure that single or married women, members of ethnic minority groups and people with disabilities would not be subject to discrimination when applying for jobs, training or promotion and that these groups would be fairly represented at all levels within High Street Retail. There was to be an end to sex-typing: all jobs were to be open to either sex. It introduced an 'action programme' to 'give the policy teeth'. In the course of 1986 the policy was presented to a directors' briefing group whence, by subsequent briefings, it was passed down the line. The major shareholder besides took it on himself to speak individually with fifty senior managers. The committee and unit together prepared plans for the five-year period to 1991.

What made this a serious attempt and perhaps unique in the private sector was that the equal opportunities unit achieved a commitment from the management to actual statistical 'targeting', made possible by the extensive computerisation of the firm's activities. The percentage of women and black employees aimed for in every grade, with cross-breaks by division, by department and in some cases by site, were set down for five years ahead. Overall the aim was to increase the proportion of black staff to 8% of the total. Women's share of directorial and senior management positions was to increase from around 2% to around 6%, of middle management jobs from around 10% to 16% and of junior/middle management from 22% to 50%.

How was this to be achieved? First, the recruitment process was to be rid of bias. Second, some practical impediments to women's advancement were removed: for instance the 'geographical mobility' requirement for store managers. New criteria were inserted into job appraisal. Women were boldly made 50% of trainees for store manager. But above all managers with responsibility for recruitment and promotion were instructed to 'think women'. It was emphasised that women had all the competences of male colleagues. It was negligence and prejudice alone that had led in the past to women being denied their fair chance. Besides, and here a sort of positive sex-stereotyping was introduced, women were now represented as bringing much needed feminine qualities to business. Positive action was agreed by the chief executive and some influential personnel managers. They felt it consistent with the new management approach. 'One can link the idea of "opportunities" to development and say "we're moving, we're dynamic"'. To personnel managers it seemed an intelligent use of skills. Some sales directors felt it made sense to have more women involved in a company selling its goods mainly to women customers. Public relations people saw it as 'a heightening of company image' in a positive way.

As far as white women were concerned, the first two years' results were good. A few high-ranking white women were brought in and a few others promoted from within. Substantial gains were made in middle management. A black, male senior manager was recruited. After that, however, progress slackened off, and no statistically significant gains were made for black people, women or men. Equality officers in other organizations report a similar pattern.

Yet the strategy of the equality activists at High Street Retail had not by any means been half-hearted.The equal opportunities manager, a socialist and a feminist, drew the management into areas where even the 'progressives' found it hard to follow her. For instance, a distinction emerged between the few top managers prepared to back her on the legitimacy of 'targeting' and the remainder of the management. 'As soon as you mention targets, all hell breaks loose' said the (black, female) equal opportunities training manager, who had the unenviable task of confronting such men in training sessions. The 'progressives' therefore found it advisable to win support for this 'women's rights' measure by legitimating it in a language of 'benefit to the firm'.

Another issue on which there was a divergence of opinion between the equal opportunities manager and the top management was the class-related issue of low-paid women's work. She recognized that underlying women's inequality in the firm was the basic nature of women's exploitation. She had emphasised in many public statements her own and the company's determination that the policy should benefit women down to the lowest grade in the firm. This proved particularly hard, however, because it ran counter to the labour market strategy involved in the management revolution in the firm. Part-timing was increased rapidly from 1984. Very few manual staff were recruited thereafter as fulltimers. While part-timing was often represented by managers as being evidence of flexible response by the company towards women's own needs, in fact the firm's preference for part-timing had other motivations. Technical developments had created some tasks (taking telephone orders for instance) that could be intolerably monotonous or stressful if performed for a shift longer than four hours. Part-timing also enabled a response to the clustering of customer shopping in both stores and telephone ordering into certain peak hours of the day. The working day had been extended to fifteen hours, worked in a sequence of part-time shifts. Part-time workers were felt to afford higher productivity than fulltimers, since output tends to fall in the fifth and subsequent hours of a shift.

A second change in the company had been from permanent to temporary employment. Like other firms of its kind the response to challenging economic circumstances was to reduce its dependency on full-time permanent staff. Some departments were moving towards a 'core and periphery' model, with a core of permanent workers supplemented by a more mobile body of temps. In so far as black women had gained employment in the firm it was disproportionately in these insecure temporary jobs. Add to these trends the fact that due to new technology and higher productivity standards, 25% of the payroll, mainly women, had lost their jobs in the early eighties, and there could well have been – EO notwithstanding – a large-scale and long-term deterioration in the prospects of the working-class female labour pool in local communities.

Despite the class-conscious EO policy decided by the major shareholder and the EO manager it was not easy to implement such a thing. There was no relevance in targeting in the case of manual women – they were already in an overwhelming majority. The issues for them were pay, terms and conditions of work – basically the value put on their jobs. The EO manager deferred any attempt to regrade or re-evaluate women manual and clerical workers because the astronomical costs of 'equal value' adjustments would have jeopardised the acceptance by male managers of the remainder of the equality plan. Part-timers continued to be excluded from the company pension scheme. They were paid at a lower hourly rate than fulltimers – a situation in which the union was as guilty as the firm. Saturday staff were particularly disadvantaged. Part-timers had little or no chance of promotion to management jobs, since most of these were specified as full-time. It was more than ever the case therefore, as a sympathetic personnel manager put it, that 'the biggest benefit you could give to women in High Street Retail would be to treat part-timers equally with fulltimers'.

The genuineness of the policy to 'benefit a wider workforce' was tested to destruction when a costly extension of maternity leave was being considered. The EO manager intended the increased benefits, albeit modest in her view, to be for women of all grades. Management decided to agree it only for management women. The union, which represented the manual women, had not been offered a seat on the equal opportunities committee and had no input to equality policymaking. 'The company made it very clear they didn't want me to involve the union' said the EO manager. After three years of equality activities women union representatives observed that no gain had been felt by manual women.

Finally, sexual politics were another hidden reef threatening the clear sailing of the equality policy in the firm. The EO manager, as we have seen, despite the difficult connotations of the word, used the term 'feminist' to describe the EO policy. She said, 'if feminism is recognising the legal, social and economic disadvantages of women and doing something to redress them, that is a feminist act, and that is what we are doing'. However, she deliberately underplayed the sexual harassment issue for fear of damaging the chances of the rest of the strategy. Her fears were undoubtedly justified. On one occasion when she proposed a meeting of women managers to discuss their special interests, the barrage of complaint from male managers led the chief executive to rule that the meeting must be held off premises and out of office hours. Despite her caution the EO manager was seen as 'a feminist'. It was only her obvious professionalism and her knowledge of EO policy and practice that saved her plausibility.

There was a clear difference, then, in the length of the EO agenda as intended by the firm's top management on the one hand and the EO activists on the other. There was a further clear distinction between committed men at the top and the more representative, hostile, male managers below them. The EO manager for her part had far-reaching intentions for organizational change in High Street Retail. She said in interview 'I'm a socialist as well as a feminist. I believe in equality *as such* and my feminism is very much bound up with that.' She had not been naive about how or how fast it would be possible to transform a capitalist business. 'I was under no illusion as to the ethos and values that would pertain. But in spite of that, and knowing the danger equal opportunities might be an exercise co-opted by management interests, I felt it was important to address it the way I would have wanted in an ideal organization. Hence the class dimension. That I shouldn't be fettered by what I knew the organization to be.' She felt, she said, that it was 'possible to achieve a more egalitarian management in the company in time, if there was a sustained commitment . . . dependent on many factors, and over a period of years, it could become a more democratic enterprise'.

Of her own accord, however, she resigned the job after three years – years she described as the most painful of her career. While the pro-equality managers were proud of their achievements, especially a modest increase of women in middle and upper management, she felt the adverse majority had won out. She felt she had failed. But this was in part because her goal had never been limited to 'rights' for high-flying women but had been a transformative one. She concluded 'The basically conservative management is retaining its hold, and that can be done by women as much as by men. It's *that* I see not changing.' Equality officers in other organizations report similar disappointments to these. It was the purpose of the research on which this book is based to explore the reasons why, and the processes in which, energetic equality strategies are curbed.

High Street Retail is only one example of many different kinds of organization introducing equal opportunities policies today. For the private sector, this firm represents a notable and serious attempt to change the organization in the name of sex (and race) equality. Being a private sector company, however, it is characterized by a motive of capital accumulation – in this it differs from a local authority or a voluntary organization that have a primarily social *raison d'être*. Yet it is a typical case of sex equality struggle in that it produced evidence of many different managerial aims and intentions. Indeed, my interviews revealed different aims among women too. Black women and white, women with children and without, manual and management women, feminists and anti-feminists, varied in their hopes and needs of the policy. The organization was typical too in throwing up two kinds of impediments to sex equality: institutional and cultural. The institutional impediments include structures, procedures and rules. Cultural impediments arise in discourse and interaction. They influence what women and men feel, think and do. The two levels are interactive. Structures can be changed in the right cultural environment. But structures predispose how people think and act. Such processes are the subject of ensuing chapters.

2

Room at the top

'Equal opportunities' in organizations, if it means nothing else to those who introduce the policy, means ending the sexual division of labour. It means breaking down the barriers that prevent horizontal movement by women into non-traditional jobs, and removing those that confine women to the meanest jobs and prevent their vertical progress to different levels and locations in the hierarchy. It says to women 'There's room at the top'. This is the first item on the agenda of positive action in all organizations. It entails opening access to the organization by fair recruitment practices; supplementary training courses for women; a review of procedures for appraisal and promotion; and ultimately an acknowledgment of the abilities and authority women thus develop, as managers, technologists, professionals.

We shall see that despite its quite transparent fairness such a policy is not easy to implement. It means confronting head-on men's sense of owning the organization. And it means intervening in the ferocious class and race rivalries that characterize male–male relations in the hierarchy. More problematic yet for women is that a focus on the right of women to a climbing gradient in the organization similar to that of men, the right to a place in the 'fast lane', is often used by employers as a device to limit positive action to an agenda that for them is relatively low cost and even has advantages. Women after all are an under-developed resource for the organization. Thus help may be afforded to a few relatively privileged women, dividing them from the remainder whom the organization continues to exploit in the manner to which it is accustomed, indeed on which it depends.

We must put aside this contradiction for the moment, however, to look at what happens when positive action for sex equality introduces to men the idea that women too can run organizations, control computers and manage men. Many women may write this off as 'mere' liberal feminism, women buying into the system. Men nonetheless often respond as though the end of the world were at hand.

As mentioned in Chapter 1, the hierarchical relations of feudalism gave way in Western Europe between the sixteenth and eighteenth centuries to a capitalist mode of production which, despite the rhetoric of 'liberty, equality, fraternity', was itself hierarchical. Workers took orders; capitalists ruled, not by virtue of birth, of course, but of wealth. The difference was that in theory all men were now free to better themselves. Relations between men in modern 'fraternal' patriarchy were *competitive*.

Capitalism has its own characteristic use for hierarchical organization. Controlling an increasingly subdivided and specialised labour force in increasingly extensive operations called for scientific management with a clear chain of command (Marglin 1976). Soon, however, capitalist firms grew too big and too complex for control by a simple hierarchy of boss, foreman, worker. *Bureaucracy* was a response to these new needs. It 'enabled enterprises to transcend the limits of direct, extensive and formal control in commerce and business either by paternalistic owners or, in governance more specifically political, the role of traditional or charismatic persons' (Clegg and Dunkerley 1980:76).

Bureaucratic hierarchical organization, then, is one face of the social contract. Bureaucracies get their authority in the eyes of those who work in them and have business with them from the sense not of dealing with some despotic ruler but belonging to a rational technical order. Max Weber, in his seminal work on bureaucracy, defined it as an order legitimated not by the charisma of a leader nor the weight of tradition but from observance of a code, written or unwritten, of rational precepts and rules (Weber 1947).

The formal diagrams of authority described by Weber, however, have long been recognized as an incomplete picture of power in organizations since they were not able to reveal the cross-weaving of the structure by less formal relations of power, the 'values and patterns of behaviour which are independent of these formal rules and which develop out of the interaction of persons in groups in the organization' (Clegg and Dunkerley 1980:132). Feminist research has shown how the sex-composition of labour force and management creates a dynamic of differential exploitation, manoeuvrability and power that affects the working life of every woman (Pollert 1981, Cavendish 1982, Wajcman 1983). In this chapter we will see something of the contrasted experiences of women and men in real-life organizational hierarchies.

Women and power: High Street Retail

In structure High Street Retail was a typical capitalist enterprise, governed by a board of directors, with a powerful chief executive and an executive group above an orderly ranking of divisions and departments. The organizational 'tree' of jobs is a misnomer, for a hierarchy is a tree standing on its head, a chief executive at the top with lines of authority and responsibility branching downwards to the mass of lowly functions at the base. In this changing business, however, formal rules were few and there was a high degree of managerial discretion. Where the chairman of the board had formerly been 'god', now the new-style senior managers were encouraged to think for themselves. It was recognised 'these are creative people who will have to be allowed to make their contribution if they're not to be very, very frustrated'. Discretion entered human resource management too. People in High Street Retail were groomed for this job or that; 'succession planning' was seen as good management. There was scope therefore for a manager simply to promote competent women if he so wished.

By the same reckoning, however, in such an organization changes occurring in parallel with equal opportunities could have the effect of stemming the erosion of male supremacy threatened by women's advance in the organization. For example, while women were being encouraged into store management today, the significance of the job in the overall power system of the firm seemed to be melting away. At one time it had been inconceivable that a woman could do the job of store manager. 'Pairs of trousers' were what was called for on the retail floor. Even after the Sex Discrimination Act 1975 there was an unofficial quota in the firm limiting women to 25% of store manager recruits. In those days this job was the classic route to power in the firm. The executive committee was comprised almost entirely of ex-store managers. Recruitment to store management was important enough to be done centrally to ensure the 'right type'. It was a white male stronghold.

By contrast, in 1988 after two years of positive action, 12% of store managers and 50% of trainees for this post were female. The personnel director was saying that as far as he was concerned 100% female store management would not be too much of a good thing. (There were a number of black store managers too. After some hesitation it had been accepted that wearing a turban should not debar a Sikh from this job.) But there were fewer ex-store managers in top jobs in the firm today and recruitment had been regionalised. The computer specialists, the marketing, advertising and public relations types, these were now the people on whom the company most depended and the attitude to store management had subtly changed. It was now acceptable that some managers settle in for long periods at that level. There was a move towards a new kind of smaller, more specialised high street shop, to supplement the big department stores. While some progressive personnel managers saw the management of these mini-stores as a great new opportunity for women (which in a sense it was) others saw women more instrumentally. Not only did women have a nice way with the customer, they could be relied on not to crowd the promotion ladder. The manager in charge of the store's expansion programme said,

> what I can't have is sixty very ambitious people as store managers. I only want ten very ambitious people. Fifty I see as being hardcore managers, permanent in the areas where they are. And what I'm looking for, crudely, is thirty- to forty-year old females, with a good retail background, who are a very effective and very efficient in their job but, because of their domestic circumstances, won't want to move.

Beavering in the bureaucracy

This manipulability of function, structure and staffing practices, characteristic of some businesses, is not, however, a feature of all organizations. I encountered one in particular where the hierarchy was so formal, the rules so bureaucratic and explicit, as to offer a productive contrast to High Street Retail. It was different in another way too. The sex-typing of people and jobs, which made possible this boxing and coxing with the nature, representation and staffing of store management, barely existed here.

A civil service department is a near-classic bureaucracy. The department in question – I'll call it simply the Service – had, in 1989, tens of thousands of employees located in a London head office and in divisional and district offices up and down the country. Its function, like that of any government agency, was directed by the will of politicians and constrained by a framework of laws and precedents. Not even the most senior officer here had complete discretion. 'There are extraordinarily few things', said one such 'of which I could say "we'll definitely do it *this* way".' By virtue of their specialist knowledge, however, the top-rankers were among the Whitehall 'mandarins', white men with power and influence as advisers.

The structure of the Service had changed in recent decades, though as with the careers it enabled, the pace tended to be of geomorphological gradualness. There had once been a clear-cut three-part pyramid. A group I shall call the 'elite corps' comprised the small top segment. They came direct from university and were put through the Service's own professional training and over a succession of exam hurdles. They were the ones who ran the Service. Beneath them was a broader and flatter segment of officers known as 'the clerical grades'. The senior clericals were executives, the more junior were administrators, all pen-pushers concerned with the mass of paper and figure work that was the staple of the Service's role. They were recruited from school at 16 or 18 years and given the appropriate training for each grade. The bottom-most segment was barely part of the hierarchy at all, since it was made up of 'unestablished' people with no civil service training. They included typists, telephonists, porters and cleaners. If the scope of the internal labour market for the clericals was limited, for the base-line workers it was non-existent.

The period between the Second World War and today has seen the insertion one after another of a number of intermediate professional grades between the clericals and the elite, providing more of a career-path for those who began without the advantage of a degree. Some of these professional posts were technical, others managerial. The invidious distinction between established and temporary staff was removed and, in theory though seldom in practice, the 'support grades' could now climb the ladder to the clericals and thence to professional qualification for the elite posts.

The position of women in this hierarchy has been the subject of bitter struggle since women were first introduced to the civil service as telegraphists in 1870. The Treasury had managed to win an exemption for the Civil Service from the requirements of the Sex Discrimination (Removal) Act 1919. It continued to operate a 'marriage bar'. Women had to choose: a career in the Civil Service or marriage, not both (Sanderson 1989). Women organized actively for equality in the Civil Service, however, and were particularly vocal in the period following both world wars. As in other employment, women were drawn into quite high grades as substitutes for the men who had gone on active service. Employment in government services, however, was seen as the natural place for hundreds of thousands of men returning from the war, especially those with injuries who could not compete adequately for jobs in industry. Those men today who say positive discrimination is 'unfair to the rest of us' should remember this instance. Women were exhorted to give up their places to these deserving men. Promotion opportunities for those that remained shrank to nil. Ex-servicemen appeared on the scene at an opportune moment, Meta Zimmeck argues, when women were in a strong tactical position due to wartime substitution and were

> threatening to translate this into solid gains. Although elite men at times found coping with their gallant allies a strain, they recognized that they were nevertheless a godsend, willing and eager cannon fodder in the war between the sexes . . . [In the years following 1914] playing the ex-service card . . . contained the most urgent threat to the gentlemen of Whitehall, that of women . . . . (Zimmeck 1988:89).

The same re-establishment of male sex-right occurred after the Second World War. Mary Tomkins, a clerical grade woman I met during my research in the Service, provides a good example of one of the submerged women. She entered the Service soon after the war but, despite an uninterrupted working life, 44 years later she had obtained one single promotion. In that career she had trained many younger people and seen them promoted over her. She was a single woman who had watched most of the young female school-leavers who entered with her marry those ambitious ex-servicemen and leave the Service. She had remained to compete (unsuccessfully) with their husbands. Mary described how, in spite of having a dependent widowed mother and young brother and sister to maintain on her meagre salary, she had been continually passed over for promotion because 'so-and-so is a family man and he deserves it more than you'. She pointed out wryly that many of these men were heavy drinkers and far from responsible family breadwinners. Eventually a maximum age barrier had caught her and held her down. Mary's story was a stark reminder of the importance even of the 'short agenda' of equal opportunities: removing discriminatory rules and attitudes that bar women from advancement.

By the 1960s, however, it was becoming more common to find a woman in the senior clerical grade and even a few women professionals were in evidence. At first both men and women were startled to encounter them, but soon they were no longer a novelty. Today 65% of the clerical grades (which account for 90% of Service jobs) are women. Women are almost half of senior clerical grade and, besides, about one in five of the various middle grades of professionals. Their numbers fall off sharply towards the top, however, with one in thirteen of the senior professional jobs. They are entirely absent from the top four grades of the elite corps and from the Service's governing body. Significantly, only half the percentage of women as of men are recruited as graduates.

Civil service women (and we are talking of course of women almost all of whom at this time would have been white) had won fully equal pay by 1961. Bucking the postwar culture of 'women back to the home' they had achieved the scrapping of the marriage bar in 1946. They had been active in lobbying nationally over the equality reforms in the 1970s. The introduction in the 1980s of a positive action policy for sex equality in the Civil Service therefore responded to the determination of women civil servants to see career barriers finally dismantled. In 1980 the National Whitley Council, the industrial relations machinery of the Civil Service, prompted by its union side and especially by women in the unions, set up a review group on women's equality (Management and Personnel Office 1982). Its report made public what women already knew: that women civil servants did most of the grafting and got few of the rewards. The report led the Office of the Minister for the Civil Service (OMCS) to issue a programme of action in which it urged government departments to set up equality committees, appoint equality officers and introduce positive measures for women (Management and Personnel Office 1984).

Embarking on 'equal opportunities'

In the Service, equal opportunities was simultaneously a policy against race and sex discrimination, for, like the Civil Service as a whole, it remained disproportionately white. The departmental personnel division was made responsible. The fifteen divisional personnel officers, quite highly graded professionals and therefore all men, and white, were designated 'equality officers' for race and sex and told they were expected to devote 5–10% of their time to this novel task. The departmental personnel officer at head office became the chief equality officer for the Service. He and his deputy were also male and again white. (It was only two years later that (white) women succeeded them in these roles.) An equal opportunities committee was set up and in this, in contrast to that of High Street Retail, the unions were closely involved. One particularly active feminist, a senior officer in the union organizing most of the clericals, was, over several years, a key figure in motivating positive action.

In 1987 an EO guide was circulated to staff, guaranteeing no 'direct or indirect discrimination against any eligible person on the grounds of race, religion, sex or marital status, or sexual orientation, whether in the field of recruitment, promotion, training or transfers'. A separate clause referred to people with disabilities. The policy included computerized monitoring of the workforce by ethnic group and sex and a recruitment campaign directed particularly to women and ethnic minorities. The number of people of ethnic minorities in clerical grades was by now 6% in the case of men, 4.5% in the case of women. There were a few among the professionals. The elite, however, remained 99% white. By now clerical grade recruitment was substantially female.

Except for the elite, there was very little external recruitment above the clerical grades. It was therefore equal chances in *promotion* that had more significance for women in the Service. The appraisal and reporting process had recently been made more open and accountable mainly as a democratizing move but also in the hope of weeding out covert marking-down of women, white and black, and black men. As one put it, what a reporting officer wanted to see in a budding professional was 'someone of whom he could say "I was just like him at his age".' White men had simply been reproducing themselves. Practical measures were introduced. Previously, promotion chances had been governed strictly by time served. This disadvantaged women, many of whom, due to child-rearing, either started their careers late or saw them interrupted. These rules were now amended. So too were the requirements on geographical mobility. Women, due to the primacy usually given to a husband's career, had more often than men been unable to comply with the ruling that professionals must accept a posting anywhere they are sent. This requirement too was modified. There was, however, at this stage, very little emphasis on changing attitudes through training in EO principle and practice. Nor was there any significant supplementary staff development training for women.

On the other hand, as a result of the equality initiative, a concern with maternity was now very much in evidence. The few women who had progressed to higher grades in the Service in the past had tended to be unmarried or at least childless. Much of the import of the EO policy was to help women with children and other caring commitments to join them. The Service introduced flexible working hours; special leave for domestic purposes; improved maternity provision; and a domestic-absence reinstatement scheme to encourage the return of women after a child-rearing break. Nursery provision was being developed experimentally at selected sites. The civil service traditionally makes little use of part-timing, partly perhaps a hang-over from 'marriage bar' days, partly because the trade unions had remained rigidly opposed to it. Now, under the EO policy it was announced that anyone might request a reduction in their hours. By 1989 it seemed likely that recruitment on a part-time basis would be introduced within a few years. There was no sign of a slackening of momentum in the Service's equality strategy. They were pressing ahead with ethnic monitoring. High-tech equipment was to be obtained to give reality to the policy on employment of people with disabilities. A programme to create crèches and holiday play schemes was in hand.

It is both cause and effect of the equality initiative that today women are acutely aware of the quite open prejudice and discrimination that operated against women in the past. Even five years previously, when applying for jobs women were routinely questioned about their domestic circumstances. It seems too that sexual harassment and pressure was common. One woman said she, and other women of whom she knew, had been held back during her young years by a reporting officer who made sexual approaches to which she was unresponsive. But above all, women had been held back by a simple assumption on the part of all managers: 'they just never thought women might *want* promotion.'

Though the marriage-bar in the civil service was long gone, informal discrimination against married women was probably the main continuing source of disadvantage affecting women in the Service. I met one senior woman who, though she had long been in a stable partnership and had reared children, had decided from the start to cohabit rather than marry, so as not to risk being penalised in her Service career. Another had deferred the announcement of her recent engagement until after her promotion was confirmed, 'just to be safe'. It was usually taken, often without asking the woman in question, that a married woman would not be prepared to be geographically mobile. Her husband's job was assumed to take preference. In practical terms of course having children has in any case held women back. The training for the elite corps, for example, usually occurs in one's late twenties. It therefore clashes with the period of a woman's life when she is most likely to have the time-consuming tasks associated with a young family. As a result of such problems, women felt 'at any level in the Service you'll find women on the whole are better than the men of comparable grade'.

The majority of women I spoke with felt prejudice against women in senior posts still to exist today, though it was, they said, less institutional than personal and therefore difficult to pin down or prove. Much depended on the officers responsible for assessing your performance each year – your 'reporting' and 'counter-signing' officer. If they seemed to 'have it in for you' you could not know if the reason was a personality clash or that you were a woman. Over the years the key point of discrimination in the Service, women's 'ceiling', had shifted upwards from upper clerical to junior professional and was now at the step between junior and middle professional grades. As you go higher the group of women gets smaller. One woman felt the higher the role the less would aberrants be tolerated – and women were still considered anomalies. 'Yet you do hear of men who are a bit – who don't quite *fit* – and yet they get selected.' A lesbian clerical told me she had had a succession of promotable reports without getting promotion. She had put in two requests for appeal but had been refused a hearing by the personnel managers. She felt, 'it still seems to be the standard heterosexual settled *man* that gets promotion'. Likewise one could say that a sari or a turban somehow just didn't fit the image. It was still the bowler-hat brigade they were looking for.

The masculine hierarchy

I interviewed twenty-six men of the Service and encountered many more. If those of the elite corps still retain the Oxbridge patina and the plummy accent, it has to be said that the middle-rank professionals today are typically rather classless, bespectacled, industrious desk-men. Politically strung on a line between *The Daily Telegraph* and the *Guardian*, many are liberals. A young woman, observing them from far below, said 'they are nice people to work with, polite kind of people'. These men do not have the machismo of the industrialist, the soldier or the engineer. Yet on talking with them it immediately becomes apparent that the civil service hierarchy they belong to is, in their minds, every bit as masculine as that of a business enterprise or the army. Though women have penetrated up its ranks, at each step they have been considered intruders. 'Not *me* of course' said one man, 'but there are *some* people, very *nice* people, who think a woman's place is at home.' Even today the Service remains in men's minds a male hierarchy with women in it.

It seems that the natural condition for an organization is to be comprised of a populous base that is not really part of the hierarchy and is the place where women are found. This reflects the finding of Annike Baude's research: that women characteristically do not move from this base – they do not operate as men do within the 'internal labour market' of the organizations in which they work. When they change jobs they change employers (Baude 1990). The hierarchy within organizations should realistically be seen as beginning at a point above this base. In the Service the base had been the 'support grades'. The hierarchy in all practical terms had begun with the bottom grade of the clericals, the GCE O-level entrants.

A second striking fact about the Service, seen through men's eyes, was the extent to which this hierarchy was in a condition of flux, in which authority was being reproduced in new forms. The upper ranks of the civil service have traditionally been the backbone of the British Establishment. As one of the Service elite put it, we were 'destined for the highest echelons of the professional life of this country'. There used to be a marked class homogeneity. A cockney accent or a lack of grooming would hold you back. It is not surprising then that members of such a class-system routinely 'pulled rank'. The kind of officer who headed the local office 'sat behind closed doors and expected to be treated as a little god'. As one clerical remembered it, 'he appeared at Christmas time, shook hands and disappeared again till next year'. There was little social mixing between the grades.

The break-up of this authoritarian patriarchal regime had occurred, it seems, in two stages. First, class privilege had given way to meritocracy. More ordinary mortals were permitted a route up the career structure, but in a process still strictly governed by seniority and qualification. The second phase, in response to the shortage of labour at certain periods, particularly in London and the South East, had been a relaxing of the entry requirements, the minimum age barriers and the time-service required at each stage. Along with this had come a new and shocking informality. It seemed to the oldsters that the young ones now were hurried up the ladder without having to prove themselves. Standards of literacy had fallen, but nobody seemed to care. 'People now are taught to cut corners and not bother if things aren't properly done.' You began to see clerical men in jeans, with strange hair-cuts and even with an earring. First names began to replace the traditional Mr., Mrs. and Miss. It all seemed a far cry from the days when it was 'very much the three-piece suit, extremely serious, very very Oxbridge', as one old hand remembered.

The computer, sweeping its way through all the Service's functions, had shaken the confidence of some professionals. 'For thirty years you always knew what you were talking about. All of a sudden someone snatched the carpet from under your feet. You sat round the table with all these computer people and you had to tell them, "treat me as an idiot!"' The computer division with its different priorities had introduced an anti-hierarchical, anti-proce-dural spirit. 'It's very free and easy here. Everyone's on first-name terms.' Its director bent all the rules he could. He said, 'I believe the most important thing is to create a thrustful, forceful environment and give people some freedom.' He prided himself on the team feeling he had built and the autonomy he had carved out for his team. Some of the traditionals feared this ethos was a virus spreading throughout the Service.

These transformations had received considerable impulsion from Thatcherism. The Treasury's 'financial management initiative' was devolving control over spending to individual departments whose divisions were made responsible for setting and meeting objectives within cost. Associated staff cuts were resulting in intensification of work. Some felt this was a source of falling standards of professionalism. The civil service was increasingly expected to adopt modern business management methods (Jenkins *et al.* 1988). 'Alternative working patterns' were being pursued with all the Conservative administration's fervour for deregulation (Cabinet Office 1987). Flexitime had long ago been adopted. If the developments in the Service's management philosophy and practice echo those we noted in High Street Retail this is no coincidence. It was the new eighties enterprise culture bearing on British management everywhere, private sector and public sector alike.

The myth of the 'end of patriarchy' analysed by Carole Pateman (1988) and discussed in the preceding chapter, suggests that the patriarchal hierarchies were overthrown once and for all with the bourgeois revolutions and the emergence of capitalist wage-labour relations, the modern democratic state and civil society. This epochal moment is symbolised in such events as the storming of the Bastille, the beheading of Charles I. But of course the process continues. The 'brothers' are obliged continually to re-enact the struggle against 'the fathers'. The reign of the Victorian autocrat was challenged by Edwardian youth, especially those who earned their manhood in the horrors of the First World War. The permissive students of the 1960s rebelled against the conformist society of their fathers. And in recent years in the drab corridors of the Service amid the filing cabinets, the red tape and the tomes on procedure, among these gentle, often kindly men, a similar slow-motion parricide had been in progress. The result of such changes was contradictory for men. A democratizing and opening of the hierarchy had clearly benefited men of the lower ranks, but the process had at the same time had the effect of diluting patriarchal authority over women and creating an environment less inimical to women's progress.

Capitalism and patriarchy in tension

The third notable feature of social relations in the Service hierarchy was the resulting rivalry between various groups of men. Promotion was and still is performed by promotion boards dealing with whole cohorts of staff. Those who had progressed sufficiently in training and qualification to warrant promotion, had served the requisite number of years and had a 'promotable' report, would watch the noticeboards in anticipation. While in a company like High Street Retail, therefore, competition pits one man against the next, the rivalries in the Service were less individual than typological.

Early in the century a civil servant in a similar bureaucracy wrote a novel in which he railed against its class distinctions. He saw, as he put it, a 'Line' separating lower and higher grades.

It's what's below *them* and above us, and it's what we can't pass. We're not good enough . . . . Do you see how we're labelled, each man with his little *Mister* and his little salary? That's official etiquette. Above the Line you're an Esquire, below it you're plain Mister and be damned to you (cited in Zimmeck 1986:161).

This bitterness lives on today. Clerical men told me they felt like second-class citizens compared to the professionals. Professionals who had gone the exam route resented the 'instant success' of those who reached the same grade as unqualified administrators. Head office staff were seen as 'a bit privileged' compared with those of the regions and districts. Those in the new charmed circle of computer division were felt to be 'the tail now wagging the dog'. But I was left in no doubt that the sharpest distinction felt by the brothers of the Service was that between the ordinary professionals and the elite corps. The elite, who have that special training and that exam, 'get looked up to. Those who haven't, however clever and quick-witted they may be, are never regarded in quite the same way.' 'One of them is never put in a position where he has to be answerable to one of us.' 'They pat the rest of us on the head . . . I think it's a shocking system.' They were speaking of their class superiors rather as women speak of men.

Patriarchy has, as we have seen, been described as 'a set of social relations which has a material base and in which there are hierarchical relations between men and solidarity among them, which enable them to control women' (Hartmann 1979:232). The above picture has shown something of those hierarchical man–man relations and the internal tension that continually threatens cohesion. Though it may impress women with its united resistance to *them*, the brotherhood has difficulty in sustaining solidarity. The hierarchies of class and organizational power are besides structured also by race. As Stuart Hall put it, the class relations which inscribe the black fractions of the working class function as race relations. 'The two are inseparable. Race is the modality in which class is lived. It is also the medium in which class relations are experienced (Hall 1978:394).' Friction between men in organizations is endemic.

The issue of 'more women' encroaching up the male hierarchy therefore arises in an environment in which a man's status and chances relative to each other are already problematised. An individual man may not feel himself to be in personal competition with an individual woman, but the presence of a whole new group in the competition for advancement was clear to all. As Crompton and Jones (1984:248) have pointed out, men's characteristic career paths in office work are predicated on the existence of 'unpromotable' categories – women, black people, older people. 'Even quite small changes in the proportion of women who achieve promotion may have a significant impact on male career patterns.' The new times in the Service therefore therefore had a painful ambiguity for men, especially white men. They had opened up a career path out of the clerical grades for men of merit. Simultaneously, however, these grades had come to be predominantly female and increasingly black.

If the changing culture had contradictory implications for men, one factor was seen as wholly negative. They believed the presence of women in the clerical grades kept salaries low. Women do not 'need' and therefore are not paid the 'family wage' a man expects from his employer. Women are not taken seriously by those with the power to determine salary levels. Besides, men believe, the unions have 'gone soft' due to their large female membership. It is a vicious circle in which men perceive themselves caught. As a result of the feminization, fewer men are attracted to the jobs, now seen as lacking importance. A similar phenomenon was observed by Game and Pringle in the Australian banking industry. 'Men will frequently say that they would not allow a son to go into banking . . . it was seen as "poofy". Bank work is now women's work' (Game and Pringle 1983:57). In any case, men in the Service's clerical grades say, they cannot afford to live and keep a family on such 'women's pay'. There is an unpleasant feeling among professionals in the Service that the 'real men' today – the Carling Black Label men – are the ones who take the training then leave to earn 'twice as much' in the private sector.

How is it then, given the disapproval of many men, that women have been admitted in such numbers to the fraternal hierarchy of the Service? First, men do not have absolute control over these things. Women themselves seek jobs and careers, and women's struggle for equality in society over two centuries has created a social environment in which it can no longer be represented as legitimate to exclude women. To a degree the social and sexual contracts that are the basis of modern society are being autonomously rewritten by women in their own hand. Secondly, however, capitalist accumulation in industry and cost-efficiency in service organizations depend on the sex-specific exploitation of women. We shall have occasion to explore this in greater depth in Chapters 3 and 4. The attractions for employers of female labour, cheapened by the domestic subordination of women to men, has always produced tension and contradiction in the complex social relation that is patriarchal capitalism.

Even in a capitalist world, profit now and then has to be subordinated to other priorities. Employers will sometimes forgo immediate profit in the interests of increasing their long-term control over the labour force. We know that they will likewise sometimes act in ways apparently at odds with their capitalist goals in order to maintain the sexual division of labour (Game and Pringle 1983:22). Why? Because employers too are men and operate within a capitalism that is patriarchal. Capitalist and patriarchal principles, class and gender relations, are sometimes in contradiction. At times the big men, those with authority in organizations, find it impossible to *both* maximise accumulation or cost-efficiency *and* stick to the terms of their hidden but nonetheless compelling deal with lesser men to guarantee their sex-right.

From the evidence in both High Street Retail and the Service we get a better grasp of the operation of that set of conventions and expectations we are calling the sexual contract, the understanding men have historically entered into with one another concerning women. I suggest it may help to distinguish two 'clauses' in this contract. The 'domestic clause', if we may call it that, is an understanding that in ideal circumstances each man may have authority over the person and labour of a wife as housekeeper, child-rearer and sexual partner in the home.

There is, however, also a 'workplace clause' to the sexual contract. Men guarantee each other rights over women in paid employment and in the organizations in which they work. In reality the domestic clause has often been flouted by ruling-class men, since the process of accumulation launched by patriarchal capitalism called for the exploitation of working-class women, not only in their continuing role as unpaid domestics reproducing the labour power of husband and sons for the employer, but also and increasingly as a specially cheap and subordinated form of wage labour. The big men, to get big, need to milk the possibilities inherent in the patriarchal control of lesser men over their womenfolk. However, in mitigation of this disloyalty to their brethren, the terms of the sexual contract are, so to speak, extended to the workplace. Here the employer and his managers have been obliged to negotiate not only with individual male employees but with the unions representing their interests. For these 'junior partners in capitalist society' (Rowthorne 1976:64) are likewise the junior partners in patriarchy.

So the employer has successively fallen back on new promises, each in turn broken as changes in production called for new labour market strategies. The deal was, first, if due to the exigencies of accumulation and cost-efficiency, women must be drawn into the labour market, it will be as far as possible unmarried women who are so used. A relic of this aspect of the sexual contract lived on, as we have seen, until 1946 in the civil service's marriage-bar. When, however, economic pressures relentlessly push the employer to break his bargain with his male worker and draw this worker's wife (unlike his own) into the workplace alongside the man, the sexual contract is revised, one might say, to read: we assure you that married women will work only on the bottom rung of the ladder, indeed in a women's sphere below the point where the ladder begins. An important additional understanding is: women and men will be employed in gender-differentiated work so as to avoid any invidious comparison of men with women and to prevent any intrusion of women into male social space. As Sylvia Walby says of the these joint practices of exclusion and segregation, 'it is almost never the case that a union which included men did not follow one of these two patriarchal strategies' (Walby 1986:244). And employers have often, when economic pressures either permitted or favoured such a strategy, observed the men's interests in this way.

Unfortunately, in High Street Retail, women were increasingly needed in merchandising, buying, even management. In the Service they were needed, especially in the two world wars, in the clerical grades. The deal with male employees then retreats one more step to the position: men's superiority will be guaranteed by the device of paying women less for the same work. Employers of course benefit *qua* employers from the existence of a secondary and cheaper labour supply. This was the state of affairs the Equal Pay Act 1970 purported to bring to an end.

When occupational sex-segregation proves a possibility, as it usually does, but where women either press for promotion or are needed by the employer in supervisory positions over other women, the employer often creates small hierarchies mainly of women, situated to one side of and a little below other pyramids comprised mainly of men, with no career bridge connecting the two paths. This is assisted by the fact that many married women work part-time and that senior jobs are invariably specified as full-time. Thus in High Street Retail even today women inhabiting various characteristically female roles were complaining that their chances 'ceilinged out' a grade or so higher, while men had the whole organizational tree to play in.

One agreement on which so far employers have stood solidly alongside their male employees is the whole issue of the value placed on work that is characteristically women's work. The provision for women to claim 'equal pay for work of equal value', which presents itself as a mere addendum to the law on equal pay for like work, is in fact a qualitatively more serious incursion on male-sex right. Employers – whether capitalist or state – here, however, share an interest with their men in resisting it because it potentially undermines the whole strategy of exploiting women sex-specifically.

A further step in the big man-little man negotiation is that, on the whole, women will be confined to manual work while men will do the mental work. Increasingly, however, women's labour power has been needed in middle management. The anticipated shortage of young recruits to the labour force in the 1990s is currently sharpening employers' interest in older women – and not only for manual jobs. Besides, as we have seen, women are themselves forcing an entry, backed by law. The deal the male employer and male employee then attempt to sustain is that a woman will never, circumstances permitting, be placed in direct line of authority over a man. Women at or near the top of organizations will be as far as possible in sex-differentiated roles. They will become the personnel managers and public relations officers rather than production managers, staff rather than line.

It should be remembered, however, that the erosion of male sex-right is assisted by the fact that recruitment and promotion decisions are always made two or three steps above the grade at which the appointment is to be made. It is bigger men who (if necessity compels) will make the decision to introduce a woman as equal colleague of certain lesser men. They may well dislike the precedent and fear for the implications. It damages the fratriarchal principle and may even cause ructions. But it will not hurt them personally.

Finally, should women by some relentless and wholly undesirable process come to dominate a field of employment, a profession or an occupation, the patriarchal relations of the external world come into play. The whole field is rapidly devalued relative to male fields. As in High Street Retail, when women are needed in the store manager job, men find better things to do. Karen Legge likewise has shown that women's widespread success in personnel management has been a hollow victory. When women have power within an occupation, she says, you can bet it is because that occupation has yet to attain power or (as is the case with personnel management) is losing ground within the organization or in the eyes of society (Legge 1987).

Cultural resistance by men

Helped, then, by a relative homogeneity and absence of sex-stereotyping in the Service's jobs, and by the priority given to the internal labour market and the formality of promotion procedures which allow for the removal of sex-bias, women, already dominant in the clerical grades, are now penetrating the professional grades and are poised for entry in much greater numbers than ever before into the elite upper reaches of the Service. Their harbingers are already in place, a handful of impressive, competent and effective women. So far, they are all white. However, in some local offices, particularly in London where an acute staff shortage has vexed the personnel managers, the race composition as well as the sex composition of the workforce has changed dramatically. I visited one district office, headed by a white woman, where a majority of the staff were now drawn from the local Asian community. The majority of these, and of the white staff, were women. The white woman in charge represented a fresh principle and style of management entering the elite corps. Her door was always open, she put human relationships first. The womanly atmosphere of the bi-cultural office was one of good humour and sociability. A white man I interviewed there not unsurprisingly felt the revolution had already occurred. It was no longer *his* place.

In a situation where the practical mechanisms assisting the retention of male control at all levels in society are successively challenged in the way described above and new devices for maintaining control are continually called for, it is not surprising that men were often to be heard affirming and reaffirming the validity of the *status quo ante*. In most studies of 'women and management', a theme of which there is now extensive analysis (see for instance Hennig and Jardim 1978, Marshall 1984, Hammond 1988, Coyle 1989), men are found to be culturally active in creating an environment in which 'women don't flourish'. Often the exclusionary practices are oblique. Rosabeth Moss Kanter for instance in her study of managers in a large US corporation found that the need for smooth communication and for the reduction of uncertainty in business life drove managers towards homogeneity and conformity: men liked working with those they were most sure of – other men (Kanter 1977). Often men are observed to generate a masculine culture in and around their work, whether this is technological or managerial, that can make women feel, without being told in so many words, 'you are out of place here' (Cockburn 1983 and 1985). In the context of Northern Ireland's new positive strategy for 'Fair Employment' they speak of 'the chill factor'. Catholics or Protestants create cultures in the workplace that freeze the other group out (Department of Economic Development 1989). Women in the upper reaches of the Service likewise often encounter a cool environment. As Patricia Walters says in her study of women in the civil service, it is a culture which 'opens itself to women and yet squeezes them out; which integrates them, yet marginalizes them' (Walters 1987:14). Men's discourse can be seen in many cases to cement relations among men, to put women down and to minimize the impact of the equality strategy.

I met a few men – very few it has to be said – who were supportive not only of women's progress in the Service, but also of the aims of the equality policy and the women's movement, society-wide. In the tolerant atmosphere of the Service it was easier for such thoughtful, unconventional men to survive than in the business ethos of High Street Retail. The predominant view, however, was very different. Most men told me women's complaints of inequality were quite unfounded. Today (men believe) women compete on entirely equal terms with men. Just look after all at the way men are being 'swamped' with women in the clerical grades. 'The floodgates have been opened.' Men feel they are up against 'absolutely fierce, energetic and competent' women in the professional grades too, though the numbers involved are less alarming. If women are not getting on in the Service today it is purely and simply 'the handicap imposed on them by nature', or because they have *chosen* to give priority to their home lives. While fairness to the sexes is right, in men's view, 'positive action for women' has now made men the disadvantaged sex. 'I really think it is getting to the stage where it is positive reverse discrimination. It is happening. And females can take advantage of it', said a very senior male personnel officer, who in title, but hardly in spirit, was now an equality officer.

Men I spoke with therefore chose to diminish the equality initiative. In terms of day-to-day work, 'it is not something one ever really considers', 'we tend to ignore it really', I don't read that stuff, I think I would disagree with it'. In the personnel sections, among very senior men with specific responsibility for equal opportunities and those who sit frequently on selection boards, the policy of course has greater salience. But among men who have no such responsibilities the initiative is little more than a source of wry humour. The woman newly created deputy equal opportunities officer for head office was pitied and teased by some of her male colleagues. 'We ring her up. "I am black, disabled, Jewish, female and lesbian. Why aren't I chairman of the board?" She gets a lot of ragging from us. I think there's a general impression it [EO] has been overdone.'

Lower-class white men, who, as we have seen, are characteristically in the support grades and clerical grades that have seen the greatest influx of women, black and white, and black men, felt particularly damaged by the equality movement. A white working-class man said 'the women are OK, the black people are OK, even the disabled people are OK. But me, I'm white, male, average height – who do I turn to?' Of only two or three men out of the thirty I interviewed in the Service would it be possible to say they were self-motivating and pro-active on equality issues. It has to be added that ethnic minority men were no less negative than white men about positive action for sex equality both in the Service and High Street Retail.

Men's resentment against women surfaced in a number of different forms. Women found some of their male subordinates unwilling to accept their authority. Most women were able to call to mind men who 'had got a chip on their shoulder', were 'awkward', who 'created undercurrents' or would comment on another man 'What? Working for a *woman*?' 'I haven't got to work for this *little girl*, have I?' Some women suspected that more hostility existed than met the eye. 'Nobody would dare express it. Because everybody nowadays is watching for their promotions. So they don't say much. But you see a slightly sulky look when they're asked to do something by a woman.'

There was resentment of women's successes. Very successful women are often made 'targets of a lot of hostility and comment'. When a successful woman fails or has a setback there is 'a lot of crowing over the humiliation'. Men readily refer to the highest-ranking women as 'tokens', supposing that they are not there because they are competent but because they are equality flag-ships. Top women are often labelled by men 'hard as nails', 'tough as old boots'. Conversely, and with blithe disregard for logic, men sometimes suppose that women obtain their successes in the Service by 'fluttering their eyelashes' at male superiors. Men, said a woman, can certainly 'bitch'.

Men show particular resentment of women for what they hold is their manipulation of the 'mobility' rules. As mentioned above, until very recently nobody was considered for training or promotion to professional status before declaring a readiness to accept a posting anywhere in Britain. Men hated this rule as much as women. What stirred the men's ire, however, was that, as they saw it, women cheated. First they often bluffed or frankly lied about their willingness to be mobile, relying on personnel department never to put it to the test; second, personnel was held to be soft on women anyway, posting men to distant places while allowing women to work near home out of respect for their husbands' more important jobs. So one man said he felt the rules were 'blatantly and provocatively' bent in favour of married women.

Men engaged in a very coherent and consistent discourse of gender *differentiation*. It is a theme we shall return to in Chapter 5. On the positive side – and one must remember that, in their place, women are really liked by men – they were described as more diligent and industrious. They point out that much of the routine output of the Service, what keeps the place ticking, is women's efforts. 'You can rely on the girls, they work harder.' Their competence too was difficult to deny. A personnel manager explained the Service's willingness to take in by now a large majority of females among school-leaver entrants saying 'The girls are *better*, aren't they. Much more competent. They perform better than the boys.' (High Street Retail personnel managers were saying just the same thing.) Secondly, women were *nicer* than men. In middle management, women were less autocratic, gave orders more 'sweetly'. 'They charm the bloody birds out of the bloody trees.' They had more sympathy with staff feelings and related better to the public. One man preferred working with women because 'you can smile at each other. With the same sex, you don't.'

What women say about 'women's difference' is, perhaps unsurprisingly, also positive. What is more they identify quite similar female traits. They say women are specially competent and practical, make better managers because of their experience of running households; that women are better at detail, are more conscientious than men, have a more caring attitude to staff and public and are less aggressive in their approach. 'As a woman and the kind of woman I am, my responses are totally different from what a lot of men's would be . . . I don't go and shout at people because people do what I want them to anyway.'

Men, however, also have a repertoire of negative representations of women and, significantly, they are criticisms of women *only* in relation to authority. It hinges on two themes, a 'belt and braces' pair. Women are not capable of authority. And they turn into nasty people when in authority. Thus, on the first count, women 'lack a bit of judgement', and 'get a bit emotional', 'are not cut out for it', 'find it difficult to be ruthless enough' and so on. On the second count women in top jobs are 'bossy', 'pushy', 'absolute bastards', trampling on others in their ambition. In High Street Retail too men positioned women in a similar Catch-22. Either women were insufficiently authoritative, or they were too authoritarian. There was a myth current there among junior men that certain women managers, with whom they had no direct contact it should be said, were 'tartars', 'ferocious', got a kick out of 'lording it over men'. Either way, women's relation to power was problematised.

What appears to be happening here is that men are warning off women, warning them not to compete with men for promotion and authority. It is a successful device since some women too come to express distaste for women who get near the top. While some women defend them, others say women in authority become 'incredibly pushy', strident and aggressive. And there is a complex reality behind these words. In the past the only women who have been able to succeed have been those without children, often unmarried. They have been obliged, or have chosen, to give low priority to domestic relationships. The environment they have joined, which is that of men of power, has threatened to repel them if they do not adopt its culture. Life experience makes us what we are and, one woman said, 'look what you have to do to get there'. Once such women have made a decision to compete with men there is a tendency for them gradually to take on masculine traits. It is not surprising they often disappoint their sisters below them.

Men thus win in several ways simultaneously. They select women with masculine virtues. They actually succeed in defeminising some women as they filter them through. They also, however, condemn even appropriately authoritative behaviour in women as mannish. And they gain a stick with which to threaten other women. 'You wouldn't want to change your nice little personality, would you?' said one reporting officer in the Service to a woman subordinate, to discourage her from seeking promotion. It is understandable that another woman had not put herself forward for professional training because she feared 'I might lose my friends'.

Men define 'women's difference' in terms that suit themselves. They play off one woman against another. Women are in a cleft stick. They do prefer what they call 'women's values' and share an idea of what they mean by that. 'I like to see a softer approach, less *self*-oriented', a woman professional in the Service said. And in High Street Retail a woman distanced herself from men who treated their secretaries like dirt, 'It's just "Do!"' Most women do not much like masculinity and do not want to emulate it. Most of them are not prepared to forfeit men's appreciation, however. Yet power and authority are defined as precisely masculine. Management and new technology are defined as masculine. It is a spiral of contradiction.

The effect of such discourse is quite material. Women are divided from each other in such a way that solidarity among them is unlikely. We will see in Chapter 5 just how ruthlessly feminism is vilified and women scared away from identifying with feminists. The equality agenda is driven back to its shortest possible length. For senior men, though forced occasionally to trample on the masculine pride of men beneath them in the hierarchy, do none-theless bear in mind the latter's displeasure. Thus one very senior personnel manager in the Service, officially an equality officer, said 'it worries me when people try to legislate for it [i.e. equality] because I suspect . . . it tends to alienate your run-of-the-mill staff'. A more sympathetic personnel and EO manager found he had continually to limit the demands he made on regional line managers in the name of equal opportunities, knowing he would quickly lose their cooperation if he overplayed the hand.

In High Street Retail the pressure of masculine popular opinion against positive action for women meant that there was an uncomfortable fudging of how you *really* reach targets. In practical terms it meant appointing a female or a black candidate in the event they were *equally* well qualified with a white candidate. But because this was something difficult to tell a white man, everyone involved was reluctant to acknowledge that two 'equally qualified' candi-dates could ever be encountered. The principle of *merit* was allowed to appear inviolate. Jewson and Mason (1986) suggest this slippage of meanings is common in equality practice and has to be seen as political. Secondly, facilities offered women in the name of positive action were quickly demanded by men too in the name of equality. Men in High Street Retail had never identified a need for an assertiveness course, but when women had one they ensured the next would be open to men too.

Transformative change

It is not surprising, given the experience women have of organizations, that some simply do not seek positions of authority within them. So what if there is only one woman chief executive among the top thousand US corporations? So what if less than 4% of the top three grades of the British civil service are women? Who wants to take responsibility for such inhuman and exploitative institutions? Other women, however, who are no less critical of the organizations in which they find themselves, retain a hope of working for change as they climb the ladder.

It would be wrong to speak of 'women' as having a philosophy of change in organizations, since many women are as conventional in their view of hierarchy, bureaucracy and management as most of the men they join. Nonetheless there is a strong voice *among* women that is characteristically *of* women, speaking for a 'different way of doing things'. It may not be well articulated and it may sometimes be utopian but it embodies a vision of something new.

Many women, for instance, prioritise a social orientation over a narrow task-orientation. 'We value other things. I like to keep my life in balance. Things outside are far more important and pleasurable.' There is a tentative democratic sense. Women, for instance, were emphatic that equality measures should be for all women regardless of grade. 'Equality, full stop', as one of them put it. Women in the OMCS, where equality initiatives for the civil service were being generated, had a longer agenda than was apparent in the formal policy. One said 'we see ourselves as one of the agents of change, the "managers of tomorrow". What we are doing is part of a recognition that an effective organization needs diversity within itself, to be open to new ideas.' Another said,

> for me it's about changing the workplace. Breaking down the division between work and home. Recognizing a whole variety of different management styles. The expectation that people will work in different ways. Lots of things [would] become legitimate that weren't before. It just seems to me, working with women, that they work in different ways.

I don't think it's innate. I think it has to do with socialization . . . the way girls are brought up, women have better interpersonal skills, often they don't have the same sense of hierarchy. They are less competitive, more cooperative. And the work environment hasn't valued those things in the past.

Men too could have those qualities, she felt. How could they be brought to the fore? 'I would start with the organizational structure', she said. A leading woman trade union activist said for her part she would 'very much like to see the whole ethos of the Service change and all sorts of more liberal attitudes, the acceptance of other ways of doing things'. She spoke of a 'radical approach', of a 'restructuring of decision-making', a hierarchy 'more open to penetration from below'. Women would change things, and 'personally' she said, 'I want that'.

These women were not alone among equality activists in looking for some quite fundamental change in organizations. We saw the EO manager in High Street Retail talking of 'more egalitarian management', 'a more democratic enterprise'. We will see in Chapter 4 women in the Union talking about a feminist practice of 'inclusion, empowering, enabling, sharing', 'going for participatory democracy', 'a different kind of union'. One equality officer said 'my passion is institutional change'. Women writing about equal opportunities use similar language. Angela Coyle says 'women need to change management, to change structures, relationships, values and ways of working' (Coyle 1989). Others talk of restructuring jobs and the relationship between jobs rather than simply getting women into jobs (Webb and Liff 1988), of 'forging a new power base' and bringing the structures and goals of the organization under scrutiny (Davies 1988; see also Coyle 1988).

To bring about such changes may seem a long haul for a civil service woman who as yet would be glad to have the grade status that confers the right to a coatstand and armchair in the office, or for the businesswoman who looks forward to her first company car. But women I spoke with continually expressed the hope that as women ahead of them climb the hierarchy they would 'not do things the way men do them'.

What is more, some men can be heard saying the same thing, a few because they support feminism, more for other reasons. In High Street Retail women in certain management jobs were, as we saw, deemed to have special uses because of assumed feminine qualities.

It was a kind of positive sex-typing. It has been suggested more generally that male management styles could benefit from 'feminizing', not for the sake of women but of the organization. There is a current school in management thinking that takes issue with the instrumental approach. Peters and Waterman for instance in their often-cited study of top-performing companies note an increasing emphasis on informality, on people, 'treating them – not capital spending and automation – as the primary source of productivity gains' (Peters and Waterman 1982:238). Besides, they say, these 'people' can differ. They are no longer expected to come out of a mould. There is a new emphasis on judgement rather than following rules. 'The rational actor is superseded by the complex social actor, a human being with inbuilt strengths, weaknesses, limitations, contradictions and irrationalities.' Given the historic association of rationality with men, irrationality with women (Lloyd 1984), this would seem to make space for the feminine. Alice Sargent has suggested that as more women come into management, organizations will become androgynous, with both sexes able to use male and female sides of their personalities (Sargent 1983). Men have created a hard world for themselves, and a hard persona. It is not surprising if, in Suzanne Moore's deft phrase, men today see advantages in 'getting a bit of the other' (Moore 1988).

If changes of this kind become widespread and long-lasting in employing organizations – and who knows whether that will be the case – it will be a gain for women and will make working life more tolerable for many men too. On the other hand, as with previous stages in the retreat from what we have called the 'workplace clause' of the sexual contract, a new line is likely to be drawn. Women may join in the exercise of power; they may even change the style of management; but they are unlikely to be permitted to change the nature of the organization. Having more women in management, even women 'doing things in womanly ways' is not the same thing as having feminists in control. It does not guarantee a feminist revision of the goals and structure of the organization, nor of its operations in the labour market. Without such a revision women will step into power in an organization which, convivial though it may be for managers, continues to exploit women as workers and consumers in the same way as before. It will be mainly white women among the men at the top, exploiting women, many of whom will be black, at the base.

It is no accident that the management sponsors of EO in both the organizations examined here had interpreted equality of opportunity mainly as removing bias to clear the way for the advancement of individual women, that they had not seen the policy as a cue to changing the position for signifcantly large *groups* of women. It is true that the enhancement of maternity provisions penetrated some way down the grade-structure, but as we shall see in the following chapter, these are a mixed blessing. If the value of the labour of women at the bottom of the organization had really been of concern, the issues raised would have been different. There would have been a big input of training for less-skilled women workers, harmonization of terms and conditions of work between full and part-timers, there would have been job re-evaluation and regrading, a narrowing of pay differentials, and above all action to ensure 'equal pay for work of equal value'. This, however, is where employers really feel the pinch, for big money is involved. These are issues to which we will return in Chapter 4, for it was in other organizations, ones with specifically social purposes, that the equality agenda extended this far.

This of course is the point at which, having confronted the patriarchal nature of capitalism, we come face to face with the capitalist nature of patriarchy-as-we-know-it. For the uses to which women's labour is put worldwide are not only or merely the uses of individual men or even men as a sex, but the uses of capital. The system can sing along with a few women in management provided the organizations in question continue to adhere to 'the main aim', whatever that may be. In the case of business companies the aim will be accumulation and profit. In state organizations it will be cost-efficient performance of functions and provision of services. Such goals are routinely given priority over humanity and the natural world. This is why, among the many women hungry for recognition and success in organizations, a few, just a very few, ask themselves whether there are limits to what they should be prepared to do as part of the job. And a few equality activists nurture the hope of not only changing the sex of the powerful at the top but bringing top and bottom closer to each other in a restructured kind of power. Such an ambition may seem far-fetched. Yet, as we shall discuss in Chapter 7, organizations do vary and it is important to test the limits of each. It may be all but impossible to turn around a multinational. It may be somewhat easier to set the terms for one's engagement in a voluntary organization, a local council, a university or a trade union.

3

Defined in domesticity

When men represent women as a problem in the workplace, whether as their employees, as professional colleagues or co-labourers, they invoke several criteria. We have seen that women's imputed temperament is sometimes hauled into question, particularly with regard to their handling of authority roles. We will see in a later chapter that women's sexuality is always significant for men. Over and again, however, what is problematised is *women's relation to the domestic sphere*. The way women do or do not fit into the schema of paid employment and organizational life is seen primarily as a correlate of their marital status and, more important still, whether they do or do not have children. This is what women *are* to most men (and to most women): people who have domestic ties. Even if the woman in question is celibate or childless she is seen and represented as one of the maternal sex. Much of the argument surrounding equal opportunities at work circles about the question: can women *ever* be equal, given their different relation to reproduction?

Pregnancy, childbirth and childrearing are matters on which positive discrimination in favour of women is permitted without any thought that it may be 'unfair to men'. Indeed to make provision for employed women to carry out these activities is not spoken of as positive discrimination at all. The state routinely provides for maternity benefit, and employers for their part are quite free to extend the amount of leave they offer to women at full or part pay and to ease women's return to work by adapting their hours or terms of engagement. Men of course do not get pregnant or give birth. They could, however, look after their children in their early months and years. Yet there is no *requirement* in the law to offer appropriate facilities to fathers to enable this. Nor do men complain that they are discriminated against on this score. It goes without saying that the practice whereby women as a sex raise the children, keep house and have less economic independence than their husbands is of far-reaching advantage to men as a sex. Indeed, as we have seen, to sustain this form of family is at the very heart of men's sexual contract with each other.

Most organizations introducing sex equality policies include within their notion of positive action a number of measures designed to make it easier for women to combine paid work with childcare and other domestic responsibilities. Where they differ, the relative length of the equality agenda, is in the generosity of the provisions for women, the range of women to whom they are offered and whether appropriate facilities (and positive encouragement to make use of them) are offered to men. It is this aspect of equality strategies that is the theme of the present chapter.

First, however, we must see how women historically came to be paid workers while remaining domestically-defined, operating in an almost entirely separate labour market from that of men, and what disadvantage that has involved. Secondly we should understand the nature of the special attraction a domestically-defined female labour force has for employers and how they are increasingly organizing production to use it to advantage. We shall begin to see more clearly the dialectical relationship between the patriarchal relations of domestic life and the patriarchal relations of work. A woman's domestic identity constitutes her as a disadvantaged worker, while being a low earner and subject to male authority at work diminishes her standing in the family. It is the effects of these processes that the equal opportunities measures discussed in this chapter and Chapter 4 address.

A domesticated labour force

It was the separation of workplace from the home brought about by industrial capitalism that caused the question of women's relative status to develop in this form. As capitalist organization drew production (the spindle, the loom, the last, the anvil) from the ambit of the feudal home and hamlet, first into workshops then into factories, the contrast in the relation of women and men to production increased. The traditional skills of both sexes were gradually made redundant by new machinery and new modes of organization. But while some men were in a position to detach themselves from the home and reskill themselves for the industrialised processes of production, women, still tied to it by domestic responsibilities, became the industrialist's ideal 'unskilled' routine hands, often at as little as one-third of male pay (John 1986).

Typically it was unmarried girls who became the mainstay of the factory workforce, but often a wife's wage, even the earnings of little children, were needed to save the family from destitution. The effect on the patriarchal status of the working-class family man was painful. Hostility to the factory system in the early years of the nineteenth century was not only a protest at the cruel conditions of work. As Sheila Rowbotham points out, 'it was bound up with the desperate defence of a way of life . . . fear of the independence of wives and daughters working under another roof with other men, coming back with their own wages' (Rowbotham 1973:29). Home and factory became twin spheres in which a working-class man's status relative to women had continually to be reasserted.

In the bourgeoisie too there was unease about the effect of the new industrial system on the working-class family. Leonore Davidoff shows the state's attempts to wrest into required shape the relationship of family, kinship and work, by means of the Factory Acts, the Poor Law of 1834, the introduction of civil registration of births, deaths and marriages in 1837 and the lodging-house legislation of subsequent decades, controlling non-family households. By the late 1830s, she suggests, the middle-class conception of masculinity had begun to permeate the working class. The notion of 'work', no longer simply the activity of whichever sex turned its hand to productive tasks, was gradually being redefined as 'occupation' and associated with manhood and independence (Davidoff 1990).

An increasing sex-imbalance in the population mainly due to male emigration meant that by the 1880s there were an estimated one million 'surplus' women. With so many unmarried females the call for married women in the labour force declined. Where a quarter of married women had had an 'extraneous occupation' at the Census of 1851, by 1901 only 13% of married women were employed outside the home (Klein 1965). At the same time, the growing prosperity of a skilled artisan class gave some reality to an aspiration to the bourgeois and patriarchal ideal of the male breadwinner earning enough to maintain wife and children. For the self-respecting working man, the 'free' wage-worker of the new era's social contract, independence had a curious meaning. As Keith McClelland puts it, 'in one aspect to be an independent man was to be not a slave, a condition which continued to be counter-posed to the "free-born Englishman" . . .' Yet what came to have dominance in the working class, and in discourses about it, was that distinctly masculine form and meaning of "independence" in which a man would be able to attain or preserve a state in which he would be able to maintain dependents within the home' (McClelland 1989:171). Independence for a man was predicated on women's lack of it.

The feminist movement of the nineteenth century was therefore much preoccupied with women's right to an education and to suitable paid employment. Campaigns were at first focused on the unmarried middle-class woman, for whom work was seen as an insurance policy, establishing the means of independent living for fear she might have the misfortune to remain unmarried or find herself widowed or divorced (Klein 1965). It was later that feminists extended their concern to married women's employment. Clementina Black, who surveyed married women's work in the period just prior to the First World War, made a positive case for married women to work, not merely when compelled by poverty, but for the sake of their own autonomy. She cites one of the women interviewed: 'A shilling of your own is worth two that *he* gives you' (Black 1983:4). But she clearly felt herself to be arguing a cause unpopular with men.

The First World War of course swept many married women into factory and office work to substitute for men on active service. They were, however, just as rapidly swept out again when the forces returned and by 1921 a smaller proportion of married women worked than at the turn of the century. The situation was different after the Second World War. Though in the 1950s a powerful ideology of femininity and domesticity pressed a housewifely role on women, and Lord Beveridge, drafting welfare policy, assumed 'most women will not be gainfully employed' (Moss and Fonda 1980:10), as a matter of hard fact the percentage of married women economically active steadily and rapidly grew from 22% in 1951 to 68% in 1987 (Office of Population Censuses and Surveys 1987a,

Table 9.4). Most significantly, these married women were often
mothers. In the 1950s it was characteristically mothers of secondary
school children who joined the labour force; in the sixties the growth
came from mothers of primary school children. Between 1971 and
1977 the employment rate of mothers of preschool children
increased at twice the rate of other mothers (Moss 1980:23). By
1984 Sue Sharpe in her study of working mothers, could write, 'most
women expect to work for many years of their lives. Becoming a
mother today rarely leads to a permanent departure from the
labour force' (Sharpe 1984:12).

In Britain many of the married women drawn into the labour
force took part-time jobs. Between 1951 and 1981 women's part-
time employment was the sole source of employment increase.
There was a fall in the number of full-time employees of 2.3 million
(1.9 male and 0.4 female). Meanwhile the number of part-timers
rose by 3.7 million (0.7 male and 3.0 female). More than 90% of
part-timers are women. Not all ethnic groups participate in part-
timing similarly, however. The sharpest distinction is between Afro-
Caribbean women, only 21% of whom work part-time (56% full-
time), and white British women for whom the percentage is 37%
(45% full-time) (Office of Population Censuses and Surveys 1987b,
Table 5.33). Of women part-timers as a whole, 87% are married
women whose reason for part-timing is to be able to devote time to
the home. Men who work part-time are different. Almost all are
over sixty years, having chosen shorter hours as a preliminary to
retirement. Part-timing has continued to grow in the eighties.
Between 1981 and 1985, while 222000 men's jobs and 100000
full-time jobs for women were lost, 600000 women's part-time jobs
were created (Beechey and Perkins 1987:39).

Part-timers are clustered in low-pay, low-skill categories of work.
The woman part-time manual worker is even more likely than a
fulltimer to work in a totally sex-segregated job. The nearest man is
likely to be her supervisor or her supervisor's boss. More often than
not the trade union official who represents her is male too – that is
if the union bothers to recruit and service her at all. The average
hourly earnings of part-timers, even when part-time office staff and
manufacturing workers are included, are not much more than half
those of the average male fulltimer. They are about three-quarters
of those of full-time women workers. Frequently the part-time
woman works too few hours to qualify to pay the National

Insurance stamp. She therefore misses out on contributory benefits
such as sick pay and maternity pay. She is normally excluded from
any occupational pension scheme. She has fewer employment
protection rights and can be laid off more readily than the full-
time worker. Because of the unavailability of full-time work at
hours she can manage, a woman sometimes does two part-time jobs
a day, often an early morning and a twilight shift (Robinson 1988,
Beechey and Perkins 1987).

Flexible, casual and cheap

While changes in women's education, in the pattern of childbearing
(smaller families, more compressed in time), and in the demands of
housework (more equipment, greater use of semi-prepared foods,
off-the-peg clothing) have increased married women's availability
for work, it is not so much women's needs as employers' labour
force strategies that have led to this massive increase in part-time
working. The cost benefits of employing part-timers are many.
They can be applied to more intensive work than a worker who has
to sustain her energies for an eight-hour shift. Mothers offer the
special attraction of being a kind of seasonal worker, paid for in
school term time, spent cleaning and cooking in school or helping
children across busy roads outside, laid off without pay in school
vacations. Part-timing thus 'reflects the responses of employers
(whether in the private or public sector) to pressures to reduce and
contain operating costs in an increasingly competitive or constrained environment' (Robinson 1988:131).

Veronica Beechey and Tessa Perkins emphasise that what is new
today is less the extent of part-time employment among women
than the fact that whole occupations and sectors of the economy,
particularly cleaning, cooking and caring work, are now being
organized on a part-time basis. What we are witnessing, they
believe, is a new form of work that is highly exploitative and quite
sex-specific. Where employers of women are looking for flexibility
they use part-timing; employers of men resort to other adjustments,
such as three-shift working (Beechey and Perkins 1987:101). It also
seems the growing enthusiasm of employers for part-time women
workers is a response to industrial protection legislation (which

leaves most part-timers unprotected), and state insurance and welfare policy (which sets a threshold level for benefits and elegibility for redundancy pay that gives employers a reason to prefer part-timers).

A parallel development has been a reversion to homeworking. Women work in their own homes, sewing or assembling products from parts delivered to them by a manufacturer or his agent. They work at piece-rates, normally very low, fitting in the work as best they can among the household's space and activities. Disproportionate numbers of Asian women in Britain, particularly those of Moslem communities, are homeworkers. They are confined to this work in part by the dictate of male heads of family, in part by the white racism that renders the outside world a dangerous place for women of ethnic minorities. Homeworking and part-timing are not freely-chosen, life-enhancing options but are the result on the one hand of ideological and material constraints on women, on the other of the profit motive of employers (Bisset and Huws 1989:38, Allen and Wolkowitz 1987:86). They are not some 'natural' result of patriarchal family patterns but the purposeful patriarchal-capitalist exploitation of those patterns. In this light Sylvia Walby suggests we should see the current trends in labour market practices as 'a round of struggle' (Walby 1989:137).

It is important to note, too, that the influence of domestication is not limited to married women. Nor does exploitation operate only through the mechanism of reduced hours. Single women, most of whom work a full day, are also obliged to sell their labour power at less than its proper value. Single women are the other side of the coin of the 'family wage'. While a man is assumed to have dependants, a young woman is assumed to be a dependant. As Meta Zimmeck wrote of the low pay afforded the new female clerical workforce in the late nineteenth century, employers assumed 'they lived at home with their families (indeed some employers demanded signed statements from families and friends with whom provincials were allowed to live that this was the case). Since they lived at home with their families, they were not self-supporting. Since they were not self-supporting they worked for pin money.' At the very least it was assumed they had nobody but themselves to support (Zimmeck 1986:103). Today the earning capabilities of young women are still held back by being channelled into jobs that offer little training and poor career possibilities, something they are too ready to accept because of a fatalistic perception that their real destiny is to leave work in their early twenties to raise a family (Griffin 1985, Wallace 1987, Cockburn 1987).

The feminization of British employment is by no means done (Jenson *et al.* 1988). A fifth of all jobs in 1980, part-timing is expected to account for a quarter by the end of the century. Married women are seen as the main untapped source of labour in a decade when, due to demographic factors, the number of young people entering the labour market is due to fall by a quarter. Nor, although Britain is noted for part-time working, is this a British phenomenon alone. A study of seven developed countries shows the female participation rate, and particularly part-timing, steadily increasing in most of them. At the same time there is no significant closing of the gap between women's and men's earnings (Bakker 1988). Most remarkable is that this growth in the significance of women in the paid labour force has occurred through two quite contrasted economic moments – the economic growth and stability of the fifties and sixties, followed by the turmoil, economic crisis and restructuring of the seventies and eighties (Hagen and Jenson 1988).

The restructuring of the economy we have witnessed in the eighties has been partly due to changing world economic conditions, partly engineered by Conservative government policy. In developed countries employment in manufacturing industry has declined, as capital has relocated production in cheap-labour Third World countries. Any growth in Western employment has occurred in service jobs – in private sector firms providing banking, insurance and other financial services to capital, in retail distribution, and in public services such as health and education. A competitive extension of retail opening hours and the need to maximise use of costly computer equipment has (as we saw in High Street Retail) led many firms to begin working shifts, often part-time shifts. Large firms are 'externalising' production, subcontracting services and purchasing goods and assemblies from plants hived-off to become subsidiaries. In the public sector government-enforced competitive tendering has often resulted in the privatisation of services like cleaning and catering. Small firms, fighting to retain their contracts in highly competitive situations, are obliged to recruit their employees on the lowest possible wages and on an insecure basis, resorting to short-term, seasonal and temporary contracts and the use of staff agencies. Employers call this flexible manning. Their employees experience it as casualisation. The Thatcher administration has supplied the ideological input and legislative backing for this 'enterprise culture'. Managers have been encouraged to take a greater licence to manage. Trade unions have been curbed, through the law, through a retreat from national to local bargaining and through loss of membership. In so far as they have found scope for resistance, often it has been male members' interests they have defended first.

The impact of these trends on women has been severe. Unemployment has not led to their withdrawal from the labour market – indeed the restructuring this time has been predicated on their labour more than that of men. Families, however, are increasingly dependent on their inadequate earnings. Cuts in social services have imposed new burdens of care on the household. Jane Humphries and Jill Rubery note, as a result of these changes, an increase in the rate of exploitation of women in the eighties. 'Their wages are keeping the wolves from the doors of many UK homes. Simultaneously, behind those doors, longer hours must be spent – and primarily still by women – in essential caring and domestic work. And these increased hours of work buy only a stagnant or even falling standard of living' (Humphries and Rubery 1988: 102).

What is clear is that this exploitation does not fall on women incidentally or accidentally. It is sex-specific and is in fact the exploitation of a worker constructed *within the terms of* the sexual contract, her subordination to husband, her responsibility for child, other dependents and home. Maria Mies has developed this line of reasoning to suggest that capitalist accumulation is predicated on the super-exploitation of three resources: women, colonies and nature. She argues that the narrow capitalist (and Marxist) concept of productive labour – the paradigm case of which is the male proletarian – has to be recast. We have to bring into view the hidden non-wage labour throughout the world of (mainly) women as subsistence farmers, as producers of under-priced commodities, and as unpaid housewives. 'Without the exploitation of non-wage labour, wage labour exploitation would be impossible' (Mies 1986:200).

Mies' analysis introduces a needed racial dimension to this history. In Britain and other European countries in the nineteenth century, women, first bourgeois then many working-class women, were progressively confined within the home. Profits of British capital from the exploitation of the natural resources and labour of colonial territories enriched the bourgeoisie and, invested in British business, raised the standard of living of the metropolitan working class. The chimerical 'breadwinner's' or 'family' wage became a reality for a privileged section of the working class. 'Thus the Little White Man also got his colony, namely the family and a domesticated housewife' (Mies 1986:110). The exploited labour of black women in one part of the world made possible the internal colonization of white women in prosperous Britain. The imperial enterprise funded the sexual contract between men of the two social classes. Besides, as and when women were needed in the metropolitan labour force, domestication of women as a sex would, as we have seen, enable their particularly exploitative treatment in the labour market. It is clear, as Carole Pateman put it, that 'capitalism and class have been *constructed as patriarchal categories*' (Pateman 1988:135, my italics). Or, as Mies puts it, 'capitalism has to use, to strengthen or even to invent, patriarchal men–women relations if it wants to maintain its accumulation model. If all women in the world had become 'free' wage earners, 'free' subjects, the extraction of surplus value would, to say the least, be severely hampered' (Mies 1986:188).

The particular merit of Mies' analysis is that she shows the sex-specific exploitation of women's labour to be not a feudal relic, as is sometimes supposed, but an essential aspect of contemporary, modernizing economies. In socialist countries the family economy and subsistence production subsidizes the socialized modern sector. Remembering the growth of homeworking for multinationals like Benetton with its zappy modern image, the massive creation of part-time jobs destined for Western housewives and the peculiarly nasty forms of exploitation reserved for migrant women in European countries and women in Third World export processing zones, it is hard to deny that the domestically-defined female sex, rather than the 'free proletarian' is 'the optimal labour force for capital at this juncture, both in the underdeveloped and over-developed countries' (Mies 1986:126). Such an understanding shows the maternity provisions in the average equality policy to be a slight addition to the costs of exploiting women's labour power, not an end to the system.

Maternity provision in equality initiatives

Some of the disadvantage women experience at work on grounds of their domesticity is nothing more than prejudice. In assessing women for a job managers think to themselves 'She'll get married and leave', 'With two children she'll never cope', or 'Her husband would never let her move to Birmingham'. In both High Street Retail and the Service women were certain that male managers used to think this way before the advent of equal opportunity policies. Perhaps they still did. Some men freely admitted that they had once thought this way and that many other men had done so too. 'The first question a woman was always asked in any reporting interview was, if she was single, was she likely to get married; if she was married, when was she going to have children. Those questions were asked every time with no inhibitions whatsoever.' Women today, however, fortified by the equality policy, are fighting back. One, now at last a professional, told me how her reporting manager had said he was not considering her for professional training 'because you're married, you've got a home to run, shopping to do'. She, as it happened, was married to a Service man in the same grade as herself. She replied coolly to her superior, 'I imagine you will be asking those same questions to my husband when you interview him next week.'

This prejudice is often unfounded: in many cases a woman could give as much of her attention to a job as a man. For some women at some times in their lives, however, the truth is that the combining of childcare, husband-care and housework with a demanding paid job *is* very difficult indeed. A woman professional in the Service described how she had been simply unable to combine the training for the elite corps with the care of two young children. 'Unless you're really brilliant there's no way you can do it without a lot of study at home. That's a lot easier for a man than a woman. He comes home and he's got a wife who puts a meal in front of him, makes sure the children are in bed or kept quiet. If you're a woman you have to come home, stop off for the shopping, see to the children, cook the meal. Obviously you're going to be at a disadvantage. It's structured for men.'

This woman, perhaps most women, *will* put the family first if it comes to the crunch. A woman senior manager in High Street Retail had for some years been held back simply because she would

not reassure her managing director that she would invariably put
the company before her family.

> I'd always made it clear to him that I was not prepared to up-sticks and
> go anywhere. On a temporary basis, yes, but not on a permanent basis.
> And the argument I always got from him was, 'Well, if I spoke to a man
> he'd say his career came first'. And I'd say . . . 'Well, I'm in different
> circumstances. I'll do a damn good job and I don't feel it's got any
> relevance whether I'm married or not'. And he always said he'd never
> promote me. But in the end he did.

It is not only the job that is forced to cede to the demands of
family in women's lives. Women are often impeded from playing a
full part in the trade union. One of my case studies was of a public
sector union, three-quarters of whose members were women. They
were mainly low-paid manual workers, many of whom worked
part-time and whose hours, both at work and at home, were
crammed with intensive work. Like some employers, the Union
had recently developed an equality policy and a positive action
strategy for its women members. They had taken steps to improve
women's representation in the decision-making structures of the
Union, to adapt bargaining priorities and campaign more actively
on women's issues.

The shop stewards and branch secretaries who ran the Union at
local level were predominantly men. The Women's Committee, a
product of the equality measures, had consequently been preoccupied with the question how to increase women members' participation. Union activism may mean a couple of nights a week out,
attendance at an occasional weekend educational conference. If a
woman has children it means her partner or someone else staying in
to mind them. But it also means a woman having a life of her own,
'getting political'. Perhaps even more than taking a job, getting
involved in a trade union or other forms of activism signifies
entering the public sphere, flouting the sexual contract that reserves
public life for the brothers and confines women to domesticity.

Quite apart from the considerable resistance such women meet
from men within the union, therefore, they face another impedi-
ment in the shape of that 'other man', the husband or partner in the
home. A male branch secretary told me 'A lot of women would be
put in a very difficult situation with their husbands at home by
wanting to take on the sort of responsibility I carry . . . . I've got to

be blunt about this. Some of the women shop stewards in our branch are only allowed a certain amount of time to attend meetings, to be active, by their husbands.' Husbands resent a wife escaping their domain. 'She'll not start that fucking lark. In and out to the clothes line's enough for her', I was told was one husband's view of the matter.

A man has to tolerate not only his wife's absence but also the intrusion of union business into the home. The phone rings a lot – and it's for *her*. A woman can only succeed in sustaining her activism, I was told, if she succeeds in 'taking *him* along'. Yet 'to have support from their partners for what they do is the exception, rather than the rule'.

The two sets of men – union men and husbands of union women – sometimes act in harmony to sustain patriarchal order, male sex-right. One male full-time officer felt it behoved the union to take care not to step on the toes of husbands. 'If you're going to promote women in the organization and if those women have family commitments, you've got to be very careful to ensure she has the support of her family and partner . . . I've perhaps got a rooted sexism myself (he admitted). If my partner did my job, I'd resent that, I couldn't handle that at home.' 'It'd make you feel put down?' I asked him. 'Absolutely. Absolutely.'

Husbands and partners may impede women becoming active in the union by making it clear they resent their engagement in union life. But they also simply make it impossible by failing to take their share of housework and childcare. The Women's Officer and Women's Committee of this union were pressing branches to organize meetings in working hours so that women could more easily attend, to choose convenient and appropriate venues, to offer childcare expenses. But of the branches, mainly male-led, few were committed to such positive steps. The Union also, like other unions today with large women memberships and some women activists, was pressing employers to develop equality policies geared to the needs of working women with dependent children (or adults).

High Street Retail and the Service had both improved on statutory maternity provision as part of the equality package. It was the Local Authority however, my fourth case study, that had gone furthest in this respect. This Local Authority is a London borough, well-known during the period 1982–87 for its left-wing Labour approach to local politics. Its generous new provision for mothers, taken with other aspects of its positive measures for women, probably put it among the most progressive of British employers in 1989. The policy began with a Code of Safe Working during Pregnancy. The guiding principle was that women who wish and are able to continue working throughout pregnancy be enabled to do so without danger. Advice was available. A woman who did not wish to continue operating a visual display unit for fear of radiation hazard might be transferred to other work. Of course the mandatory provision for time off without loss of pay to enable attendance at ante-natal and relaxation classes was taken for granted.

Maternity leave might start, as in the statutory regulations prevailing in 1988, 11 weeks before expected confinement date. The Local Authority differed from the official norm, however, in waiving the two-year qualifying period for eligibility for maternity benefits. All that was necessary was for the woman in question to be a permanent (not casual) employee of the council before the expected week of confinement. Before going on maternity leave the expectant mother had to state her intention to return to council employment and to remain back at work for a minimum of two months. She was given until seven weeks after the birth to confirm this decision. (If she failed so to return she would retrospectively forfeit some of her maternity pay.) Both the length of leave and the level of pay were a considerable improvement on the statutory provision. The first sixteen weeks of absence were paid at full normal salary, deducting the amount received in statutory maternity allowance. Following this, twenty-four weeks more leave were available to be taken, at the woman's choice, either in their entirety at half-pay, or the first 12 weeks fully paid, the second without pay. The mother might thus remain away from work for a total of 40 weeks. Similar provisions applied to parents adopting a child.

The council also provided *paternity* leave of ten days at the birth of a child. This, however, was termed 'nominated carer leave', to reflect a mother's right to choose a relative or friend as substitute for the father. Besides, all employees, regardless of length of service, were entitled to special paid leave for the care of dependants who might be sick, or whose normal care arrangements had broken down. Up to ten working days could be taken in any one period of absence, to a maximum of fifty working days a year. Further extensions were allowable on manager's discretion.

On return from maternity leave the mother had the right to come back to her own or a very similar job on terms and conditions no less favourable than before. She might, however, request to return as a part-timer, or to turn her job into a shared post. Indeed, quite independently of maternity rules, an employee of the council could at any time request to convert from full-time to part-time working, or to turn her or his job into a job-share. There was no job in the council that was ruled out as a possibility for job-sharing, including that of chief executive. Part-time employees of this Local Authority, so long as they worked sixteen or more hours a week, lost none of a fulltimer's rights and benefits.

Flexitime had long been worked throughout the council and more recently extended from a weekly basis to that of a nine-day fortnight. Free annual cervical and breast cancer screening was provided. Fifty-five places were available in staff day nurseries. In protest at the government's ruling that the benefit of a nursery place be assessed with a parent's income for tax purposes, the council was currently allowing its employees to use the nursery facilities virtually free of charge. A mother-and-baby room had been established in the town hall so that women might change and feed their children while visiting the council offices. A 'return to work' or 'career break' scheme was in process of being introduced.

The women I talked with in the Local Authority appreciated the maternity provision perhaps more than any other aspect of the EO policy. Having more senior women officers visibly pregnant or with young children was encouragement to juniors thinking of combining work with babies. One said 'The personnel officer who's advising me about my maternity leave is also a pregnant woman who is in the same position as me. That's one of the kinds of things that's kept me in this local authority.'

Though they could always use more – more nursery places for instance, a women's rest room – the dominant feeling among women was that the provision in the Local Authority was good and that it was, moreover, not a perk but a basic necessity and should be standard in all workplaces. Their main concern was now to defend it against the cuts in council spending. A problem recognized by women was that of finding temporary cover for the absent woman at a time of critical staff shortages. In these circumstances even women managers admitted they were finding maternity leave difficult to handle.

Things have got so bad from a staff morale point of view, people feel so strained and stressed that they aren't in a position, or able, or want to take on someone else's job [as well as their own], or even a part of it.

Observing with malicious pleasure the council juggling the claims of its various functions on an ever-tighter budget, the local newspaper crowed 'Baby Boom Hits Libraries'. However, the characteristic woman manager's point of view was summed up as follows

I suppose you're involved creatively making equal opportunities work. It gives you the extra administrative problem of interviewing and so on, but I don't view it as a problem but as their right. You just get on with it as far as I'm concerned. And if people are negative about it, you put them down for it.

Equality policy had certainly strengthened women's arm here.

There is a curious conflict of intentions concerning working mothers in Britain at the time of writing in 1990. The Conservative government is determined that working parents should make arrangements for their childcare and pay for it in full out of their own pockets. It is the role neither of state nor industry, in this view, to subsidise the family (Coote and Hewitt 1980). The British government is also alone in the European Economic Community in vetoing a draft directive that would give equal rights in law and equal pay and conditions (*pro rata*) to part-time workers.

Employers, however, are increasingly alarmed by 'the demo-graphic time bomb' – the anticipated 25% decline in numbers of young people leaving school and entering the labour market by 1995. Especially in London and the South East, where labour is already hard to come by, they are now intent on competing with each other for older female recruits. They are also considering ways of retaining young women already in their employ. We are now seeing companies, whose directors would not so long ago have castigated the Local Authority, and others like it, as 'loony leftists' for offering wildly generous maternity provision, currently issuing press releases announcing similar provisions they themselves are now making. Within one week in June 1989 *The Financial Times* carried articles on a plan by British Rail to set up a network of nurseries near rail depots around London; Mercer Fraser's scheme to give their employees vouchers to pay their childminders; and

J. Sainsbury's proposal to open up many more jobs to part-timers, develop promotion possibilities for them and for total harmonization of part-time and full-time terms and conditions. Midland Bank in the same year announced a plan to open 300 day nurseries in four years. The bank was employing seven people just to plan and establish this provision. Meanwhile two other banks, National Westminster and Barclays, were polishing up their 'returner' schemes (Boyden and Paddison 1986). Women everywhere were startled to find themselves suddenly wooed in this manner by the big men of the big corporations. But how were the lesser men responding to the incursion of labour ward and nursery into the workplace?

Accommodating motherhood

The issue of maternity provision highlights a tension between men at the top of the hierarchy, particularly those senior personnel managers with responsibility for labour market strategies and human resource management, and men, particularly line managers, down the line. The former, with the organization's overall competitiveness in mind – and when we are talking of competitiveness in labour markets this applies as much to public sector as private sector employers – are identifying the special value of domestically-defined women employees and adapting personnel policy to make better use of them. The hapless line managers have to deal with the contradictions. For them, all this increased maternity provision that arrives in the name of equality of opportunity for women is a bit like a blow to the funny bone, leaving them midway between pain and mirth. On the one hand it is a severe nuisance. It makes practical difficulties for managers, increases the proportion of women in the labour force and brings a unwelcome domestic odour, a whiff of kitchen and nursery, into the workplace. On the other hand the more women are permitted various kinds of flexibility in relation to work to enable them to cope with motherhood and other domestic responsibilities the more they can be dismissed as 'different', less serious than male employees.

In the Local Authority there were many male managers who were 'fed up to the back teeth' with the continual absences of women for 'one thing or another'. Now it's the clinic, now the baby's due, now her youngest has the measles. One chief officer made it clear he felt he had adapted nobly to all this coming and going as far as his clerical and administrative staff were concerned. Now that women of childbearing propensity, supported by the equality policy, were entering his *professional* team and they too were needing 'cover' for months at a time, that was altogether too much and he felt aggrieved.

Annoyance with the managerial implications of maternity leave and related provisions such as special leave, part-timing and job-sharing, seems to be widespread. In High Street Retail too men were embittered by the disturbance caused, for example, to the orderly ways of the buying department. One manager said he would frankly prefer pregnant women to leave and not return. Others felt confused. Yes, of course 'the girls' ought to be allowed back, provided they gave adequate warning and kept their word on the matter. But how could the department manage in the meantime? You train up a temp and no sooner has she learned the job than the original employee returns. One young man, new to employment and its laws, was simply astonished at the extent of the adaptation called for in a company to meet the needs of pregnant women. To him employees had just been undifferentiated people. He had never imagined the *physical* reality of women employees.

In the Service, too, many managers felt maternity leave and flexibility were 'too generous' today, had 'gone far enough', and managers were being 'hemmed in'. Service rates of pay, held down by government policy, were falling behind the private sector. Top managers knew they needed to compete with the private sector for women recruits. 'We're losing them to industry', they complained. They had to use the only incentive available to them, better terms and conditions. Maternity leave, for instance. Pregnant women, said one personnel manager in a startling metaphor, 'they've got us over a barrel'. Because provision in local authorities and government departments therefore tended to be more generous than in companies, 'there is, I regret to say, a tendency for the public service to carry the can in circumstances of conflict between domestic and work obligations'. If one spouse worked for a private company, the other for a public service, 'the chances are it's the public sector that takes the cat to the vet. That's the way it is. And it's wrong.'

The irritation noticeable in all three sites had been exacerbated by a tendency for maternity leave to be exploited as an occasion for reducing staff levels, simply by failing to provide cover for the absent woman. So managers felt the problem with maternity leave was 'the financial tag attached. How the bloody hell do we do the job without a replacement?' And colleagues complained 'those who are constantly here have to bear the burden for those that aren't'. Top men are called on to impose the new flexibilities on middle managers below them. It is the latter who pay the price in inconvenience and whose complaints ring loudest. A particular source of scandal is women who 'con us' by saying they will come back and then fail to reappear. They 'hold us to ransom while they are away'. There is a deep-rooted feeling among many men at all levels that pregnant women and new mothers are 'cheating', 'taking us for a ride' or generally 'messing the organization around'. Yet sick leave, which is more frequent and less predictable than maternity leave (Daniel 1980) does not incur the same blame.

Underlying some of the resentment against the maternity provisions is a widespread view that mothers of young children morally ought to stay at home with them, should not attempt to 'have their cake and eat it too'. 'If you want to have babies, go and have babies. If you want to work, work.' Several men in the Service, for instance, had wives who, they were happy to say, had 'chosen their priorities', had dedicated themselves to their families because 'they felt it was important'. 'I find it a bit surprising' one such man remarked, 'the rather *detached* attitude some ladies have to farming children out'. Having made the housewife\breadwinner decision for themselves and sacrificed that second salary, some resented the better standard of living of some of their colleagues whose wives had remained in employment.

Men are experiencing disturbance in two spheres simultaneously, provoked by changes in women's economic and domestic behaviour. As Carole Pateman put it, 'paid employment for wives threatens both the husband's right of command over the use of their services and the fraternal order of the workplace itself' (Pateman 1988:139). First, men's wives, mothers of their children, are leaving the home in increasing numbers for at least part of their day. This is making women, in men's eyes, more uppity, less ready to accept a husband's authority. We have seen that a woman who gets involved with the union may be even more troubling. One who had become a shop steward found 'I can talk to anyone now. It gives me a wee bit of power.' Being involved outside the home reduces the priority a woman places on domestic responsibilities. One woman shop steward I interviewed looked at her watch as it approached 5 p.m. and observed,

> If I hadn't been in the union now I'd have been thinking, I'd better get home to put the dinner in the oven. Now I'll say I've got other things to do. You'll have to wait for your dinner. I think my husband's changed too, because I'm in the union. He can't say things as heavy as he used to. He knows I've a mind of my own now. I'd have been just . . . having dinner ready for a certain time and having his shirts done and that. Now I couldn't give a hoot. I do something when I want to do it. I'm not neglecting them [she added], they're just getting something different.

Secondly, at middle levels women are a growing source of competition for men in the workplace. In some cases they spoil the fraternal relations of a formerly all-male work group. They come in trailing evidence of domesticity, for not all women will or can pretend they do not have to hunk plastic bags full of vegetables back from their lunch-hour shopping, lie down for half an hour because of menstrual pain or phone the school about a child's truancy. A top woman manager at High Street Retail reported a curious exchange with a senior male colleague who had been staring at her during meetings, behaving in a way she found unsettling. Eventually she asked him, 'What's the matter?' He said, 'I'm sorry, but I can't help it. Everytime I look at you I see *my wife*.' She answered curtly, 'That's your problem.' But she commented to me on men's confusion in their experience of women in two worlds. 'Men do have difficulty in seeing a woman as anything other than a secretary, a sex object or a wife.'

Men are angry with women who try to be both mothers and employees. They are, however, used to reckoning on women being less of a threat to male career chances because they are held back by pregnancy and childcare. They therefore *also* feel angry with women who cheat by remaining single or childless. A male professional in the Service said bitterly, 'To get on in this place you need to have had a divorce and a hysterectomy.' He was referring directly to a woman who had experienced both things and been promoted over him.

If dealing with the interaction of work and motherhood is a source of stress between male managers, it is also a source of division among women. There is some mutual resentment between women who combine care of children with paid work and those who do not. Like men, many women have a strong conviction that mothers should stay home with children. 'This is why there's so much violence and unruliness in children nowadays. Because years ago the mother was at home, they went to school, they came home and had a proper dinner. There was no junk food. And there was discipline.' Some women I met felt they had made a costly choice in deciding not to have children in order to pursue a career. Some women managers simply reacted to maternity as an administrative problem. 'I think when a woman has children clinging to her apron strings, she's got to be helped, yes. But it's hard on the rest of us who haven't got children.' 'You do sigh inwardly when you hear of another one pregnant. Here we go!'

Ambitious women without children, some of whom are unmarried besides, know full well that having all these 'mother's privileges' serves to confirm men's belief that women as a sex are unreliable employees who have their mind half the time on domestic matters. Though part-timing, job-sharing and career-break schemes are now sometimes available to women to help them through the childrearing years, they know full well that this route is a succession of career impediments. In the Service, for instance, women told me one would be ill-advised to go part-time if serious about a career above the clerical grades. The career-break or returner scheme being introduced by all three of these organizations is a particular example of this ambiguity. To many women and men it was a welcome scheme precisely because it enabled women to fulfil their motherly duties by staying with their children for four or five years. For that very reason it was, of all the maternity provisions, the least controversial among men. Yet there were few who really believed that five years away from work would not put paid to their promotion chances. A double standard is clear when men praise the career-break scheme as enabling the progress of women while saying that *men* could not afford to make use of it because to do so would 'damage their careers'.

Domesticating men

As things are, maternity and domesticity are undeniably a hazard dashing women's hopes of equal chances in the hierarchy. Only a few women will slip through the rapids, those who trim their shape by avoiding encumbrances, real or apparent. For the more typical woman, life must involve juggling both domestic and employment responsibilities. There is of course no way to transcend the contradiction experienced by both sexes over the attempted integration into the organizations of paid employment of women as homekeepers and childrearers, the basic challenge of equality of opportunity, so long as change relies on the actions of either the employer or women. It is only men, as men, who can take steps to square the circle, make possible the impossible.

This is the necessary conclusion from recognizing the social contract for what it was – a restructuring, for the new era of capitalism, of pre-capitalist patriarchy. When a woman, a child on either arm, attempts to claim as hers a citizen's place in the public sphere, aspires to be a party to the social contract, she finds her entry ticket is unrecognized. When put to the test, the social contract reveals itself as an understanding between men from which women are excluded. Indeed it is precisely a compact underpinned by male sex-right. It is a silent accord between men to grant each other equal status and independence defined precisely as the rendering of women dependent. Until the symbolic man-as-citizen has his mind on the cooker, his eye on a toddler and a hand on grandad's wheelchair, no constitution will guarantee social equality.

For women to escape subordination to men the relationship of home to work has to change beyond anything yet envisaged in the name of equality policy. Men have to be domesticated and in the workplace (to use Joan Acker's phrase) the rhythm and timing of work must be adapted to the rhythms of life outside (Acker 1987:27). For women, getting into the workplace, becoming workers, earning their own money, has proved a necessary but insufficient step towards liberation. A further necessary condition is for men to move the other way, get into the home, start nurturing, become domestics. For *that* to happen their relationship to work and career has to change. Like women, they must begin to see employment as something you pick up and put down, contingent on the needs of other human beings. There is no room in this scenario for fetishized masculine careers. A requisite of course is that employing organizations make available to fathers too these flexibilities that some are just now offering to mothers. More, however, they have to direct their personnel policies towards the expectation that men will really use them.

I asked men in all three employing organizations whether they would value the extension to men of some of the provisions mainly intended for women. For instance, would they want a week or more of paternity leave at the time of birth or adoption of a child? Some countries of the European Economic Community have adopted voluntarily a draft directive on paternal leave that has long been vetoed by the British Government. High Street Retail and the Local Authority had both, in fact, introduced paternity leave as part of their equality package. Secondly, would men value the right to share in the longer maternity leave – to make it truly *parental* leave? In Sweden, for example, man or woman may take leave for the nine months after childbirth at 90% of normal pay, followed by three months on fixed grant and optional unpaid leave until the child is eighteen months old. Either parent has the right to reduce their hours to a six-hour day thereafter until the child is ten (Svenska Institutet 1987). In High Street Retail any man whose partner worked for the company and became pregnant was theoretically entitled to take at least half the maternity suspense. Third, I wanted to know whether men would consider using the proposed career-break or returner scheme to enable them to be away from work for longer periods with reinstatement rights.

A few men do now positively welcome the idea of a full, or at least a much greater, share of parental work. They are, however, a small minority and they seldom practice what they feel to be right. Family finances, they say, preclude it because their own earnings are so much higher than those of their partners. In this way subordination of women at work spirals around to reinforce their subordination at home. In two hundred interviews I met only one case of a woman whose husband looked after the children while she was at work. They were a young Asian couple and she earned more than he. They felt driven by necessity to a practice both would have wished to exchange for normalcy.

Most of the men I spoke with, like most men today perhaps,

welcome a week or ten days' childbirth leave for fathers. Some, it has to be said, felt 'any excuse for extra days off can't be bad'. Others felt they had done it out of their annual holiday entitlement – so should the rest. The question of sharing in the longer maternity leave was swiftly dismissed by almost all men. The arguments were mainly essentialist: women are the 'natural' child-rearers. 'It's biological, it's women's role.' The mother is the 'one the child naturally turns to', 'the paternal link is not so close'. The father's role was to 'assist in all the little jobs when he's around'. As to the career-break scheme, these men showed less enthusiasm still. Except, it must be said, that one or two supposed the provision, if it was to apply equally to men and women, as in all these organizations was the case, should mean a man could take a sabbatical now and then to visit Australia or write a novel.

Some men simply acknowledged that they would not wish to play a more domestic role. They frankly preferred their work, not only for the economic independence it gave them but for the sense of having a place in society, belonging to a men's club. Interruptions to a career 'would have spoilt it'. One said he would never have considered it because of the loss of continuity in his reporting record. You built up a reputation with a reporting officer. They kept looking back at your reports. 'If you get out of that and let someone else go past, you've lost the momentum – and momentum is everything.' The whole idea of such an added career handicap was perverse. 'You are pulling back the man to have the same problems as a woman' said one man in disbelief.

Like the British Government, the Confederation of British Industry is on record as strongly opposing the EEC paternity leave and parental leave proposals. It considers it would undermine industry's competitiveness, be counter-productive to reducing unemployment and fail to recognize the importance of an employer's right to choose (*Equal Opportunities Review* 1985:5). Do senior managers and personnel managers who administer these new rules for their part really intend men to behave like women? I found no evidence of it. A senior man in the Service elite gave a not untypical answer.

Oh dear me [he sighed]. I haven't really addressed my mind to this at all. And I confess to having a prejudice against it. [His irritation increased as he chewed the matter over.] I can see the case for giving a few days' leave at the time of birth. That would be humane and desirable, and it wouldn't cost much. If you go beyond that – I admit it's irrational, it's prejudice – but I like to see men who give *proper* priority to their job . . . *doing* the job for forty-six weeks in the year with six weeks leave. A half-hearted commitment whereby he's here part of the time and fulfilling a domestic function the rest doesn't seem to me to show an ideal attitude towards the job on the part of a male employee. But there we are. I accept that's improper, irrational and prejudiced.

Geographical mobility, which, as mentioned in Chapter 2, was a live issue to men and women in both High Street Retail and the Service, usefully illuminates the contradictions between the domestic and the workplace clauses of men's sexual contract. Women find the requirement of mobility hard to meet. This is because their husbands often require their own job to take precedence – he earns more, his career 'matters' more. Men for their part find mobility hard to sustain. Their wives and children often complain at being uprooted from their communities. Men must discourage their wives from developing an attachment to a job so as not to add to this family inertia. Personnel managers are thus placed in a difficult position. If they move a woman against her husband's will they are flouting the male conjugal right. If they do not do so and move a married male employee instead, they are guilty of favouring the conjugal right of one man (their female employee's husband) over the career interests of another – their own male employee.

Public and private: sources of separation

The men of High Street Retail, the Service and the Local Authority are not exceptional in their resistance to change. There is no evidence of men's attachment to paid work modifying in response to married women's entry into paid jobs. Indeed, men in the UK work longer hours in their paid employment (an average of 43.5 per week) than men in any other EEC country, and their commitment of time to paid work actually increased by 40 minutes per week between 1984 and 1986 (Central Statistical Office 1990). The sexual division of roles, with men making the economic input, women giving the labour time, intensifies with parenthood. Peter Moss finds that the longest hours are worked by men with young families.

They need to compensate by overtime for the loss of their partner's earnings. Married men under thirty with children work four times as much paid overtime as similarly-aged but childless husbands. Even among the relatively few men who are single parents, 86% work and most full-time. Their average weekly stint of 41 hours is only one hour less than that of fathers in married couples (Moss 1980:48). Later British studies confirm such findings (Sharpe 1984, Martin and Roberts 1984). Nor does being unemployed appear to drive men to the kitchen sink (McKee and Bell 1985).

Political context seems to make little difference to the likelihood of men becoming more domesticated. In social democratic Sweden only one in five fathers uses parental leave and those who do on average take only 41 days to care for their baby (Svenska Institutet 1987). This is in spite of the fact that a proportion of the leave is forfeit if the father does not take it. In Norway men reduced their paid work time by five hours a week – but increased their household work by only 12 minutes per day. The rest became increased leisure time (Lingsom and Ellingsaeter 1983). Women in the Soviet Union have recently developed a new policy approach involving a controversial critique of men's neglect of domestic, caring and educative roles. They write of the 'mono-functional man', with his limited perspective of breadwinner (Zaharova *et al.* 1990). In China, during the revolutionary period of the Great Leap Forward, some housework and childcare was socialized. By 1960, however, the woman was once again, in practice if not in ideology, the main domestic worker. 'The Chinese Communist Party has heavily emphasised equal status in the home, but it has been far less insistent on achieving interchangeable roles' (Adams and Winston 1980:217). Finally North America confirms the pattern.

> Men do very little housework . . . Whether men are asked to estimate the time that they spend at housework, or wives are asked to estimate their husbands' time, or outside observers actually clock the amount of time that men spend at it, no-one has ever estimated men's share of housework at anything higher than one and a half hours per day. Housewives who are not employed in the labour market spend, roughly speaking, fifty hours a week doing housework; housewives who are employed outside their homes spend, again roughly speaking, thirty-five hours on their work in and for their homes. Men whose wives are employed spend about ten minutes more a day on housework than men whose wives stay home . . . (Cowan 1989:200).

There is a vicious circle here, of course. Women's relatively low pay prevents men giving up their salary to care for the home, while women's domestic confinement limits their chance of earning a salary on which they could, wholly or partly, support man and child.

Many feminists have identified the separation of public and private spheres as constitutive of male power. Michelle Rosaldo for instance, on anthropological evidence, suggests that the more closely associated the institutions surrounding motherhood with those of the wider society, the more egalitarian is that society likely to be (Rosaldo 1974). Recent theoretical work by Mary O'Brien offers a sustained account of men's relationship to paternity that enables us to see these separations, of private and public, nature and culture, the domestic and the economic, in historical context (O'Brien 1981). Once a Glaswegian midwife, now a Canadian political theorist, O'Brien draws on the practical experience of many births, many paternities. She considers anew the Marxist understanding of production – labour in response to the necessity of individual subsistence. She shows how our theories have neglected *reproduction*, another kind of labour in response to another necessity, that of birth and the survival of the species. Children are the product of conscious labour, she argues, both the labour of parturition and that of domestic life.

O'Brien suggests that an early turning point in human history – indeed the beginning of human history – was the slow dawning on humankind of the practical facts of paternity, the relationship of coition to pregnancy and birth. This new knowledge brought a transformation in male reproductive consciousness. Men became aware of being alienated from their seed in the act of insemination, divorced from genetic continuity and from the cyclical time of the natural world. While a woman has always known her own child, for a man paternity has been fraught with uncertainty. 'Nature' says O'Brien, 'is unjust to men. She includes and excludes at the same moment' (O'Brien 1981:60).

In an attempt to mend this alienation, to establish certainty and mediate time, men *appropriate* the child. They claim, however, more than the child alone. They claim ownership of women's reproductive labour and labour power. Patriarchy was the constitution of the family as a private realm in which men established conjugal right to control women, to segregate them from other men and lessen the doubt that haunts paternity. To achieve such control 'requires a community of actively cooperating men and the creation of social institutions to buttress the abstract notion of right. Man the procreator, by virtue of his need to mediate his alienation from procreation, is essentially man the creator' (O'Brien 1981:56). In the space among and between men, men create culture and politics, make history and assure, artificially, their own mode of continuity.

Like Pateman and Mies, O'Brien is insisting that we cannot see the subordination of women as a vestige of a bygone age, soon to be modernized out of existence, but must see it as the bedrock of 'democracy' as we live it. The project of building civil societies and creating democratic constitutions in Eastern European countries following the events of 1989 has made painfully evident that men expect women's subordination to continue: after all, what has women's liberation to do with democracy?

The distance separating this grand schema from the banal realities of the lived relationship of contemporary men, managers and employees of the retail trade, clerks and professionals of the Civil Service, officers of local government, is not too great for the analysis to throw light on their behaviour and discourse. As I have shown, men continue, with verve but scant imagination, to assert their right, legitimated by appeal to nature and to history, to a woman who will attend both to their own domestic needs and the rearing of their children. They continue to express themselves as uneasy with the emergence of those women from the private realm into the economic and political world of men. They play their lives as the deft administration of the sexual contract, maintaining the proper gender-relationship of its domestic clause on the one hand, its workplace clause on the other. They dedicate their creativeness to the public sphere, to production, politics, governance.

Many men feel a sadness and an anxiety over their alienation from women and domestic concerns. They regret their dependence on women to bear their children and link them to reproduction, to the species. They suffer from the increased independence of women and the growing volatility of marriage, which often removes their children from them. Increasingly too men are recognizing the costs they pay, tied to the rat race to earn their breadwinner-wage. Yet the gap between themselves and women is not easily closed. If they are to come closer, really share our lives, contribute their own labour of love (as opposed to their money) to childrearing, to the care of the ill and elderly, to the sustenance of life, men will have to renounce their male sex-right and with it their masculine identity as it is currently constituted. Some men know this. A few are willing to do it, but individual voluntarism is not enough. More and more will be forced to think about it. The dilemma for men is intensifying as women – with advances in contraceptive technology, access to a salary, backed by this pervasive ideology of 'equality' and with feminist ideas always within reach – become new people.

Meanwhile, however, 'mothers' privileges' are highly contradictory for women. It is not surprising that any opposition to them from men is muted. They are beneficial in bridging the gap between work and home. But they benefit only some women and for a relatively short span of their working lives. If they are not extended to men and used by men, so that men too come to lead more 'womanly' lives, increased support for women's domestic role could drive women even more firmly into a distinct, domestically-defined, place in the labour market. What in the long run has to change is the pattern of men's lives. A forty-five hour week, a forty-eight-week year and a fifty-year wage-earning life cannot be sustained by both sexes. It should be worked by neither.

4

Woman's worth

The domestication of a single sex, then, producing women as a category on the labour market distinguishable from men, opens to the employer the possibility of a special form of exploitation. While some women for some part of their lives may manage to escape into pay and conditions not greatly inferior to those of men, the paradigm case of the woman worker-with-domestic-ties is the woman part-time low paid manual or office worker. These are the millions of women, characteristically but not exclusively in the public services, who cook and clean, wash, make and mend, type and tidy, tend and care. They include a disproportionate number of black and ethnic minority women.

This chapter looks at what 'equal opportunities' means in the case of such base-line women workers. Some may value the chance of promotion to a supervisory post or training for transfer to some more skilled, traditionally masculine, occupation. To propose a managerial or professional career perspective, however, of the kind discussed in Chapter 2, is to ignore both the nature of the constraints on such women and that employers need and intend to hold on to some such super-exploitable category of employees at the bottom of their organizations. To propose 'equality of opportunity' through the twin policies discussed in Chapters 2 and 3 – that is, first, enabling a few women to escape the women's work ghetto and, second, providing more generous maternity leave provisions to help them and those they leave behind cope with the pressures of domestic life – is not enough. The ghetto walls have to be brought down. A relevant policy for the majority of women really has to be about changing the structure itself: ending low pay; breaking job segregation by redesigning jobs or retraining staff or both; re-evaluating and up-grading their occupations; and restructuring grade systems to reduce differentials. Few employers will make such changes voluntarily. They are not even on their 'short' equality agenda. They are, however, as we shall see, sometimes pursued by equality officers as part of the equality project and also by trade unions, when women are strong enough within them to overcome the resistance of male members. The story can conveniently be told through the sex equality strategies of the Local Authority and our Trade Union, whose actions were, in some of their phases, interconnected.

Tackling women's low pay

Local councils in Britain are responsible for the delivery of services such as housing, schools and environmental maintenance, activities dependent on the repetitive manual effort of large workforces. A study published in 1982 showed the painful extent to which women in local government employment were concentrated within the lower grades. Male manual workers characteristically occupy upper manual grades (Local Government Operational Research Unit 1982). The resulting difference in rates of pay, given the 'public service' nature of these organizations, is spectacular. A *pro rata* factor of ten is not unusual between the senior council officers (almost all men) and the lowest grade employees (almost always part-time manual women).

In 1979 the Local Authority and the Trade Union in my study had together agreed a pay deal in advance of the national settlement giving the council's low-paid workers a minimum wage of £60 and a 35-hour week. This decision was subsequently challenged in court but the council successfully defended their decision on the grounds that, had they not settled, the ensuing industrial action threatened by the Union would have damaged local ratepayers' interests. A similar partnership-in-conflict between these two Labour-oriented organizations occurred in 1983 when a further claim by the Union prompted the Local Authority to commission an independent report on low pay among its manual workers. Following the report's recommendations the council introduced a minimum earnings guarantee. This raised the level of the lowest-paid absolutely. But also, being graduated, it diminished the differential between top and bottom manual grades and thus between the sexes. The measure was woman-friendly in another way too. It boosted London weighting, sick pay and maternity pay, important to women, while not increasing overtime payments, which mainly accrue to men. The Local Authority was not alone among London boroughs in the eighties in using as equalizing measures such devices as low-pay supplements, minimum earnings guarantees and the consolidation of bonus pay into basic pay.

The Local Authority also initiated an independent performance review of certain base-line women's jobs in the council. But in 1985 a nationwide re-evaluation and regrading affecting one million local authority manual occupations achieved something much more far-reaching. Progressive Labour-led authorities and the three major manual work unions had been influential in this exercise. A new job evaluation scheme had been introduced, designed to remove sex-bias. For the first time women's characteristic 'caring' skills were recognized. The job of home help, for instance, was now acknowledged to entail not only a high degree of initiative, mental and physical effort, but also a new quality: 'responsibility for people'. Working alone in the client's home, without direct supervision, was seen as calling for a high degree of trustworthiness. Such factors lifted home helps (almost all women, many of them black) to a grade at which they drew level with the 'male' jobs of school caretaker, gardener and refuse vehicle driver. In addition to such gains for individual female occupations, the review reduced the number of grades and thus levelled overall differentials.

The manual unions argue that, while job re-evaluation and regrading on these lines can help women in the lower grades it is at best a redistribution of resources among the poorest. *All* manual workers are low-paid and their work as a whole should be re-evaluated and its conditions 'harmonized' with those pertaining in white collar work. This would certainly benefit a larger group of working-class women and is a strategy often legitimated by an appeal to sex and 'race' equality. A study by a London shop stewards' combine argued,

apart from economic expedience there can be no rational basis for perpetuating a system whereby one group of workers (the group which includes the fewest ethnic minority workers and, in most boroughs, the lowest proportion of women) works shorter hours, gets longer holidays, and is subject to more lenient grievance and disciplinary procedures than another group, simply because it happens to do work which is labelled 'white collar' (London Bridge 1987:39).

Harmonization also, of course, benefits male manual workers and for this reason is rarely controversial with the male-dominated manual unions. Pressed by the latter, the Local Authority had in fact taken some steps towards harmonization, introducing a 35-hour week for all employees and a unified disciplinary code giving manual workers much greater protection than before against dismissal.

Many of the gains for manual workers, however, in this local authority as in others, were threatened by the increasingly vicious financial constraints imposed by central government and by the consequences of the Local Government Act 1988, which compelled councils to put services such as cleaning and provision of school meals, many of them staffed by low-paid women, to competitive tender. Whether a private contractor won the bid or the council succeeded in undercutting the competition with its in-house team, the result was usually a deterioration of the situation of the employees concerned. If they did not lose their jobs they were likely to experience wage cuts, a reduction in hours, greater intensity of work and sometimes loss of benefits. Increasingly, as the eighties wore on, formerly left-Labour councils shifted from the red to the blue end of the political spectrum. Equal opportunities went 'out the window' and the partnership between the councils and 'their' unions, always rocky, deteriorated into more serious conflict.

Equality and the unions

In the Local Authority it had been the management side in the name of equality policy for council workers that had instigated the performance review that reconsidered the structure of typing and some other female jobs. The council's equality staff had been involved in prompting training schemes for women to help break down sex-segregation. These had included, for instance, courses to enable women in the housing department to become caretakers, and apprenticeships for women in the building department's trades. Ethnic minority women had been offered professional social work training and courses were organized for young unemployed black

women in clerical skills to help them compete for council jobs. On
the other hand it had not been through an autonomous initiative by
the council but rather through the *industrial relations* mechanism
that the initiatives on low pay, grade levelling and harmonization
had been generated. These were, for all that, 'equality' initiatives.
As we shall see, the unions, like employers, have their women
activists, their equality policies and their positive action programmes (Equal Opportunities Commission 1983, Trade Union
Research Unit 1986, Ellis 1988, SERTUC 1989). Woman-friendly
bargaining ploys therefore may be seen as reflecting eqality
initiatives in the labour movement. We saw another example in
the Service, where the running was from the start made by the
union. At best, positive action for women converges from both
sides in the industrial relations process.

How much unions do commit themselves to 'equality bargaining'
is of great importance to women. Although union power has been
systematically undermined, evaded and localised under the Thatcher government of the last ten years, and the unions have suffered
a decline in membership, joint regulation still determines the basic
pay and conditions of the majority of British workers. Over half of
all establishments in private manufacturing in 1984 recognized a
trade union for negotiation on behalf of at least some of their
workers (Colling and Dickens 1989:5). All public sector organizations do so. The unions besides share a responsibility for
implementing the Sex Discrimination Act. The amendment of
1986 made illegal any outcome of collective bargaining which
constitutes direct or indirect discrimination on grounds of sex or
marital status. Just as collective bargaining can perpetuate inequalities so potentially it can do much to dismantle them.

There is, however, frequently tension between equality officers
and equality units, on the one hand, and union branches on the
other. Seldom do they raise quite the same equality issues or press
for quite the same gains. In most private sector equality projects, as
in High Street Retail, unions are discouraged from involvement, if
not actively excluded. Employers do not want equal opportunities
to become yet another stick for the unions to beat them with. But
then, trade unions operating in the private sector are often negligent
or even opposed to raising equality issues. A recent study showed
that union negotiators, mainly men, accorded the equality legislation scant importance as a factor in collective bargaining and

showed little understanding of concepts such as 'indirect discrimination' (Colling and Dickens 1989:46). In the public sector, though the unions nationally have more actively espoused equality issues, this does not guarantee local implementation. Equality officers report often finding themselves up against white male shop stewards or officials at local level who are hostile to equal opportunity measures. Problems of this kind were 'a very common theme' among respondents to a study involving 25 local council equality officers inside and outside London. The animosity was reported as being particularly acute in the case of manual unions, on occasion amounting to sabotage of equality initiatives. Women equality officers, their loyalty divided, felt themselves put in 'a somewhat unclear position somewhere between management and unions and . . . liable to be resented by both' (Stone 1988:56).

The unions' ambivalence to sex and 'race' equality is in part the result of the individualist approach to equality of opportunity preferred by employers, in contrast to the collectivist traditions of the labour movement. Often, however, the ambivalence of the unions has to be read as a negative male response to women's activism. Trade unions, like workplaces, are male-dominated and have historically given priority to the interests of their male members. Women were once altogether excluded from some skilled unions (Boston 1987). They were admitted to the engineering union, for example, only in 1942. In others, such as those organizing in the printing industry, women were restricted by union rule to certain lowly occupational groups (Cockburn 1983). It is not surprising therefore that women have found these skilled unions the most resistant to equality policies. Even these unions, however, have had to recognize that structural change in the economy compels a new response. Between 1961 and 1981 manual employment fell by 2% while non-manual employment increased by 20%. Women's presence grew from 33% of the economically active population to 40%. In the ten years 1970–79 alone, the number of women in trade unions doubled, to reach 3.5 million, involving a 42% increase among women workers against only 6% among men (Central London Community Law Centre 1987). Even in the years of union decline since 1979, while overall membership was falling back from 12 million to 9 million the proportion of women in the membership went on growing. By the late eighties a third of all union members were women (Cockburn 1987). Nor was this a product only of changes in employment, it was also a matter of motivation. The sixties and seventies saw women becoming more committed to unionism as men lost interest. In those two decades a 4% decline in union 'density' among male workers was matched by a similar increase among females (Bain and Price 1983). Black women were particularly supportive of unions. A study in 1984 showed that 57% of West Indian and 38% of Asian women employees were union members, against 34% of white women (Policy Studies Institute 1984).

Unions, then, even those representing male craftsmen in declining manufacturing industries, were having to recognize that if they were to survive, let alone to prosper, they must actively look to recruit women in related occupations – even if it meant poaching from rival unions. The public sector unions and white collar unions, however, hardly had to search. It was in their domains that the growth in women workers was occurring. As we have seen, much of the growth was in part-time work. The unions recruiting in these areas were forced to realize that their bread and butter depended on genuinely seeking to understand and represent the interests of women, even of the despised part-timers. 'Their enormous contribution in caring and productive jobs is undervalued, misunderstood and unrecognized', admitted Rodney Bickerstaffe, General Secretary of the National Union of Public Employees (Central London Community Law Centre 1987). It was becoming clear that the paradigmatic union member today was not the coalminer nor the railman but the female hospital ancillary worker. The truth was gradually dawning that the old bargaining priorities would no longer serve.

Male unionists' ability to keep men's issues at the top of the bargaining agenda has been assisted by the exclusion of women both from full-time official jobs and from the decision-making committees and councils that govern unions. A study in 1981 showed that the degree of women's under-representation in this respect had changed little since a TUC survey a quarter century before (Ellis 1981). If women's interests are better represented by trade unions today it has not been because of any natural trend but because of a concerted struggle by women themselves to defeat male self-interest (Beale 1982, Hunt 1982, Central London Community Law Centre 1987, Ellis 1988). As women, encouraged by new-wave feminism, became more active in the unions they successively won at least a formal commitment to positive action from some individual unions and from the TUC, which in 1979 published a ten-point charter for women's equality (Trades Union Congress 1979). By the late eighties many of the trade unions had appointed women's officers and many by now had active strategies for their women members. In the best of these, notably public sector and white-collar unions, women had begun to influence collective bargaining.

Women active on women's issues in the unions, however, have reported meeting opposition from some union 'comrades' at every step. A recent study of more than one hundred full-time officers in 39 unions found that eight out of ten felt a woman 'had to fight harder to gain the same respect as a male in the job'. The resistance occurred, it seemed, almost equally among male colleagues, superiors, members and employers. Some of the women officials were 'clearly very angry with the way they had been treated by men' (Heery and Kelly 1988:47).

Representing low-paid women

Many of these trends apparent in the labour movement at large were visible in the particular Trade Union that enabled me to make a case study of its equality policies. In its recent history we can see some of the somersaults male trade unionists were being obliged to turn in order to present a progressive face to new circumstances.

The Trade Union in question organizes manual workers in the public sector where it has almost two-thirds of a million members, three-quarters of whom are women and three-quarters of those part-timers. It operates through eleven regional councils and offices, has 1200 local branches and as many as 25000 elected shop stewards. The Union's women members are characteristically school meals cooks and cleaners, care assistants, nurses, nursery staff and home helps. Men are mainly school caretakers, parks and gardens staff, refuse collectors, ambulance staff, porters and ancillary workers of various kinds. The jobs of both sexes are primarily manual and low-graded, though women tend to be on yet lower grades than men. This grade disparity is reflected in their average hourly gross pay, which is only 80% that of their male counterparts.

Democracy is an important variable in organizations, and one with a considerable bearing on women, clustering as they do at the base of most. The four organizations included in this study differ as environments for equal opportunities activity due to variations in the degree of democracy that springs from their structure and function. In High Street Retail the autocratic effects of a hierarchical system of control needed no legitimation. This was simply the natural mode of a profitable business in which top managers answer only to the board that represents the interests of the owners. In the Service the effects did require negotiation and, as we saw, both men and women had appealed at different periods and in different ways to fairness and 'opportunity' in order to open up career paths. In neither of these organizations, however, was democracy an active concept.

In the Local Authority, by contrast, an elected council did see itself as formally representative of the community and even, ideally, of its ethnic and sex diversity. It was felt right that not only the elected members but also, to some extent, the officers working in the town hall and neighourhood offices should 'stand for' the local people. The multicultural community visible on the streets and in the shops should be self-governing. Apart from democratic principle, this was seen as the only way of ensuring appropriate services. Here, too, the hierarchical nature of organization was at least open to challenge. The women's unit, for instance, had successfully argued for operating as a collective.

The Union was different again in being a membership organization. Here the hierarchies both of lay representatives and of paid officials were continually called on by the membership to justify themselves. The high proportion of women in its membership and the sexual division of labour reflected in it resulted in a situation in which to represent women in union strategies clearly meant also to represent a set of interests characteristic *of* women. They included the defence of local and health services and promoting the value of caring skills. In this sense the Union was obviously more vulnerable to 'women' than the other three organizations.

In the seventies the Union had called in academic consultants to devise an appropriate structure for maintaining 'democracy and efficiency' in the organization. The changes flowing from the consultants' advice reflected a belief 'in the crucial importance of democracy and humanitarianism', in a time when a massive increase in membership was threatening to render the leadership more and more remote. The thrust of the proposals was to strengthen the involvement of the membership and the role of lay representatives, to decentralise the Union and to render it less dependent on its paid officials. The resulting structure with later amendments was embodied in today's 'rule book'. It was a system of indirect representation, based on a network of shop stewards and branch secretaries, delegated upward into a hierarchical system of district, area, divisional and national committees and councils, all ultimately answerable to national conference.

One thing the survey exposed was the serious numerical under-representation of women members at all levels in the Union. Basically this, like every other union, was run by men for men. Women members, numerous though they might be, were seen as little more than a source of subscriptions. It was not for some years, however, that a serious intention was signalled to change things. In 1981 national conference resolved on a women's working party to advise the executive council on means of encouraging women's greater participation. In 1982 the first women's officer was appointed at head office and divisional women's advisory commit-tees were set up, followed shortly by one at national level.

An important element in sex equality policy in the Union was a set of positive measures to improve the representation and activism of women members. Steps were taken to recruit some women as full-time officials. Branches were pressed to reduce procedural formality and organize meetings in work hours or provide child-care to enable more women to become active and get elected as lay representatives. A substantial proportion of the education budget was allocated to 'schools' for women and about women's needs.

The most urgent reason to improve the representation of women in the Union was of course to ensure that women's interests were adequately reflected in negotiation with employers. Most pay-bargaining was done nationally, involving this union as one of several making joint claims as the 'staff side' of various negotiating bodies. Certain principles introduced by the Union into its annual negotiations were a direct response to the recommendations of the women's working party and were a notable break with precedent in the trade union movement. Especially beneficial to women's interests was the emphasis on ending low pay and narrowing pay differentials, in particular through the demand for flat rate, rather than percentage, pay increases. Second the Union adopted a goal of reducing the number of grades and the differences between grades. Third it set about negotiating improved terms and conditions for part-timers, most of whom are women. Equal pay for work of equal value had also been an important issue in the Union in recent years. There was, however, as we shall see, disagreement as to the best way of progressing towards this.

Despite these steps towards sex equality women activists in the Union remained dissatisfied with the slow pace of change. Many believed that little more would be gained without a bolder commitment to positive action, and some wished this to include the setting of firm quotas for a representative proportion of women among paid and lay representatives at all levels in the Union. A demand so directly threatening to men's position, however, could scarcely be raised in the prevailing climate. The women's officer made it clear she felt that, despite their overwhelming majority in the membership, women were still no more than a 'pressure group' in what continued to be a male union. This could not yet, by any stretch of the imagination, be called *a women's union*, and nothing less was appropriate.

Union men: standing in women's way

What then were the impediments to change? As I made my way around the Union talking with women and men from shop steward to general secretary it was possible to see clearly that the difficulties emerged in an interaction between the beliefs and behaviours of individual men and the structuring of the Union as an institution. This process of dominance, for that is what it is, is best exemplified by reference to two important roles in the union, those of branch secretary and full-time officer.

The reshaping of the Union had had a contradictory effect for women. On the one hand, in giving heightened value to the representational process it had prompted a growing perception that the membership *was*, after all, largely female and that their representational needs might differ from those of male members. Any democratization tends to favour the interests of those at the base of an organization. However, the particular system adopted here had been one in which the power lay less with members as such

than with lay representatives. Being a system of indirect representation involving progressive delegation from one tier to another, it
had created of the branch secretaries 'a clique', a 'major power
bloc', with a tendency to restrict the involvement of the ordinary
member. The clique had become self-perpetuating. They 'nominate
each other for this and that', so that the same faces appeared year
after year on committees, councils and at national conference.

Of these 1200 branch secretaries three-quarters were men. Men,
naturally, represented male branches, but they also frequently
served as secretary to branches with mainly women members.
Worse, sometimes the branch secretary was both the women's
spokesperson and their 'gaffer', as when a school caretaker represented school cleaners. Women, I was told, find it more difficult
than men to put themselves forward for election, to think that they
could do the job as well for the members as an experienced full-time
male who, first, has few domestic duties to eat up his free time and,
second, is accorded more respect by employers. Women have less
facility with the jargon and procedures that male trade unionists
have developed over the decades. When they first attend meetings
they hear technical terms being thrown around – 'are we quorate?',
'let's refer it back' – and they feel the men who deploy them with
such facility are the natural leaders. I met several male branch
secretaries who had been re-elected for continuous periods of up to
ten or fifteen years. One such justified his position by saying 'I'm
part of the geography of the Union. That's the way the Union
works. It works through me as far as [they] are concerned. I'm a lot
more skilled than them'. Given these perceptions, it is perhaps not
surprising that many women, as well as men, vote for men to
represent them.

The life of a branch secretary in this Union can offer many perks
that he (or she) comes to take for granted. First there is a financial
incentive, the ethical implications of which are worrying. Branch
secretaries receive a percentage commission on members' subscriptions that in 1989 could amount to as much as £500 a month. That
is hard to let go. Then there is time off with pay from what may be
a boring, hard and menial job to do the more attractive work of the
union. There are regular trips to attend committees or conferences.
Above all perhaps there is the appeal of 'being someone'. 'There's a
lot of ego involved' said one male branch secretary frankly, 'When
you go into a negotiation and the employer has to take you

seriously. When your members always listen to what you say. When you have a strike and can bring the whole city to its knees. Yes, it does make you feel powerful.'

The result, as many women told me, is that too many branch secretaries, especially men, 'assume they have a position for life'. A bad branch secretary can be a source of inertia and obstruction. 'You come across branch secretaries who like to keep all of the information and all of the work to themselves. It cripples them, but they won't give it up.' A branch secretary may treat the members and shop stewards (especially women) as 'his flock', taking all initiative out of their hands, blocking women's progress. At worst, such a representative can become a tool of the management, closer to the employer with whom he habitually deals than to his members. Several of these men were quite honest about their permanence. 'So long as no one complains I'll go on standing'. 'I can't see any woman standing against the general secretary. I can't see any woman standing against me.' 'I'm very selfish in a way. I want to hang on to the job and I don't want to have to share it with others who may come and compete for it. I have to be honest about that.'

The preponderance of men in the role would not be so damaging if they adequately represented women's interests, but women felt men knew little and often cared little about 'women's issues'. 'It's partly ignorance. Their wives are the ones who experience domestic problems, not them. Nothing in their experience tells them.' So they have hidebound ideas about what the union is for. One woman had noticed that among delegates to national conference 'the men never spoke on women's problems. And when the women spoke it was *only* on women's problems. Some men spoke against us.' The result has been a far more cogent rendering of male than of female interests in the Union. 'It's all filtered through a male brain.'

There is a good deal of frank misogyny and sexism among the men. It is not so long since, as one woman put it, 'county roadmen were the heart of the Union', men who had their union get-togethers 'in the pub of a Sunday morning while the wife cooked Sunday dinner'. There are still men in the union who believe that part-timers should have only half a vote, who believe that pay claims should be based on 'the male breadwinner and the family he supports', and that men's jobs should be protected at the expense of women's. These are the men who disagree with the Union's policy of flat-rate pay increases, grade levelling and equal value, and are frequently heard these days exclaiming in exasperation 'Bloody women!'. For such men's spleen is exacerbated by the disturbing sensation of being a diminishing minority in the membership. 'Men will soon be a rump', one grumbled. 'Women will dominate the workplace, the union and bargaining practices, the lot.' Whilst few men today would be rash enough 'to get up and say openly sexist things at conference' there is no doubt that many men felt the equality strategy was out of order, the Union had 'gone too far on women'. 'We represent some of the most working-class people in the country, and working-class men look after their wife and kids. If the woman earns, great. But it's the man who's *expected* to earn. The Union ought to temper a little sensibility into their arguments.' One man had given up being a shop steward because he 'couldn't stand' the activity around the women's committee. 'When it comes to positive action for women – that's where you lose the men'.

> I see it creeping in. I see it creeping in . . . [said one branch secretary bitterly]. People voted for the best person, the one who was going to be able to do the job. But now I've this sneaky feeling we're getting away from that. Whereby a woman is getting voted on just because she's a woman. But who's going to do the best job? 'That doesn't come into it. We want a woman.' And in many cases the candidate is being pressurized to put herself forward. 'Go on, you have a go at it.' I think it's bad for the Union. It's bad for the Union.

A woman who had unseated a male branch secretary had to survive a campaign of vilification against her. He cut her dead, spoke ill of her behind her back. The hurt, she said, 'it's dreadful. It goes very deep. You can't believe it's happening to you. When you're only trying to do something well.' If these were the responses only of the old guard they might be expected to die out with time. But it is not only masculine traditionalism. One woman said, 'the new ones are shittier than the old, hanging on to what they can in the face of our revolution.'

There are more practical measures that could be taken to encourage women forward into lay representative positions. Women point out, for instance, that there is nothing in the rule book to restrict the number of shop stewards. Two could work in tandem, sharing the role. With a simple rule-change, the branch secretary job too might be opened to job-sharing so that an experienced branch secretary could train a less experienced person. Using such a team approach, 'when this wonderful man does in the course of time move on, it's clear to everyone there's a woman there capable of taking over from him'. A further rule reform discussed by women is restricting the period for which an individual may continuously hold office. 'There'd be huge opposition. That's where the explosion would happen. But if it were accepted, change would flow through the union.' As she ruefully pointed out, however, the men who dominate national conference where rule changes are agreed, are 'unlikely to die at their own hand'.

Given the prevalence of such antagonism among men, the leadership are cautious about alienating the male member by too much equality activity. Men might desert for a rival union, or become embittered and inactive. 'If you give the impression that most of the men in the union, including me, are going to lose their job to women in five years . . . people would become very defensive and worried about it. So you've got to handle it very carefully.' The pressure from some men, and its management by other men, together effectively restrict the extent and pace of positive action for sex equality.

Full-time paid hero

The full-time officer has a key role in the Union. Despite the formal democracy of the Union's structure, 'it's the officers that hold the power. Not the executive council, national conference even less.' Operating from head office, from divisions and area offices, they are the ones who support and advise lay representatives, maintain the continuity, deal with crisis and conflict, and do much of the negotiation with larger employers, taking national agreements and 'fleshing them out' locally, in the detailed job descriptions, duties, hours and equal opportunities clauses that make all the difference to the circumstances of members.

Because men dominated the Union's decision-making bodies, it was largely men who were in a position to select these full-time officers. Partly for this reason they too remained, as in other unions, overwhelmingly (89%) male. In the spirit of positive action for sex equality the Union had recently urged divisions to consider women candidates more favourably for officer posts. In the name of better representation it had also shifted to a policy of recruiting more officers from the membership, in place of professional trade union officers from the movement. The two aims were apparently compatible, since the majority of members are women. Such positive action had recently resulted in the appointment of a handful of women officers.

Some existing male officials, however, deplored the new trend. Representation would be hindered rather than helped by this move, they said. First, the women so appointed were likely to be from the middle-class para-professional groups in the membership, such as nurses. These would be less representative of working-class women than the working-class men they supplanted. They also feared the members, women and men alike, would be short-changed by a fall in the quality of officer. 'We are cutting ourselves off from the great influx of fulltime officers we had in the late sixties and early seventies where we benefited from people from engineering, the mines, transport, factories, the whole range of the British trade union movement. We were recruiting the best.' They clearly had in mind as the ideal officer not only men, but the real McCoy, industrial labour movement aristocrats.

The work of a trade union officer is very demanding. He (or she) will be out at meetings two or three nights a week and will have commitments many weekends of the year. The job involves fostering branches and servicing representatives. It means being endlessly on call, ready to respond to every kind of crisis – victimisation, disciplinaries, redundancies, disputes. There is conflict with the bosses but there is also an element of rivalry with other unions locally in the competition to recruit new members, have a local reputation, be a local force.

The job has traditionally been an arena for masculine heroics and this was reflected in the men's portrayal of it. 'First and foremost you need commitment. Twenty-four-hour a day, seven-day-a-week commitment.' 'You need leadership. You need to put up with flak both from officers and members. You need to have a thick skin.' 'The first skill you have to have is an unwavering belief in yourself and what you stand for . . . . In other words you've got to be a bit of an egotist, basically, to cope.' Men felt women 'hadn't got the bottle' for the job. 'How would she deal with a crowd of drunken bin men?' They set up the job for women as something like an assault course for trainee marines. 'Once they've proved themselves, once you've seen them operating in the mire and dirt where people are kicking each other to death and you've seen they can survive without crumbling . . . [then] they'll have respect.'

In many ways the full-time union officer was clad in the same glory as the hero-manager of modern business. And women's response to this ethos was similar. While men relished the combative element of the job, women problematised it. They described the work in other terms. 'You must be patient, resilient, able to take criticisms. You need to be well-organized, able to handle many things at once. You need to be able to get on with people.' For women, communication skills rated high. 'You have to be able to talk to people. You have to take people with you . . .'. Even with the employer there was scope for developing relationships. 'I don't mean you have to be friends with them, but you have to relate to them on a professional basis.' Women defended their own way of doing the job. 'I don't think I'm any less effective than any of my male colleagues', said one young woman. 'You can only say a woman's ineffective when you've seen a woman and a man performing the same job. And we've not yet had a chance to see many women doing the job.' A new woman officer was distressed by the lack of collective working in the divisional office. 'The ethos is one of individualism. You work alone till you do something wrong, then they come down on you like a ton of bricks.' It was, she pointed out, a curious ideology for a nominally collective movement.

The women of one divisional women's advisory committee had made a written submission to their divisional council appealing for an equal opportunities recruitment policy. They complained of the 'male grey-suited image' of trade union officers and of men 'boasting about the number of hours they worked and talking continually about their achievements in an aggressive and obsessional way [which] put women full-time officers under further pressure to keep up with and perform the same as their male counterparts'. They argued that the job could be humanized. Patches could be shared, officers cover for each other. Their proposals got short shrift, however, from their male divisional officer.

Women who had been rash enough to take on the role of fulltime officer reported being systematically undermined by male colleagues, employers, lay representatives and members. Senior men had many ways of holding a woman back. 'They intimidate you by contradicting things you say.' 'Men can push you back quite gently'. 'They are extremely clever at keeping you in the background.' One described how her male colleagues would be scrupulously polite, 'treat you like a queen, then undermine you behind your back.' In dealings with employers, also mainly men, she found 'they play all the tricks that you would get from men in everyday life . . . . They'll flatter you. They'll patronize you. They'll try and put you down in front of your own members in a way I don't believe they'd ever try to do with a man.' In meetings, when you express a justifiable anger that would be not just tolerated but admired in a man you are told: 'don't get emotional'. Many men show you scant respect, will not hear you out, shout you down. A group of manual workers had told one of these female officers 'we don't want any more women at our meetings'. Another woman officer obtained her position in direct competition with a male branch secretary in her division. He was so angered by being passed over for a woman he threatened to leave the Union, taking his entire branch of 3000 members with him. The difficulty for the incoming woman officer of building confidence and cooperation in her new patch in the wake of such divisiveness can be imagined. Some women members too prefer their male heroes and can make life hard for a woman officer. 'My ladies will never accept a woman.' The men relish this, saying 'women often prefer to discuss their problems with a man'.

The full-time officer job places intolerable strain on family life. The men's wives tell them 'the Union's seen more of you than your children have'. One man's wife had cited the Union in her divorce petition. But still men would say 'my job comes first with me'. Clearly the job leeches out more from the domestic situation than it puts in. Few of the women officers I met had dependent children. Those who had partners often depended on them being more flexible and supportive about the home than the traditional man, certainly than the traditional male union officer. Women struggled to sustain something like a 'normal' life alongside this demanding job. They thought sometimes the job ought, now and then, to give way to domestic need. A man, by contrast, when asked if he would consider such a reprioritising, replied sardonically, 'I doubt very much if some of my colleagues would tolerate the argument from someone in my position that "I can't see you this week because I've got childcare responsibilities".' Instead, the characteristic man thrives on the outward pull. 'It's competitive, succeeding. Very much so. I wouldn't be happy with a job I didn't have to give everything to. A job that was dull.' To do the job differently would be, they feel, to do it worse, for the member, for the Union.

There was, however, a very small minority of men who, in resonance with women colleagues, were able to envisage the possibility of something different. One said

> I've loved my time in the union. I love the union. But . . . I wouldn't do it again. I mean you can't live your life twice. I've lost all the strengths and rich experiences that would come from being closer to the children and helping to bring them up. I think you've got to shift the practice, to look at a practice of trade unionism which isn't as hyperactive and elitist and vanguardist as trade unionism has been in the past . . . . [It would be] a movement that reflects the members' needs, not just in [their work]. You'd say straight down the line this isn't a special, privileged job. Your members want leisure time and to spend more time with their families. This should reflect back on *your* role [as a union officer] as well.

With so much resistance to women from the average full-time officer, women often ask themselves how sincere are those less-average men at the top in their apparent project of transforming the union to meet women's needs. The Union, after all, is publicly and energetically committed to the advancement of the woman worker, of women in society and to equal opportunity in all guises. But is it just rhetoric? Just as the leadership is known to be ambitious to carve out a place for the union on green issues, and to be in the forefront of the labour movement in the fight against privatisation, so perhaps instrumental advantage is seen in being the acknow-ledged leader on 'women'.

The average woman member, I was frequently told, was devoted to the male leadership. The general secretary for instance,

> from the member's point of view is beyond criticism . . . I mean they *love* him. One of my branch secretaries said, 'I'd trust him with *my life*'. And meant it. They know if he's had a hand in things the best possible will have been achieved for them.

A minority of women, however, particularly those active on women's issues, were more sceptical. They felt 'a thing isn't nec-essarily done because it's right. It's done to be seen to be doing it.'

The senior officers were using women's issues like rungs on their ladder of personal advancement. 'It's popular. It's the flavour.' So you do it. 'The men have learned how to swim in a women's organization. They know what sort of language you can use and what you can't. It doesn't change the feelings.' Even the most supportive men couldn't imagine a union in which men would actually step down from power. A man said 'I can't see men sitting back and letting women go forward and run the whole thing themselves . . . . I don't think any man would say "we'll be in the background".'

In the last resort union men, just like the men in the business firm or the civil service, look after their own. You have a vacancy coming up. The next person in line is a man, someone who has given years and years to the union, someone who is loyal, hardworking, does the job well. How can you appoint a younger, more junior woman over his head, out of positive action principle? A man would take that hard. And indeed one said,

> as a man you can sometimes feel a bit threatened by it all. For instance I'm not sure that I'd happily step aside in my job to allow a woman to come into it. Or if I had the opportunity of becoming, say, general secretary that I would *not* do it because I thought a woman ought to come through.

Women do observe that sometimes deals are done over jobs within the leading group of senior men. People's feelings are saved. Failure to get one post is compensated by appointment to another. 'That's how women's interests are sold out to save a man's ego.'

Women end by feeling that 'equality' is a frail plant grafted on to sturdy old stock. Were they to stop cultivating the men they would immediately revert to kind. And men indeed admitted that much does depend on women's pressure. If one year the motions on women at national conference were to dry up, that would be one thing less to attend to in the ensuing year twelve months. A senior officer saw his job as searching for 'straws in the wind' boding future trouble. If he acted it was because 'I want to avoid a situation where we have fourteen angry women fighting for the microphone at conference'.

There are men, then, among the supporters of equality in the Union who veer towards instrumentalism and pragmatism, operating on a limited equality agenda. There are by contrast just a few who want the changes many women want, and want them as much for themselves as for women.

> This equal relationship between men and women is growing. The unions have got to be able to accommodate the change in people's lifestyles. In the future you can't expect from men and women what I gave to the union when I was a young man. Because that doesn't provide equal opportunities at work or at home. It results in a distorted kind of lifestyle where the man goes out and runs the union while the woman stays at home and runs the house and brings up the kids. That's not any longer acceptable.

Think of the most disadvantaged

Despite equality moves, then, the Union continued to be led mainly by men at local, divisional and national levels. Only one division was very different from the rest in this respect. Northern Ireland division possessed the Union's only woman divisional officer. Indeed, three out of four of the full-time officials here were women. This breakthrough by women and what the women had achieved was a source of some astonishment among the men, and admiration among the women, on the mainland. Northern Ireland's 'difference' arose not only from the fact that women were in control but also from the particular energy and talents of women officers and local women members and from the way they thought through the politics of their situation. The division provided a heartening example of an equality strategy taken to its logical conclusion, the longest agenda: an alternative concept of power.

An important decision taken by the Northern Ireland divisional council some time in the middle-eighties had been to prioritise what they called 'participation and democracy'. This meant, for example, committing its education budget less than usual towards existing lay representatives, the activists, and more towards the ordinary member. The idea was that while activists are important it is an involved and informed membership that creates a strong union. The fact was, of course, though women in the divisional leadership did not stress the point, 'member' is more likely than 'activist' to be a woman. The aim was to produce members who speak for themselves with the support of the union. They state their own case in front of the media, health and education authorities and at union conferences. This in turn has empowered other members to believe they are capable of action and intervention.

They had found that membership involvement produced different kinds of requirements of trade union organization. It had required a 're-examination of the structures of the division to ensure they serve the needs of the membership rather than the structures themselves dominating our activity'. They monitored branch by branch just who was getting involved – was it women or men, high or low grade workers, full or part-time workers? Not surprisingly they found the participatory approach involved 'exhausting, detailed and meticulous work'. But it paid off in women's self respect. Whereas before you thought of yourself and other women in the way everyone thought of you, 'it's only the cleaners', you began to see your job as useful and yourself as having value. 'I suppose in every woman there's a sense of her own worth. It only takes an issue, or someone else, to bring it out.'

Women on the women's advisory committee began what they called their 'women's health and history project'. Regular meetings involved a kind of consciousness-raising exercise, though such a phrase could not have been further from the ordinary member's mind. It meant sharing stories of your own lives and those of your mother and grandmother before you. The women found this did wonders not only for their mutual relationships but for their understanding of their situation in the NHS and local government today, for which many of them worked and of which all were clients. For example, when home helps got together to talk they realized they were all experiencing a health hazard in tending clients' noxious coal stoves all day. It taught representatives and officers to 'attend to the small things', listen to 'all the small humiliations' of daily life for such women and not to forget to include them in collective bargaining.

An active link with the community was high in the division's priorities. They recognized that women members' problems do not begin and end with work. Poverty is a low wage but it is also bad housing, poor services. Particularly in Northern Ireland, as for many black women on the mainland, poverty means community violence and oppression. The unemployed too deserve a union's support. The aim here therefore was that a union card should be regarded as 'a social weapon'. Knowing the Union needed community support in union struggles (against privatization and hospital closures, for instance) they put union strength in turn behind community struggles, which were often also led by women. They joined tenants and other groups' actions 'on an equal basis, empowering those who have less power than ourselves'.

'Participation and democracy' had led to a consultative approach to bargaining. The normal process is for national committees to 'mark up the priorities' for the coming round. Negotiators get together with those of other public sector unions, usually also male, and 'cobble a list together'. In Northern Ireland, by contrast, instead of the divisional council simply endorsing national proposals for the collective bargaining agenda, they set in train extensive discussions down at the grass-roots 'with the most invisible sections of our membership'. Members' needs were rethought 'from the point of view of the most disadvantaged worker in every workplace'. No need to say a woman – it always turned out to be so. When they examined the outcome of recent pay-deals they found that gains to the higher grades had in many cases resulted in a deterioration in the situation of the lowest. 'Women are paying not only for their own pay-rises but for everyone else's', women discovered. 'We are the acceptable sacrifice in their eyes'. Over and again it turned out that employers were clawing back what the union was forcing them to give in an annual pay-round, in a shorter working week or in a regrading scheme, by cutting part-timers' hours and intensifying their work. Often their earnings as a result would fall below the level for payment of National Insurance contributions or their hours be reduced to a point at which they would be ineligible for superannuation or lose protection from dismissal. Neither did reduction in hours mean any less work. A home help (one told me) used to be allocated by her employing authority one hour for each home visit. This was little enough, given the travel time. Since last year, however, the authority had cut back the length of each visit to half an hour. But 'nobody told the old folks that'. The home helps still found the same amount of work waiting to be done in the shorter time allowed. Much of the work is responsible: checking that a person's nebuliser is filled, ensuring a client takes their tablets. And much is social: often you are the only person the client has to talk to from one day to the next.

You do much more time for them than you're supposed to do, because you take their washing and things. You run out to the shops for them. They'll say to do the half-hour and no more. But you can't. You can't walk out and leave them . . . So you only get paid for the half-hour but often enough you still work the hour.

It emerged from this democratic process that what was needed was a 'genuine shift in bargaining priorities'. What is the point of a minuscule pay rise if it is immediately lost in benefits? What is the use of a reduction in the standard working week for someone who only works part-time? What good are improved bonuses and over-time provisions when 90% of part-timers are excluded from bonus schemes and 100% from overtime pay? Pay is important, yes, but what about holidays, maternity leave, childcare, health issues? It was increasingly clear that for women you 'cannot divorce pay from conditions and in many cases conditions have become the priority'. The traditional package of demands that had constituted, in essence, 'the family wage' should no longer be the focus of union bargaining. The divisional officer said, 'if you accept the concept of a family wage you accept that there is such a thing as a breadwinner who should earn a decent wage and other people who shouldn't. Those other people are largely women and part-time workers.' These were perceptions that could just as easily have been generated in any division of the Union. They only occurred, however, in the one where women were in control, where women were empowered to listen and women empowered to speak.

Using the law on equal value

When in 1984 the British equal-pay legislation was at last amended in line with European law to give women the right to equal pay for work that could be shown to be of value equal to higher-paid work done by men, women in the Union began to think of strategies for making use of this new possibility. They were, after all, the archetypal case of the undervalued woman.

There is nothing more fundamental to sex-inequality at work than the grading structure, usually based in the case of larger employers on some formal job evaluation scheme. As Joan Acker points out, job evaluation is a key factor in the retention of hierarchy. 'The rules of job evaluation, which help to determine pay differences between jobs, are not simply a compilation of managers' values or sets of beliefs, but are the underlying logic of organization.' That logic represents itself as gender-neutral. In fact jobs are conceived from the start as gendered (Acker 1987:16). Just because established evaluations are so fundamental to cost efficiency in the public and voluntary sectors, to surplus value creation in the private sector and to the retention of male advantage in both, nothing is more fiercely resisted by employers and, unfortunately, by their male employees, than upsetting this neatly-stacked applecart.

For employers, equal-value cases threaten enormous financial penalties. In early 1989 a tribunal ruled in favour of an evaluation case affecting 5500 Lloyds Bank secretaries and typists. Beatrix Campbell, reporting on the case, pointed out, 'if women in the banking system in Britain were paid the same wage as male employees for work of equal value the banks would have to find an estimated £17 billion to cover the cost. That is the amazing arithmetic of wage equality' (Campbell 1989:20). It is not surprising that the bank in this case quickly reacted by reorganizing its internal grading structures to prevent such contagion spreading to another 50 000 women clerks, while announcing that it would appeal against the judgement, all the way to Europe if necessary.

Their pocket is not the only place employers feel the effect of equal-value cases. Another source of trouble is the disaffection of male employees faced with a threat to masculine status. Unions representing both sexes likewise fear the potential divisiveness in equal-value claims. Equal-value cases, as Beatrix Campbell puts it, 'blow apart the historic compromise between capital and labour that has cost women a fortune' (Campbell 1989:20). What is suprising, then, is not that the male leadership of the Union were cautious about supporting cases at industrial tribunal but that they were willing to flout the male rank and file by espousing an equal-value strategy at all. Their ambivalence was about the correct approach. They felt recourse to the law, case by case, too individualist for a trade union. They preferred to use the existence of the new law as a weapon in traditional collective bargaining, pressing employers to revise job evaluation schemes to remove bias against women's skills and making a case for upward regrading of women's work.

It was perhaps not surprising that dissent from this line should have come from the women officers and members of Northern Ireland division. Over there they doubted both the will and ability of male negotiators to make equal value the main focus of collective bargaining. They carried out a far-reaching education programme on the new law. As a result, hundreds of women were inspired to wish to bring cases. A case had to be approached intelligently, however. There were advantages in striking while the law was new. Gains from equal-value cases might be only a shortlived boost, until employers learned to insulate themselves against future claims, for example by subcontracting work. Equal value therefore should be part of an overall equality strategy pursued by the Union. By bitter experience the women knew that getting women upgraded and better-paid was no earthly use unless their hours of work were protected and a minimum level of earnings guaranteed. There would be the danger that taking a grading structure through the courts might do no more than create for the wily employer a structure proof against further claims. And they had to watch out for the men who had tricks up their sleeve for preserving the differential in final take-home pay by boosting shift pay, weekend pay and productivity bonuses.

These manual women of the public sector, however, were already back on their heels. Their jobs were threatened with privatisation and their services with expenditure cuts. They felt it was better to step from defence to attack, and, as the divisional officer put it, 'compete upwards', forcing issues of equality of opportunity, health and safety and standards of service into the open as a matter of public debate. A carefully-chosen, high-profile equal-value case fought through the courts would challenge the existing job-evaluation schemes and open the door for new structures to be achieved by collective bargaining. An exemplary case, even if it failed, would raise awareness and add to pressure for a stronger law. It was decided to support the case of five women domestics in a hospital. Their male comparators would be a groundsman and a porter in the same hospital and the same union branch. The tortuous legal process began.

By 1990, as this book went to press, the women had won an interim victory, but the employers had appealed and the case remained unconcluded. The applicants and others supporting them had, however, learned a great deal in the process. They had dealt with lawyers and judges. They had flown to London to lobby parliament. They knew now how the legal process put you down, 'making you an outsider even in your own case'. If once they had felt 'It's built in. Women are in the lowest grades because it's the natural order of things', now they had learned that in the first place it had been a deal between the NHS and their male-led union that had stitched them into low pay. The five women and members with whom they came into contact in these years would, as an official put it, 'stay mobilised for a long time to come'. As one respectful male colleague observed, the equal-value case had 'turned little mice into lions'.

The women of Northern Ireland division saw the equal-value case as just part of an all-round strategy in which the key word was value. It was about 'the value of our members as people, the value of their labour, the value of the services they work in and their value in the community'. The fight for equal value, they said, was all one with the fight against privatisation, bad housing, poor social benefits and every other community issue. It was aimed at making the most disadvantaged woman visible, a public issue. Beatrix Campbell, reporting the case in the *New Statesman*, called it 'an audacious strategy, based on the belief you can't defend services without valuing the workers who provide them. This of course does violence to history. Equal value for the least valued workers challenges not only employers' cavalier contempt but the labour movement's historic indifference' (Campbell 1990:18).

Women, democracy and power

The Union whose equality strategies have been described here is a profoundly working-class organization ('everyone in this union is below the poverty line') and the instincts of many of its lay representatives and full-time officers are class instincts. 'Class is the great issue', people said. There is a fundamentally democratic ethos. There was, though, a confusion of interpretation. Was it representative democracy or participatory democracy to which the Union should aspire? Did democracy just mean, as the traditionalist men thought, that everyone should have a vote? Or did it mean everyone should be enabled to activate their belonging in the Union in other ways? There is in any case a historic hole at the heart of 'democracy' where women should have been. Although there is no one more working-class than a working-class woman, women have all too often been subordinated in or absent from working-class 'democratic' organisations. Many women in the Union believed there was an intrinsic link between achieving a 'real democracy' in the Union and the empowering of women. As one woman said, 'Will they go for democracy? That's the crunch.'

The committee structure created by the consultants had successfully integrated branch secretaries into the superstructure above them but at the cost of a rift between themselves and the members below them. The bodies near the top of the representational hierarchy, national committees and the Executive Council, tended not to consult the base but to act directly on their legitimacy as elected bodies. The formal processes could be hard to grasp. A woman full-time officer regretted this gap between her members and 'their' structure.

> A complicated structure like ours, if you look at the 'map' of the union, it can be very offputting to women. In the types of jobs [our] members do they don't tend to be involved in a lot of complicated organisational structures. And the union presents them with precisely that.

Some pointed to the vital role of the women's advisory committees as proof of the inadequacy of representative democracy in the Union. If women's interests had been adequately represented in the formal bodies there would have been no need for such supplementary structures.

Discussions about democratic structure and processes logically engaged with the question of power: who wielded power in the Union, on what terms, in what way? Some women felt the existing system – committee structure, rule book, traditional practices – played into the hands of those whose aim was to remain in office year after year. 'If you want to hold on to power, the structure offers you the means.' There is a tendency to 'a politics of position', as one woman full-time officer put it. Holding the position becomes important in itself, rather than the work you do in it and through it. It becomes a matter of self-regard. 'If it's a matter of ego or your members' needs, it's no contest. Ego always wins . . .'. And she added, 'you can't develop your ego and democracy at the same time'. She wondered at the fact that, though some women do play into the politics of position, it is more often men who do. 'I'm always surprised how little the men will settle for. Perks, position. A pat on the head from government ministers. They do it all for so little return. It's such a narrow view of being human.'

So long as democracy had meant no more than formal and indirect representative democracy it had failed to empower women, despite their numerical dominance in the Union. The conventional set of processes governing trade union life is, as a product of labour movement history, a masculine way of doing things. However, once the concept of democracy was extended to participation and involvement of the membership, women showed themselves very likely to introduce (and respond to) new ways of doing things. As a woman full-time officer said, 'to turn the union over to women would be the death-knell of the union-as-it-is'. She meant: there'll be new lines of communication, decentralisation, power will reach out beyond the divisional office.

Northern Ireland Division seemed unique as a place where a language of power, participation and democracy was in common use. This may arise in part from the link between 'equality' and the decades of civil rights struggles in which the same women have been active, forced to learn political skills. However, that may be, there are practical differences in this division of the Union. It was often cited as a division where there was a higher proportion of women shop stewards, more divisional council members were women and women had a bigger share in the divisional delegation to national conference. The woman divisional officer had clearly been an important influence in the development of other women's confidence and activity. But women always referred as well to the equally-respected woman assistant divisional officer and the other area officers, emphasising that within the divisional office there was no 'personality cult' but rather a strong working team. It was woman-led, profoundly influenced by women's thinking, but not exclusively female. A woman officer in London said of the division:

I think it's in the nature of the full-time officers there, they seem to mix socially and they seem to have a kind of understanding about things. They don't seem to be frightened of the members over there. They regard them as friends and colleagues, people to share information with rather than tell things to . . . . They seem to be in tune with what the members want. And I think that's because the division is run by two women and so much of the membership over there is female . . . . They discuss and explain union policies to their members. They are seen to be part of the community. I don't get that feeling anywhere else.

The divisional office in Belfast is seen as a resource not only for activists but for ordinary members. A woman lay representative said, 'you can come right in and feel you're on the same level with them. They don't consider themselves important like men would. I wouldn't come in if it was men. They think they're the big boss and sit behind their desks.'

The officers talked explicitly about *feminist* ways of doing things. By this they meant 'inclusion, empowering, enabling, sharing'. 'The more you feminise the methods the more difficulty an individual man has in holding on to power.'

Northern Ireland division made a clear distinction between 'good representational politics and good democratic politics'. It was part of the effort to reach down below today's activist, believing in tomorrow's: 'always the involvement of the ordinary member'. They said, 'head office is basically centralist. We run in the opposite direction. We're the only division that does everything through the members.' They identified the role of the branch secretary as a key problem. They held the view that to hang on to a post for many years at a stretch dulls your own creativeness and blocks the way for others. You should 'move over and give someone else the chance you've had'. So it had been a motion from Northern Ireland division that was adopted at national conference limiting to two terms the period for which the reserved seats for women on the executive council might be held. They would have liked to see such a rule extended to all the Union's committees and councils. And in the meantime some Northern Ireland women were practising that voluntarily. They tried, they said, to see their position 'as *a* seat, not *my* seat'. It was hard. 'Back into the branch. I won't like it. But it's the only way.' This was a conscious dismantling of 'the politics of position', seeing power-holding as 'greater responsibility, less perks, more sweat'. A woman shop steward said,

Male members have been used to power being taken and used in the one way. The traditional way, the male way. Obviously they must have found it strange when other things started to happen. I mean, we don't so much take power, what we do is start working. That is the difference, we start to work. It's only when people start to come to you about different things that you realise that you've in fact taken some power. But you worked before you took the power. You didn't just take it and leave. You don't take it in fact, it's given to you. It can't be demanded, it's got to be earned.

When you take power, in such a context, you 'bring others with you'.

Women can rise phenomenally given the support. Every step you take you turn your head and pull someone else along. Not ask them; *pull them*! And as you go you demystify the process at each stage.

Some might think that a focus on women and on democracy, good as it might be for internal relationships, would weaken the Union in its external struggles in a hard world, where a Conservative government was set on destroying union influence. But Northern Ireland division is acknowledged even by male officers on the mainland to be 'efficient, effective and tough' both in negotiation and campaigning. As one of the Northern Ireland women pointed out, 'if you only have a politics of position you can easily be handled by the employer'. A member-based organisation largely female and led by women, the Union in Northern Ireland is more, not less, likely to hit back with protest and disruption at the attack on local communities through cuts in services, privatisation. 'We have had a thousand women on the streets to stop the contractors . . . . Warm, angry women, linking arms.'

The grass-roots orientation, however, cannot evade the fact that the power game has to be played also at the highest levels, where the fight is often dirty. The officer who referred to 'kicking each other to death' was barely exaggerating. The women of Northern Ireland division were carrying the struggle for democracy, for the lowest-paid and for women, into the Irish labour movement, where the behaviour was far from gentlemanly, 'breaking corrupt male power as viciously as they hold it'. But a distinction was continually drawn between taking position and taking power. *Position* was often refused. But 'you engage, you take space, so as to be further engaged'.

A big factor in the success or failure of the strategy for women adopted in Northern Ireland division was their ability to forge alliances with men who might otherwise feel angered, alienated or rejected by the Union. They went about it through appealing to male trade unionists' best political instincts. They explained:

You are . . . about trying to get more for those who have the least. That doesn't mean you are in opposition to those who have more. But you have to decide where your resources will go. You make it clear that people who have the most have to change the most. Men, who have a little more, thinking first about women who are on the bottom. Questioning 'why should there *be* a bottom?'

For a man whose interests had till now been given priority in the union this might be hard to take. 'You have to help him reconstruct his identity.' It was not impossible. Though some men would resent the women's emergence till their dying day, in others there was much goodwill to appeal to. The men who had acted as comparators in the equal-value case had overcome their masculine pride to support the women wholeheartedly at the tribunal, on the streets and outside Parliament. One explained how giving evidence had convinced him of the justice of the women's case.

When I went to court I just couldn't believe it, you know . . . . They asked me, 'What do you do?'. And I answered, 'I empty wastepaper baskets and lift tins off the green.' What does the lady do? 'Well, she makes sure the operating theatre is spotless so people can have operations. She makes sure the kitchen's spotless so people don't get diseases from the food.' And to me, like, it was an open and closed case. To be honest with you, what I began to see was, it was the *opposite* to what I'd thought. Everything had been stacked against the woman.

At the same time, such a man and such a woman have common interests. His interests too, if he can only see it, are best served by a high steady basic wage and less need to work the overtime that keeps him from his family. If the women's interests are protected, so will his be: the employer will be less likely to replace him with two part-timers. Besides, as the divisional officer put it, 'there's more to being human than enjoying the prestige from being a little higher, having a halfpenny more than someone else. When they think about increasing the value of someone else they may come to see that that increases the value they have themselves.' And when a man responds to this kind of politics, 'you can get a glimpse of what it might be like'.

Sex-equality struggles, then, can be class and race struggles too if their agenda stretches to issues of women's worth, democracy and the empowerment of low-paid women. As Joan Acker found in her participant research in an important 'comparable worth' case in the

USA, labour relations are structured in such a way that women's interests may appear as 'only' gender interests, which are devalued and displaced. Men's interests, on the other hand, are often seen and acted on by men as representing general class interests (Acker 1989:218). The women whose interests are marginalized are often black. The men that have the power to define men's interests are usually white. The processes in which women's worth are continually denied and in which women are excluded from self-representation are the processes in which class, gender and race inequities are simultaneously reproduced.

5

Sexuality and difference: on whose terms?

While men in powerful positions in organizations may well see good reason to introduce fairer practices in recruitment and promotion, special training for women, or more generous maternity leave, it is seldom men who raise the issue of sexual politics. That is left to women. Indeed, in many organizations it has been sexual harassment, incidents in which men have annoyed, persecuted or abused women sexually, that have prompted women to become more conscious of disadvantage and to organise spontaneously, in a union or without one, for positive measures for women at work. Flowing from a concern with sexual harassment are some wider issues. One is the sexualisation of social relations in organizations and what that means for women. Another is the heterosexism of much workplace culture and the significance of homosexuality in the struggle over male sex-right in the workplace, which will be discussed in Chapter 6. Sexuality is more likely than any other issue to spark off arguments for and against separate organization by women, separate provision for women and whether or not the equality project is 'feminism'.

Sexual harassers: everyone knows one

Sexual harassment was, in a sense, a discovery of new-wave feminism. Though women had complained, from the moment they entered the male world of paid work, of men pestering and threatening women sexually, there seems to have been no specific

term for the practice until the early 1970s when women in the USA
first labelled the problem. Though women are clearly the objects of
sexual harassment everywhere from the beach to the bedroom, the
phrase has been taken up particularly to refer to a phenomenon of
organizational life. It has been defined as

> all those actions and practices by a person or group of people at work
> which are directed at one or more workers and which: are repeated and
> unwanted; may be deliberate or done unconsciously; cause humiliation,
> offence or distress; may interfere with job performance or create an
> unpleasant working environment; comprise remarks or actions associa-
> ted with a person's sex; emphasize a person's sexuality over her role as a
> worker (Hadjifoutiou 1983:9).

I will describe briefly two recent incidents that were reported to
me by women in interview that appear to me appropriately termed
sexual harassment. Due to the sensitivity of the subject I will report
them in disguised form, not indicating the organization or
organizations from which they are drawn and changing the
unimportant details a little to avoid any possibility of the women
in question being recognizable.

The first concerns a young woman in a junior position in office
work. When I asked her whether she had ever experienced here
anything that she would call sexual harassment, she surprised me by
flushing deeply and saying '*All the time!*'. Wendy Wilkins said that
the group of men she worked for in a junior role were making her
working life unbearable.

> I get remarks all the time. [What about? She paused.Then, with an
> embarrassed laugh] Most men comment on my boobs. They say things
> about them to each other. I walk past and they're just like *that*. [She
> mimicked someone staring at her chest.] This man [she named a senior
> person], I was talking to him and he was just standing there staring at
> me. He didn't even look at my face, he was like *this* the whole time. I just
> feel like punching them. I get comments all the time. This man [she
> named a different manager] he gets on my nerves. It may sound funny.
> But he makes so many comments, like 'Every time you walk into the
> room we all swoon at you.' And whenever I go into the filing room he'll
> squeeze in there and pretend to try to get something out of a file. And
> he'll *say* things. Well, I've got a pair of jeans with a pattern on the pocket
> and he'll say 'Oh, it must be nice to have a flower on your bum.' One
> time I had a T-shirt on with some writing. [She indicated her chest.] And
> one of them peered and said 'What's that?' Then all of a sudden I had

about six men over me, all staring, saying 'Oh what's that, what's that.'
It's *every minute*. I hate going into that room for any reason because I
get it all the time. If I wear a skirt I get comments about my legs or
something. 'You've got nice legs.' I just dress scruffy, I dress in black so
that they won't say anything. I sometimes, I could really swear at them.
My mum says to me, ignore them, don't say anything. But I want to say
something. I want to tell them to shut up and go away and leave me
alone. I could nearly scream sometimes.

I asked Wendy if she had felt able to go to anyone for advice or
help.

I wouldn't want to complain about a silly little thing. My actual boss,
he's nice enough. But I'd feel too embarrassed to tell him. If I said
something to the other girls about it they'd have a giggle and say 'You're
the lucky one!'.

Without my asking any direct questions, subsequent interviews
confirmed Wendy's story. Several of the men knew that Wendy's
breasts were the subject of banter between the men but assumed
that she did not notice or even that she liked it. One, for instance,
volunteered that there was this young woman in the office 'she had
certain very noticeable characteristics which have been commented
on by the men. [I looked questioning.] She's got big breasts [he
laughed] . . . . But I'd be surprised if anybody has made her feel uncomfortable.' Another observed that 'comments were being thrown
around [about her] that some people wouldn't have understood, it
would have gone over their heads . . . . But others would have
known what was meant . . . and been embarrassed.'
     Older women in this workplace were too far removed from
Wendy's situation to suppose that such harassment could be
occurring. Wendy had confided her distress to two close colleagues,
younger men of her own grade. One of them told me he felt
she was to blame for her handling of the situation. She was over-
reacting because she had taken a dislike to a couple of the men. The
other, however, was sympathetic. He often did jobs for Wendy to
enable her to avoid having to walk into the room where these men
worked. He felt the men, who were old enough to know better, were
'making fools of themselves . . . . They are trying to be funny, and
they're not.'
     The interaction between Wendy and the men in the office
involved a little touching, but no compulsion, no threats. It is the

kind of thing that passes for humour, the sunny side of office life for the men she works for. It was, however, consistent with the definition of sexual harassment cited above. It was repeated and unwanted. It was causing humiliation and distress. It was unwanted sexual attention. It was making her working day a misery. Consequently it was affecting Wendy's chances at work. She talked of leaving the job before long. She would look elsewhere but inevitably it would be for similar, junior employment. There was no reason to suppose she would not encounter the same kind of treatment from men wherever she went. Young males of comparable grade meanwhile might well start their climb up the ladder to professional status. Who knows how many young women move from one low-status job to another not only because of the acute boredom of such jobs but because they cannot face up to the men in the office one more time?

Harassment, like rape, is generally understood in feminist theory to be an expression not of men's unbridled desire but of *power*. Hierarchies are expressions of differential power, maps of the distribution of authority and subordination in an organization. Though conventional organization theory represents this power-tree as neuter, it is in fact a structure of gender power. In the main, men are in the locations where power resides, women where there is none. 'The notion of organizational structure as an objective, empirical and genderless reality is itself a gendered notion' (Sheppard 1989:142). Men's treatment of a junior woman such as Wendy is a clear instance of the exercise of sexual power.

The second example, however, shows how emergent and potentially powerful women too must be cut down to size by sexual means. In one organization they had recently recruited a woman to a very senior post. A confident, good-looking, stylishly-dressed single woman, Pamela Gray had been a kind of shock-therapy for the male establishment. She described herself as 'pretty aggressive, very direct. I don't pussyfoot around. I don't swear at *people*, but I do swear.' She was no friend of the equality policy, and said she felt there was a tendency for women in the organization to 'go overboard' in the way they were talking about men as a problem. Sexual harassment? 'I don't really know what that means.' Sexual innuendo? 'Infinitely childish, you just ignore it.' Yet, she admitted, 'They certainly saw me as a huge threat when I first came. They made me feel very, very uncomfortable for six months. The woman bit. Men don't like it. They don't feel comfortable with women as superiors.' Besides, her newly-defined job was destined to impinge on the roles of some of the powerful men. She took an aggressive approach from the start, was not afraid to get into rows with male colleagues. Underneath, however, she was feeling 'horribly lacking in confidence, a bit lost, friendless, in an alien culture'. And then, one day as she walked up the stairs to a top-level meeting among her senior male colleagues, in a situation where he knew she could do nothing about it, one of them covertly pinched her bottom. 'I couldn't *believe* it,' she said, 'I was so stunned that I didn't even react'. Later she felt mortified that she had not said something then and there. It long continued to rankle with her. Their shared knowledge of the incident, of her defeat or even her imputed connivance would have intruded into her working relationship with the man in question. And who else might he have told?

Here again we see sexual harassment as being a male intervention for the assertion of power. But this time it is a warning to a woman stepping out of her proper place. It is a controlling gesture to diminish any sense of power she may be acquiring and to remind her 'you're only a woman, that's the way I see you. And at that level you're vulnerable to me and any man.' As David Collinson and Margaret Collinson (1989:107) say, at the conclusion of a British study in six industries over ten years that revealed extensive sexual harassment, 'men's sexuality and organizational power are inextricably linked'.

Thus we see again how women's presence in the workplace is a highly political issue for men. In the original terms of the sexual contract a woman's proper place is at home. If she is drawn into the paid workplace, then her proper place is in clearly-defined women's work at or near the bottom of the organization. Women's claims to economic independence and an equal place in organizational life, to a rewriting of the social contract, call forth new measures of exclusion, a reassertion of male supremacy. The means range from the administrative to the physical. Among the physical, they range from the dangerous to the ludicrous. Male violence drives women off the streets. Innuendo and *double entendre* polices women's discourse.

It is sometimes suggested that sexual harassment derives specifically from the power imbalance in the organization (Kanter 1977, DiTomaso 1989), and this connection is clear. However, the relations of the workplace and the world beyond it interact. Men's power in the extra-organizational world, in the family, the state and civil society, enters the workplace with them and gives even the most junior man a degree of *sexual* authority relative to even senior women. Nor is sexual harassment only a process of subordination and resubordination of women as workers in a hierarchy. It has to be seen as an individual appropriation, a 'taking' of women's bodies, in the terms of the original sexual contract, of male sex-right. When women escape the dominion of father and husband and enter the public sphere they become fair game for the fraternal gang, a threat which tends to enhance for many women the attractions in the long run of coupledom, marriage and domesticity.

A sex equality policy, in blowing the whistle on sexual harassment, potentially exposes these issues of power. Positive action usually includes good housekeeping gestures such as removing pin-ups from the office wall and cleaning-up spoken and written sexist terminology. The real test of the policy, however, is over the encouragement given or not given to women to bring cases of complaint against men and the action taken to discipline those who are found to be offenders.

The equality policies of all three of the major employers represented here – High Street Retail, the Service and the Local Authority – acknowledged the problem of sexual harassment, defined it, noted that it would be treated as a disciplinary offence and set out a complaints procedure. Thereafter, however, there was a considerable difference in the energy with which the policy was executed in the three organizations. In High Street Retail few cases were brought and they were dealt with in a low key manner. The equal opportunities manager, feeling it to be an explosive issue, deliberately played down sexual harassment. The hostility elicited there by a simple request for the removal of some offensive pin-ups gave her reason to fear a backlash damaging to the more far-reaching policy of 'targeting' women for recruitment, training and promotion. At the other extreme the Local Authority launched some highly controversial disciplinary hearings against racist and sexist transgressors of their policy, in which the local press found, as usual, occasion to mock the council. It became part of the 'loony left' furore that caused local Labour Parties to back pedal on all equality measures. In both these cases therefore we can see male reactions pushing positive action for sex equality back to its shorter agenda.

Most women I interviewed had at some time in their working lives experienced some kind of embarrassment or discomfort due to the sexual behaviour of men at work. Many women I talked with told of incidents involving themselves or other women, could point to some man who had the reputation of being a problem. They often took for granted that sexual discomfort is an unavoidable fact of organizational life. A woman just learned what to wear, whose eye to avoid, which rooms to stear clear of, places you should 'always go in twos'.

The Service, for instance, seemed at first glance an all but sexless organization. People shifted paperwork, head down to the desk, from nine till five. It was a pedestrian, rule-bound world. There were no exaggeratedly sex-typed roles, no dressy receptionists, no Sierra-driving salesmen here. All the same, I was told by women, and frequently also by men, who know very well what goes on among their colleagues, of many incidents in which men had been widely observed to 'take advantage' of women colleagues and juniors.

First, men told me, there was a good deal of 'woman-objectify-ing' talk among certain groups of men. There was also, they said, 'loads of evidence' in earlier days of women being marked down for refusing sexual favours. Elite officers in charge of district offices 'abused their position terribly and made a real nuisance of themselves. They couldn't keep their hands off women.' Among numerous stories I heard, a man of professional grade 'sat in a chair and pulled this girl on to his lap and shoved his arm round her just under the breast and started tickling her ribs'. The 'girl', this observer noted, was 'getting a bit flushed' and clearly did not like what was happening to her. Another man was 'always pressing himself up against women. He did it all the time in a loud and open manner.' A third would 'put his hand up a girl's skirt and snap her suspenders, or smack her on the bottom'. And so on – the accounts, from men themselves, became repetitive and depressing.

Many of my women informants in the Service were no longer young and felt themselves less at risk of harassment today. But many referred to incidents in the past. One had felt confused and guilty when an older man she had allowed to befriend her in a fatherly way pressed his attentions sexually and became difficult to deal with. There was a tendency, though, among both women and men in the Service, to say that things were different *today*, different in *our* office. Of course there were those men who were always 'twisting your words', turning everything you or they said into sexual innuendo. But young people could look after their own interests better today; men had learned how to behave, the equality policy had caused them to clean up their act.

In the Local Authority women activists had taken a strong line on sexual harassment and sexism more generally. This had occurred partly because the equality policy was inspired by feminist councillors and employees to whom such preoccupations came naturally. It was also partly due to the content of the organization's equality policy. Positive action here involved, for instance, introducing women alongside men in skilled trades in the building and works departments. It extended to according women greater consideration as clients of social work, housing and other services, which automatically generated issues of the proper nature of interaction between, for instance, male caretakers and women tenants.

How did men respond? Some top-level officers felt too much was being made of these issues by the feminists. They were embarrassed by the excuse they afforded the local press to make snide comments. 'Mother-in-law jokes may cost you your job!' More junior men, especially manual workers, who were particularly incensed by an injunction not to call women 'love', 'dear' and 'duck', reacted bitterly. Several made it clear they felt a 'thought police' operated in the Local Authority. It was 'Pol Pot-ism, the Local Killing Fields'. You no longer knew how to behave. 'Like, sometimes you open the door for a woman, to be a gentleman, as it were. They might say "I don't want that. I'm equal to a man. I'll open the door myself". It goes too far and causes a problem, are you with me?' Men had had to become paranoid, cautious about their every word and move. 'Girls can spread malicious rumours about a man.' 'Say you get in a lift together. You get people [i.e. men] who stand in lifts today with their hands in their pockets in case they accidentally catch somebody with their hand and get accused of something. Employees of the council have got this uncomfortable feeling.' The same thing was occurring over racism. White men in charge of black male workers in particular represented themselves as going in dread of contravening proper non-racist behaviour.

Some women too felt the backlash against the new policies outweighed the gains. But many others, both men and women, said they felt the standard of behaviour had greatly improved since the equality policy had raised issues of sexism and harassment. A woman in quite a high technical post said,

> I realise I'm spoilt [in this Local Authority]. Because of the equality policy men seem more accepting here. I work with a lot of builders, but I'm never made to feel awkward by the men for being a woman . . . I just know that being here I'm not going to be looked down on and will be treated equally with other people.

In High Street Retail and the Service, in contrast to the Local Authority, there were more instances where women's claims were considered insubstantiated or 'over-reactive'. There was a noticeable preference for dealing with sexual harassment informally, hushing things up, 'having a talk with the fellow' and warning him that 'he's making a fool of himself'. The preferred treatment was to move the man quietly to some new office where he can 'make a fresh start'. The only incident I heard of in the two organizations that actually resulted in a man being fired was not where a woman employee had complained about him but where an unseemly 'romp in a strip club one lunch time' had threatened the organization's own reputation.

White male senior managers, including personnel managers responsible for implementing EO policy, are cautious about challenging the behaviour of men below them in the hierarchy beyond the point demanded by organizational 'propriety'. Many individual men, of course, respect women and behave courteously towards them. Such men are often pained by other men's obscenities and 'pranks'. One, for instance, said 'Some men have a horrible perception of women . . . . Scorn, sexual scorn. "Women are there for . . .", "give her one", this sort of thing, you know. They wouldn't dare say anything like that in front of their wives.' It is almost unthinkable, however, among men, to take issue directly and personally with other men's sexist behaviour. 'You'd bring a ton of bricks down on your head', said one young man in High Street Retail. 'If you said, "Let's discuss women's place in society" they'd look pretty – yuk! – and be off to the pub.' Women too, though they think they are standing up to abuse, seldom do more than fall silent, turn their back or respond with mild sarcasm. Men who are habitually sexist very often get away with it unchallenged.

Sexuality and feelings at work

When women in the 1970s started drawing attention to the problem of sexual harassment in the workplace it seemed as though they were forcing a conceptual connection between two phenomena that had nothing at all to do with each other: sex and organization. Sexuality was something that arose between consenting adults in private, in leisure, at home. Organizations by contrast were places where one worked in exchange for money or of which one was a client. They were rational task-oriented environments with no room for emotion, sex or indeed any bodily needs. Organization theory portrayed organizations as formal hierarchies with definable rules and procedures, peopled by employees who were not only without gender identity but also devoid of sexuality, a bundle only of specifiable functions and skills. The expression of sexuality in the form of sexual harassment thus appeared as an occasional pathological aberration in the organization.

The 'scientific rationality' perception of organizations derives at root from early apologists and analysts of capitalist industry (eg Taylor 1947). It reflects the forcing apart of the private from the public, the personal from the political, employment from home life on which patriarchal capitalism is predicated. Rational management, however, was shaken by the innovatory 'human relations' approach to management in the 1920s which began to expose beneath the formal structures and processes of the workplace less predictable factors. People's feelings could be shown to have a bearing on organizational outputs. A successful organizaion had to take account of, and respond to, the psychology of its employees (Mayo 1933).

Today these two approaches remain in tension with each other. In most organizations personnel management in practice pursues the tough instrumental line, partly because managers do not trouble to employ or develop the skills that would enable them to do otherwise. Nonetheless 'human resource management' has growing resonance. Books such as *In Search of Excellence*, in which Thomas Peters and Robert Waterman make an explicit critique of the rational model, find great popularity. 'The exclusively analytic approach run wild leads to an abstract heartless philosophy' warn these authors. 'Treat people as adults. Treat them as partners; treat them with dignity; treat them with respect' (Peters and Waterman 1982:238).

The emotional life brought to light by these and similar management theorists is nonetheless still somewhat narrowly defined. It is about boredom versus enthusiasm, aspiration versus discontent, about the difference between commitment to and alienation from the job (Blauner 1964). Gendered behaviour and sexual desire continue hidden from view. In a different genre, however, a cross-fertilising of Freudian psychoanalytic theory with the Marxist understanding of capitalist class relations has produced insights into the link between sexuality and institutional behaviour. Marcuse, for example, recognized the ways in which sexuality is repressed in the interests of 'civilization' and exploitation (Marcuse 1955). The work of Michel Foucault too has generated new awareness of the way our bodies and our desires are constituted and controlled in and through institutions (Foucault 1973, 1977, 1981).

Once stated it becomes quite obvious that some kinds of organization are designed to govern both the physical and mental behaviour of their members. Such total institutions as the armed forces, prisons, boarding schools and mental hospitals must repress sexuality and to achieve this they must continually subdue, shape and sanction feelings. In this tradition Gibson Burrell has argued that capitalist organization has systematically suppressed sexuality, eliminating it from the workplace in the interests of production and control (Burrell 1984). Worker resistance sometimes therefore takes the form of an assertion of sexuality in the workplace. In earlier work I have shown how working men bond with each other through sexual banter and exchanges. Men's morale and solidarity in their struggle against the boss is sometimes achieved directly at the expense of women (Cockburn 1983).

It is only recently, however, that contributors to organization theory, inspired by feminism, have begun to explore and expose the full significance of sexuality in employing organizations. Jeff Hearn and Wendy Parkin demonstrate that sexualised social relations are not an exception but a normal part of the functioning of organizations. In a study of 'organization sexuality' in the public sector, in local councils, hospitals and universities, they concluded, 'Enter most organizations and you enter a world of sexuality' (Hearn and Parkin 1987:3; see also Horn and Horn 1982). The 'sexual regime', as Hearn and Parkin call it, sustains the male power system. The heterosexual construction of certain relationships, such as that of boss and secretary, the management of spaces and movement, the deployment of imagery, language and dress, all foster a male authority.

It is important then to hold in view a number of different dimensions in the interaction between people in organizations. The expression and repression of feelings of all kinds are involved, as well as sexuality in a limited sense. Employers sometimes make profitable use of our sexuality. The 'sexy' uniform of a club waitress, for instance, exploits for profit both her female sexuality and the male sexuality of the client. Ironically, a woman in the labour market may be simultaneously both domestically and sexually defined. The boss–secretary relation, for instance, is organized around heterosexual and family imagery (the 'office wife') (Pringle 1988:84). Employers also, however, need to control and limit the independent expression of sexuality (Cockburn 1985). Sexuality is simultaneously a force of production to use and a threat to social order. 'Organizations have historically become a series of sites where the danger and pleasure of sexuality can be both repressed, and exploited within forms of oppression' (Burrell and Hearn 1989:5).

Likewise employers both repress and make use of our feelings and emotions. Arlie Hochschild points out in her perceptive study of airline flight attendants and debt collectors ('the toe and heel of capitalism' as she puts it) that much of the work we are paid to do calls, over and above mental and manual work, for emotional effort. This emotional labour 'requires one to induce or suppress feeling in order to sustain the outward countenance that produces the proper state of mind in others' (Hochschild 1983:7). Sold for a wage, labour of the emotions has exchange value; in private life it has use value. Both commercially and privately women do more emotional labour than men. Hochschild reckons that 50% of women's jobs and 25% of men's involve a substantial element of emotional work and 'for each gender a different portion of the managed heart is enlisted for commercial use' (Hochschild 1983:163). Women are wanted for jobs such as receptionist and social worker, where behaviour must affirm, enhance and celebrate the well-being and status of others. Men by contrast tend to be engaged for jobs requiring them to be cool, impassive or stern – as in policing or bank management. Such 'masculine' occupations, however, are no less a process of controlling one's own and others' feelings.

The sexual regime in business

It is interesting to dwell on some of the ways sexuality, emotions and the representation and use of bodies enters into the life and labour processes of a company like High Street Retail. First, certain jobs have a clear emotional labour content in Hochschild's sense of the term. Consider, for instance, that of the sales assistant in the company's shops, who must please; and that of the store manager, who must impress, placate and control. Second, the company's advertising and shop window displays are full of idealised, 'attractive' women, men and children wearing the company's clothes, using the company's consumer durables, representing now a caring and domestic lifestyle, now a recreational and carefree one. (Some of the fashion models today, in response to a greater sensitivity to ethnicity, are chosen with care from the 'visible minorities'.) The company's open-plan offices, like those of other firms, may have been consciously designed with person-management and psychological effects in mind. Where there are no closed doors there is no private space for hanky-panky. Finally, every year the company has a talent contest at which Miss High Street Retail is chosen and launched on a year of public promotions. In this equality era there is embarrassment among some managers about the continuation of this beauty contest – for that is what it is.

The company operates a strict dress code for its office and sales workers. (Manual women have more freedom.) Women are made to feel ill-at-ease wearing trousers, if they are not outright forbidden to do so. What would happen if a woman turned up to the office in trousers? I asked. 'Oh, there'd be eyebrows raised', 'there'd be a colossal amount of talk, totally disproportionate'. Even wearing flat shoes can make a woman feel out of step here. The dress required of a woman office worker or manager is a skirt or dress with a high or medium-heeled shoe; blouse, jersey or jacket; an overall feminine, though not sexual, appearance. For men the suit, usually grey, the necktie and a trim haircut are *de rigueur*.

In workplaces such as this we have travelled little distance since the nineteenth century moralists condemned women pithead workers for wearing trousers, 'unseemly dress and with those unseemly manners which indicate an unsexed mind' (John 1986:21). There are no unsexed minds in High Street Retail. To sit in the staff canteen at head office and observe the employees deliver their lunch trays before returning to their offices is to witness a kind of ritualised daily ballet in which gender is the organizing principle. The men move together, a solid mass of grey, conversing in deep tones. The women by contrast tap-tap along, chatting and laughing, colourful as a bunch of flowers. Gender differentiation is total. At one level it is mandatory, for strong sanctions govern behaviour here. At another level, however, it is elective, a pleasurable self-expression, a negotiated achievement.

These are some of the facets of High Street Retail's sexual regime, of which we shall see more below. Clearly the management have regard, for their own purposes, to sexuality, bodies and emotions. Their employees too, of course, have personal needs they introduce into the workplace, despite the management. For many people, women and men, work is the arena in which they are most 'in the public sphere', most feel themselves to be social, expect to meet new friends. It has been suggested that up to a quarter of marriages are made at work (Hearn 1985:113, Hearn and Parkin 1987:14). For women, work may be hard or boring but it can also be a sphere free of some of the cares and responsibilities of home. The Marxist analysis of work has led us to focus on the exploitation of the worker. Feminism has alerted us to the gender-specificity of that exploitation. But work can be a path to pleasure too.

All organizations must generate policies for handling sexual affairs and marriages among their employees if they are to avoid disruption, loss of output and failure of managerial control. In High Street Retail until fairly recently if a male manager began a relationship with a female employee, the woman was required to leave the firm. One woman manager told me she was warned by her male boss on promotion to a new site 'Don't you *ever* have an affair with anyone here. If you do I'll get to hear about it and you'll be in trouble.' She was advised by older employees never to get her money or her affections tied up in the firm.

Women as well as men have a stake in a degree of openness and sociability in the organization. Sexual harassment shows only the negative side of organization sexuality. It does point nonetheless to a contradiction in which women are caught. Sex is often represented as totally 'natural', as something in which women and men participate as equal beneficiaries. Sexuality, however, like other aspects of gender relations, is socially constituted and gender asymmetry prevails here too. Male power and male sexuality are linked. Indeed power itself is eroticised, and power is male (Hacker 1989:57). When men, as they often do, claim that women as often as men are sexual harassers at work, this has to be read as bad faith. A woman may take a fancy and embarrass a man. But women very rarely possess the combination of sexual inclination and power that would turn them into harassers of the damaging kind that men are.

There are two important ways in which the gender dynamics of the social life of High Street Retail disadvantaged women. First, male managers and office workers had over many decades generated a male social world within and outside work from which women were *excluded*. Men (especially men of similar grade within a department or team) would frequently drink and socialize together at the end of the day and over the weekend. Women told me they felt their absence from these all-male gatherings impeded their process, cutting them out from important sources of information. 'There's a lot of "in" things I don't get to find out' said one young manager. And indeed the men affirmed the value of their socializing. 'We have a phrase: you'll learn more in the pub than you will in the store.' Some men clearly felt women were incapable of relating, even to each other, in the same social way as men were wont to do. 'I just don't envisage that – they are just – they operate on a different level altogether', said an older man. 'It's a level that obviously appeals to *them*. But I don't see them as having the same informal camaraderie, if you like.' The socializing among the predominantly white male workforce may sometimes exclude black men. Yet black men too can value the male bonding process. Thus a young black junior manager said that for him too socializing with male colleagues was the important thing. 'I'm not being anti-woman,' he said. 'I suppose ladies may feel they've got things *they* want to talk about.'

Women in any case felt on false ground as far as mixing with the men went. One said she avoided all social contact with male colleagues, 'it can lead to difficulties – people assume things'. Another said, 'they won't invite me [to dinner at] their homes because I'm not married. And I'm a woman. And I don't have children to talk about. So yes, I'm marginalized.'

An all-male golfing fraternity was an important source of male bonding in the firm. The golfing society 'is very, very strongly supported' said one male manager. 'When golfing days come my chaps vanish.' Why is it men only? I asked.

> Well, there was a girl [sic] here once who was a very, very good golfer. I think she did apply to join . . . . The difficulty is in golf there are women's competitions and men's competitions. Yes, there *are* mixed foursomes, but that doesn't – you have a different set of tees for ladies. The average man can hit the ball a lot further. How would you go about catering for the women competing? Her handicap was based on her separate female circumstances. How would we arrange to play? It's complicated.

Such energetic rationalisation seemed to conceal a deep reluctance to spoil the male–male relations by introducing a female. It is an expression of what Valerie Hey has called 'the taboo against male un-bonding' (Hey 1986).

Sexual humour as male control

A second source of disadvantage to women is the heightened heterosexual and sexist culture generated by men within the workplace. In contrast to the exclusion of women by male clubbing this culture *includes women but marginalizes and controls them*. An incident illustrating this point had recently occurred in High Street Retail's Computer Division, giving rise to considerable conflict. The middle and senior staff of the Division had gone away together at company expense for a weekend's conference in a hotel. The occasion was intended to review the Division's work and build *esprit de corps*. The first morning's business opened with a presentation by a senior manager. He had prepared a 'visual aid' in the form of a lifesized photograph of a bare-breasted model. In the photo she appeared leaning against a rock with a hole in it. In this space the senior manager had had superimposed a second photo, of the divisional director's face. He opened his talk as follows. 'We are lucky to have [the director] with us this morning. He's just risen from a sick bed. [Pause for effect] His secretary has flu.' This drew a laugh, not only from the audience but from the director – and from his secretary who was also present at the time. There followed other sexual allusions and jokes from this and subsequent speakers.

Later this same presentation was repeated back at head office for the benefit of a larger group, this time including quite junior programmers and other divisional staff. Some of them were young women, including a group who had joined the company part-time as a result of a new policy to relieve the skills shortage by attracting women 'returners'. This time the jokes were not universally well received. Later some of the young women, who told me they had felt angered and alienated by the tone and style of the event, wrote a letter of complaint to the director for which they canvassed signatures. Some male colleague who shared their distaste also signed the letter. The equal opportunities manager was approached and she took the matter up with the director of the Computer Division. At first he reacted tetchily. He felt the complaints had failed to understand the humour. He was annoyed that the serious side of the weekend conference, the technical presentation into which a good deal of preparation had gone, had apparently been wasted on these women who saw nothing but sexual suggestiveness. He reluctantly agreed, however, that, given this inexplicable degree of sensitivity among the women, he would ensure such material would be avoided at conferences in subsequent years.

The manager who had given the talk, on the other hand, justified himself. He said in interview he 'liked to liven the proceedings in this way'. He had found his off-the-cuff remarks had 'gone down well in the last twenty years. It was a surprise to me that people found it offensive.' He saw no reason not to do the same thing another year. If he were to be censored he might prefer not to do it at all. The divisional personnel manager too had been defensive, though he was obliged, given the equality climate now existing in the firm, to agree that some 'reinforcement training' for some of the men might be appropriate. The young women remained unreconciled. But some began to fear they might have 'gone over the top' and spoiled their career chances.

As did several of the men in discussing the incident in interview later, the director appealed to popular culture. 'If you look at newspapers there are naked women in those, that's sexist. If you look at TV you have comedians telling sexist jokes . . . . OK, we've got to be careful. But personally I think it was blown up *completely* out of proportion, because it was an attempt at humour.' He explained to me that sexual jokes are the stock in trade of management training – you were *taught* to drop 'icebreakers' and 'liveners' into your delivery to 'get the audience relaxed, keep 'em interested'. Besides, he said, his secretary had not been at all upset by the reference to her in the joke. 'Because [she] likes to be flattered constantly about her appearance. She likes to wear sexy clothes and parade around the department sticking her chest out, and encourages sexism, right . . . . So I don't know what the offence is.'

The divisional personnel manager also excused the men by reference to expectations in the extra-organizational world. He perceived a problem for men in knowing when to 'switch modes' from the 'natural' pursuit of the female – always prone to lead them on – to a behaviour more appropriate to the modern office.

> In this building you will have women who are definitely dressed to titillate and that is their objective. They are perhaps not dedicated to work as work. The social side of it is very, very important . . . . Now the male going around the building, you know, he's got to pick up all these signals all the time. This woman *wants* me to admire her. This one doesn't. It can be difficult for men to handle.

I was unable to interview the secretary, to verify her manager's representation of her feelings. It is true enough that many young women do play into men's hands in this way. Some young women know of no other way to behave. They receive confusing messages from men and the rules of behaviour in the office are unclear. Some women actually delight in the heterosexual play of working life. They feel well able to survive in a highly sexualised atmosphere and to operate in a flirtatious and provocative mode. The price they pay, of course, is that they are not taken seriously as colleagues, they are personal ornaments and playthings for their bosses and other men. They make things more difficult for the women around them. And unless they are deft and clever in handling men they may suffer emotional and sexual exploitation.

One point made by the director and other men in the Division was that it would have been better if the young women, instead of complaining, had 'given as good as they got'. Why had they not thought up some witty and equally sexy riposte to put the men in their place? The young women said, however, 'Why would we *want* to do that?' It would in their view just exacerbate the problem because the difficulty they encountered was not one particular slur against women but the entire *sexualization of the working environment*. For the truth is that, though women want to be free to be their fully sexual selves, at work as elsewhere, they find that, because of the power-relations of heterosexuality they are unable to do this without risk. I saw a good example of this. One young woman in Computer Division had clearly tried to take part in this male culture: she was known for sending sexy birthday cards to other members of the department. Her male senior manager, however, saw this as distasteful. 'I've one [woman] out there who's a shocker', he said. 'Sends people cards that I think, God! Oh dear!' A woman cannot operate by men's rules and get away with it. What is funny coming from a man is obscene coming from a woman.

New men, new oppressions

Some of the personnel managers and others who were thoughtful about the position of women in High Street Retail and keen to see 'equal opportunities' firmly established there told me they were confident that progress was now assured because the whole culture of the company was changing for the better. It was, they felt, the older traditionalist men in the firm, relics from the previous management regime, who had been the chauvinists in High Street Retail. I did indeed meet several men of this kind. Some clearly felt women's place was in the kitchen. Some saw womankind frankly as sexual material for men's delight. 'I actually believe women are feminine creatures who are there to be admired. End of story.' As the traditionalists reached retirement age and left the firm, these more thoughtful managers said, women would find themselves in a more hospitable culture. The 'modern' executive or manager often had a working partner at home, he expected to work alongside women and knew how to treat them as equals.

Experience was showing this optimism to be misplaced. The new men, though certainly different from the old guard, were little better from a woman's point of view. The Computer Division was characteristic of the new regime. Its managers had deliberately sought to make it a 'flatter' hierarchy than the rest of the firm, with fewer status differences. There was a conscious preference for informality, using first names. 'We're all very pally, everyone's on a par.' In these things it was strikingly similar to the Computer Department in the Service, generating the same iconoclastic, fast-moving, 'fun', expanding zone in what was seen as a stuffy, rule-bound, old-fashioned organization. However, the relations in both areas were competitive, and the competition centred on technical expertise and career pace. It was no coincidence that women's statistical position was inferior in the information technology divisions of both organizations compared with their position in the labour force of the organizations as a whole. This was partly because of the national scarcity of women with IT qualifications. That absence itself, however, had to be seen as generated partly by the masculine appropriation of technology and its associated skills, a cultural exclusion of women effective in both training and employment (Cockburn 1983, 1985 and 1987). There is some affinity between the 'technological' and the 'young manager' culture.

Women had identified this new type of male not only in High Street Retail and the Service but also in the Trade Union and the Local Authority. What distinguished him was an overt and confident machismo. Women everywhere made reference to the 'cod-piece wearing jocks' of the policy unit, the 'new men' of the advertizing department. This masculinity does not share the woman's-place-is-in-the-home mentality of the old guard. These men expect to find women in the public sphere. Nominally at least they welcome women into this exciting new world because their presence adds sexual spice to the working day. The equality of women can never be actuated, however, for the women are placed continually in a double bind by the new sexual regime. They are expected to be as sexually combative and amusing as men, yet their ability to be so is undermined by the asymmetry of heterosexuality. Heterosexual relations are not as consensual as they are popularly represented as being. They are gendered and unequal. Women are in a no-win situation. When they try to join equally in the sexual relations, like the young woman of the birthday cards, they burn their fingers. When they ignore the sexualized culture they are in turn ignored and marginalized. When they resist it they are labelled spoilsports, lacking in a sense of humour. The complainants in the incident above were defined as a 'minority opinion', lumped in a pot with 'feminists'. It is not so far from the school playground, where girls are trapped in the damned-if-you-do, damned-if-you-don't discourse of 'slag' and 'drag' (Lees 1986).

Male power is not dying out with the retirement of the old traditionalist men. It is being reproduced in new, one might say literally 'virulent', forms that are appropriate and effective for the late twentieth century. The discourse that was typified in the Computer Division incident was not an exception. Nor is it coincidence that the weekend conference at which it occurred was intended to cement relationships in the department, bringing together employees of different levels. Such sexualized discourse is a necessary part of the cementing activities with which senior men seek to bond men beneath them firmly into the fraternity, healing the contradictions of patriarchal and class structures that threaten to divide them. The ploy came unstuck because women had by now intruded as colleagues into their technical world.

Bodies, then, are used in many kinds of process at work. They are put to work to perform manual and mental labour. They are also 'dressed' and presented for work according to organizational norms. Uniform may involve deliberate sexualizing of the body or its desexualizing. Informal dress is also governed by written and unwritten codes. Bodies and sexuality are sold to the employer and by the employer – literally in the case of the sex industry, less totally in the case of the 'attractive' secretary or 6 ft black security guard. This exploitation is by no means all enforced. Much of it appeals to, as well as reinforcing, our own sense of identity and what for us is pleasurable. It is always an open question how much we present ourselves and behave as *they* want us to, how much we use work to develop and express a bodily and sexual identity we cherish. Young women, for instance, avoiding technical training that seems to diminish their femininity, may choose hairdressing precisely because it enhances it (Cockburn 1987). This, however, is not to suggest that such choices are free choices. We develop our identities in response to patriarchal pressures and are acutely conscious of the rewards offered for conformism and the punishments awaiting deviance. As Rosemary Pringle says, 'men control women not only through rape or through forcing them to do what they want [them] to do, but through definitions of pleasure and selfhood' (Pringle 1989:165).

Equality policy faces a problem, therefore. The short agenda in most organizations includes a bid to instil respect for women – but the approach usually amounts to effectively banning sexuality from the workplace. This is not a popular move with all women. It is in any case all but impossible to achieve. First, it runs counter to the new 'liberated' management style. Second, only superficial behaviour is accessible to policy and that which remains inaccessible (organizational uses of our bodies and sexuality) is more extensive, significant and damaging.

The problem is that while male-dominated organizations use our bodies they also deny their true materiality. Women's menstruation, PMT, pregnancy and menopause for instance, to say nothing of lesbian desire, are censored out of the workplace. How many workplace toilets have a lockable space with a bidet where a woman can wash herself in private? How many workplaces afford a woman a place to lie down? Horizontality is as prohibited at work as it is on railway station concourses.

One aspect of women's taking of space and authority in organizations has to be a reassertion of our bodies 'in the round'. We must also be bold in knowing and asserting our likes as well as our dislikes. 'Opposition to sexual harassment is only one component of a sexual politics in the workplace. It needs to be supplemented with analyses of the ways in which sexual pleasure might be used to disrupt male rationality and to empower women' (Pringle 1989:166). Men's sexuality is traditionally treated as unproblematic in the workplace. It is women who are, as the Victorians put it, The Sex. Men can play almost any power game with women and still maintain an acceptable identity as true organization men. Women have to act asexual if they are to avoid being seen as sexy (Gutek 1989:61). What needs to change is not the sexiness of women but the vulnerability of women. The long agenda for the women's movement in organizations must be to strengthen women's position and confidence in many different ways so that we can re-introduce our bodies, our sexuality and our emotions on our own terms.

Women, separateness and difference

Closely related to the idea of embodiment, of course, are ideas of specificity and 'difference'. For women at work, especially for women who want to be taken seriously for their skills and career potential, it is a continual problem to know when to hide their difference from men and when to assert it. The question often arises in acute form when positive action for sex equality gives rise to suggestions for *separate provision* of training or other facilities for women. The difficulties can be illustrated by reference to High Street Retail.

The equal opportunities manager with the agreement of at least one other senior woman manager and the major shareholder who was, as you will remember, a key figure in equal opportunity developments in the firm, decided to initiate two 'women-only' activities. The first was a meeting for 'women in management', the second an assertiveness course for women. It was hoped that both might become the first in a series of such events. As recounted in Chapter 1, the meeting was held, twenty-six women attended. No more ensued, however. The assertiveness course was held too – but it was decided that all subsequent sessions were to be open to men too. Why did these women-only initiatives fizzle out?

The answer was the opposition of men and the ambivalence of women. From men I heard very few expressions of support for the concept of women-only activities. While progressive personnel managers accepted the idea of women's assertiveness training as part of the equality strategy, it was ridiculed by more typical men. And there was profound suspicion concerning the women-only meeting for women managers. At best it was felt permissible so long as it was intended to be the start of mixed-sex networking. Justifiable if it were to be a question of 'a few gin and tonics', or 'a drink, a bite and a natter', it would be illegitimate if business matters were on the agenda. All too easily, men felt, this sort of thing could tip over into 'discrimination against men'. For some men the whole idea was frankly a joke. The fellows 'fell about laffing'. It was 'absurd', not 'natural', 'forcing things'. It was women saying 'I'm a woman and I'm privileged', creating an 'us and them situation' and was equated by one man with a trade union for women's vested interests. One said it smacked of 'a little gang behind the scenes'. Men would 'wonder what was going on behind their backs'. Even a personnel manager supportive of equal opportunity initiatives felt these would be damaged by women doing things on their own.

It is not surprising then that, when they heard about the proposed women managers' meeting, some senior male managers (as previously mentioned) made direct representations to the chief executive to have it stopped. He felt obliged to refuse permission for the meeting to be held in the office in working hours, so that the women had to make the venue a local bistro after work. Some senior men sent 'their' women along to the meeting to report back on it.

Even the men who support equality initiatives tend to get annoyed at the point where they are excluded by women doing something on their own. Separate activity by women is clearly perceived as a threat by men. They fear the creation of cells of disloyalty, women 'telling tales' about 'their' men (Hey 1986). Men do face a contradiction here. They do not want women with them in the male sphere, yet they need to hold women close enough to them to ensure no loyalty develops between women. This may explain the similar responses by men to women's separate activity and organization in the other three organizations. The language in which the opposition was voiced was often colourful. More reasoned arguments tended to take one of two lines: either such separatism was damaging to women, or it was damaging to men. Or both at the same time. Underlying much of the discussion was the argument that if women want to be equal they must abandon any idea of 'difference'. 'You can't have it both ways'.

We need to hesitate here and explore this question of *difference* – for on it hinges the future of women's politics. From the beginning, new-wave feminism has debated with energy and sometimes with fury the question of whether women are essentially, naturally and for ever different from men. If such difference were a fact, it would arise from our biology: women's and men's complementary roles in reproduction. The political implications of 'difference' have been well spelled out by Anne Phillips. Advocates of 'no difference' have argued

> once feminists admit the mildest degree of sexual difference, they open up a gap through which the currents of reaction will flow. Once let slip that pre-menstrual tension interfered with concentration, that pregnancy can be exhausting, that motherhood is absorbing, and you are off down the slope to separate spheres ... But those who have argued for a feminism grounded in sexual difference have their own very plausible case. The politics of equality directs energies to the spheres that are occupied by men .... Why shouldn't the world be made to change its tune? (Phillips 1987:19).

As discussed in Chapter 1, a further real danger in subscribing too heavily to 'difference' is the implication that if women are all different from men they are all similar to each other – which is palpably not the case and leads to the marginalising of black and working-class women's interests by the dominant voice in Western European feminism, that of white middle-class women. This strengthens the preference of some feminists to represent the social process of gendering as diverting us from an equally 'natural' similarity with men (Epstein 1988). Gayle Rubin, for instance, says 'far from being an expression of natural differences, exclusive gender identity is the suppression of natural similarities' (Rubin 1975). In a similar anti-essentialist approach, other feminists see our constitution as self-conscious and gendered subjects as occurring continuously, and only, in discourse (Weedon 1987).

By contrast, I tend to share the view that 'the problem of biological difference refuses to go away', that we do not need to reduce women's subordination to biology but equally 'we do not need to ignore biology without good reason' (Ramazanoglu 1989:40.) The social practices that construct gender relations neither directly express nor are they without reference to natural biological differences. Rather, to use R.W.Connell's phrase, 'they negate them in a practical transformation' (Connell 1987:79). This dialectical approach can be seen too in the work of Nancy Hartsock who points out that women experience greater unity of mental and manual labour. 'The unity grows from the fact that women's bodies, unlike men's, can be themselves instruments of production: in pregnancy, giving birth, or lactation, arguments about a division of mental from manual labor are fundamentally foreign.' This could result in more women than men having a world-view to which dichotomies and dualisms are alien (Hartsock 1985:242). Mary O'Brien (1981), as we saw, has argued that the whole process of reproduction from ovulation to the bringing up of the child to adulthood, is conscious labour on women's part, comparable to productive labour, and has generated its own 'reproductive consciousness'. Men's alienation from this labour – they lose their seed at the moment of ejaculation and have no further biological part to play – has resulted in a different reproductive consciousness in men. This usefully puts the emphasis on men's, not women's, 'difference'.

Whatever the cultural connectedness of women to their biology, and whatever the shaping of women's bodies by their social gender, I would argue that for political reasons we need to retain a concept of 'women's difference', problematised but available. Carol Bacchi has argued, I believe correctly, that feminism only gets caught up in sameness/difference debates in certain historical moments when they are forced by external circumstances to limit their demands. 'The women's movement . . . has not debated constantly whether women are the same as or different from men, or at least not always in the same way. Serious disputes about woman's sex-specific function, whether all women should mother, did not arise until the inter-war years. Serious debate about women's character, whether all women share a maternal, caring nature, is more recent still. It is important to identify the historically specific conditions in which divisions appear in order to understand their causes' (Bacchi 1990:258).

That the position taken by feminists on sameness and difference is influenced by the socio-political context is demonstrated by the way women are obliged, on the one hand, to shun 'difference' when a fascist or conservative discourse is exploiting the concept, on the other to espouse it when escaping (as in the Soviet Union and Eastern Europe today) from a dogmatic socialist imposition of sameness.

What we see in the bitter reaction of men to 'separate organiz-ation by women', even in the harmless guise of the occasional assertiveness course, is a controlling practice: *men will say when women's difference is relevant.* High Street Retail affords an example of men's use of women's difference, routinely reinforced and exploited. We saw that masculine and feminine dress codes were in force. Women's skills, imputed and actual, were set to work and undervalued. For the company, therefore, women's domestically-defined, sexually-defined, differently-perceived labour power was an important source of capital accumulation. Individual men used difference in their arguments against women's equality. 'I think that's something women will have to live with all their lives and in future generations', said one young man. 'But in these [feminist] groups they are saying "I don't *want* to live with that". They have got to accept they are a liability. Women will always have that burden on their shoulders.' Yet when it came to women saying, for themselves, 'for some purposes we are different and have different interests', this was ruled illegitimate. Men's argument then was: if you want to join men as equals in the public sphere you must leave behind womanly things, you must be indistinguishable from a man, you must, in short, *assimilate*.

Politically, especially in the context of positive action for sex equality, we need to keep 'difference' in play. For many of the women I spoke with, feminism was problematic precisely because it seemed to seek *sameness*, as well as equality, with men. They did not wish to abandon what they felt the better things in life. 'There are some lovely things about being a woman.' As feminists we need tactical flexibility. We need to be able, now to assert the true value of 'women's work', now to claim the right to men's work. We need to be able to state our needs concerning pregnancy, menstruation or menopause without being written off as biologically inferior. We need to be able to claim women's 'different way of doing things' without being stereotyped as the caring face of management or hearing it said that 'women and technology are incompatible'. It is the idea of difference, whether rooted in biology and culture, or in history and culture, that gives the feminist project its world-transforming potential.

Feminism and hegemony

While women's career chances, better maternity provision and equal pay for work of equal value are themes that can, at a stretch, be represented and debated without recourse to 'feminism', discussion of sexuality and separate activity for women unavoidably pulls down this ton of trouble on a woman's head. If you challenge sexist language, protest at pin-ups or ask for a self-defence course you immediately risk being tagged 'feminist' and, to maintain credibility in the organization, are obliged to develop a strategy for responding to this.

Feminism was a theme on which I engaged the conversation of both men and women in High Street Retail and elsewhere: what did they see feminism as being, what did they feel about feminists? Most men distinguished clearly between 'equality at work' and 'feminism'. Equality was held by most to be legitimate. Women should 'get a fair crack of the whip'. However, many men believed women were already equal – positive action was quite uncalled for. Many simply felt true equality to be impossible 'in the nature of things'.

If some men could talk the language of 'equality of opportunity', however, the language of *feminism* was altogether another matter. While fortunately it was not felt to be as 'rife' in Britain as in the USA, feminism was labelled with a long list of pejorative terms. 'Women's libbers' were, I was told: harsh, strident, demanding, uptight, aggressive, vociferous, dogmatic, radical, zealots, crusaders and overly ambitious. They are the extreme element, the Greenham Common type, the burn-your-bra mob. Feminists bash people over the head with their ideas, they ram things down your throat, take things to ridiculous lengths, niggle about semantics and, not surprisingly, given all this, put people's backs up. They are always going on about women having a hard deal. They are more assertive than other women for equal treatment. They feel men are all enemies and that they must undermine them. They make snidey comments about men's sexist jokes. They have no sense of humour. They are a minority group, shouting and screeching. And they wear lapel badges – at worst badges that say 'I am a lesbian'.

The fear and distaste felt by men for feminism is not limited to those of the older generation. A young man in his early twenties, of junior manager status, had bitterly anti-feminist views that he expounded at length, illustrating his points by reference to 'a girl in his department' who had, among other things, rejected his courtesy in holding a door open for her. He had encountered a similar rude young woman who had refused his offered seat in a bus. These things implied, he said, 'a feminist attitude'. He saw feminism as 'these little groups popping up over rights for this and that', taking advantage of a social atmosphere in Britain that possibly afforded too much individual liberty. He felt feminism was running against the course of history and of nature.

The response of men to the women's movement and women's organization amounts, I would suggest, to a sustained *anathematizing of feminism*. The majority of men put their weight behind this process. It has, I believe, a profound influence on what it is possible for women, and for other men, to do, think and say on the issues of gender.

For there is a minority of men who are supportive to change in gender relations, both for women's sake and for their own. Some of them, in High Street Retail and elsewhere, had been influential in furthering the equal opportunities strategy from key positions in senior management, characteristically in personnel. One man, a trade union officer, expressed particularly clear ideas concerning the damage their systematic subordination by men was doing to women. And he felt, besides, that being held forcibly himself to the treadmill of a demanding job, being separated from the more human side of life, had been damaging to him personally. 'It's a source of unhappiness from my point of view', he said. 'I wouldn't do it again. I mean you can't live your life twice. [What did you lose?] All the strengths and rich experiences that would come from being closer to the children, helping to bring them up.' He also felt that the damage went beyond the personal to the societal. 'The world's run basically by men who haven't had that experience . . . those experiences should be shared and the world should be run by people who have shared them.'

The organizations I studied differed more than in anything else, in the space their culture allowed for pro-feminist ideas and practice. It was in the two with a basis in socialist politics (the Local Authority and the Trade Union), in which there were active anti-racist strategies and a positive position on lesbian and gay rights, that I found enclaves in which both women and men were able to explore, experiment with and try out the effect on practice of feminist ideas. In the Trade Union, as we saw, particularly in the Northern Ireland Division, women had made just such a space. In the Local Authority I found in the Housing Department, where I carried out many of my interviews, not a few women and men who talked in a new and refreshing way about the welcome changes feminist ideas were bringing both to relations in the department and the kind of service being offered to tenants.

Most women, however – and this applies particularly to those in the less progressive environments of High Street Retail and the Service – have mixed and contradictory feelings about feminism and indeed about any action by themselves or others that would identify them as a group called 'women'. In the former, for example, with the exception of the equality activists, none of the seventeen women I interviewed were prepared unequivocally to call themselves feminists. Twelve said quite firmly that they would not. The remainder positioned themselves along a spectrum with three saying that, with certain disclaimers and in some circumstances, they 'might'. Women often oppose to feminism a better way of going about equality: being 'sensible and logical', taking 'a more moderate view', a 'mature and responsible attitude' and not 'doing a trumpet voluntary' about women's oppression. One felt women already experienced enough isolation at work from men's distancing of them – feminism simply aggravated the alienation.

The negative set of feelings expressed about feminism should not, however, be read as an indication of passivity. Quite a few of these women were strong-minded, strong-willed and some of them quite angry. Harbouring suspicion or dislike of feminism did not necessarily mean that one was not pro-woman. It was significant perhaps that several women said they would not call themselves feminist because 'they had never needed to do so', they had 'never come up against anything' – implying that feminist consciousness is a product of experience. Some had become more conscious of equal opportunities, more self-respecting and 'had their eyes opened', in the course of time. Husbands leaving them, undermining their confidence, or failing to do their share of the housework – these had changed some women's attitudes. One had learned, she said, from her sons and daughters. Some had felt swept along by 'a general atmosphere of change'.

It is significant that the most common reason stated for not wanting to be associated with feminism was not women's disadvantage, which was recognized by most women, but simply that 'feminism has got itself a bad name'. It was a matter of how feminism was seen, the meanings attached to it. There were two particular associations of feminism that gave women difficulty with the concept. First was that it was seen as 'political', with a big P, as associated with leftism. Second it was linked with lesbianism, and the taboo against same-sex desire is still one of the most powerful in contemporary society. In politically conservative environments to espouse either of these identifications immediately puts women at odds with male colleagues. The anathematizing of feminism imposes a penalty on it that most women cannot afford to pay. Basically men make it clear: *you have to choose – be a feminist or keep my respect. You cannot have both.* Men persistently drive wedges between women, saying 'You are someone I can work with, get along with. You are not a feminist. You are not like *her*.' A senior woman manager told me that on taking up her post she had been informally warned by a senior male colleague that she would be well advised not to make the mistake of a certain other woman colleague who had got involved with equality politics and thereby had damaged her long-term chances. What is and is not feminist, on men's lips, amounts to what is and what is not acceptable and desirable in women.

Women therefore do not make a free choice. Of course we must ultimately bear responsibility for our own ideology and politics. All the same, just as the choice we make between a discourse of 'difference' and a discourse of 'sameness' is made under pressure from men, so men lean heavily on our choice as to whether or not we use a discourse of feminism. The anti-feminist discourse of men has to be seen as a policing of women's consciousness and an important mechanism in the reproduction of male power.

A term that seems appropriate to describe these processes is 'hegemony'. It is masculine sway exerted over women and men alike, not by legal coercion or economic compulsion but by cultural means, by force of ideas. Since it helps us to understand why women rather rarely break free of patriarchal ideas and patriarchal relations, a brief exploration of the origin and political uses of the concept of hegemony may be worthwhile. Though the idea of class hegemony had been current among Russian Marxists in the late nineteenth century, and Lenin too had written of the need to build up proletarian hegemony in the process of creating a revolutionary movement, it was Antonio Gramsci, the Italian Marxist, whose development of the concept in the 1920s was to seem specially relevant to those engaged in the social movements of the left in Europe fifty years later (Gramsci 1971). Gramsci's concern was with the way the various fractions of the ruling class were together able to produce a social and cultural environment in which capitalist relations of exploitation appeared quite normal and acceptable to ordinary people. How was it that certain interpretations of reality, that logically could be seen to be in the interests of a dominant class, could appear as 'common sense' to those they ruled? How could it be that, despite exploitation, class rule could be achieved in many cases and for long periods without compulsion and coercion? When and why did people reject this 'common sense' and start to think contrary thoughts?

Hegemony, then, is moral and philosophical leadership, an apparent right to govern accorded a dominant group by the active consent of the governed (Bocock 1986). The term has been used to characterise the compelling ideological sweep of Thatcherism and the New Right from the mid-1970s in Britain, even influencing with its 'enterprise culture' the ideas and identifications of many working-class people. Conversely, the question is asked, how the new social movements of this same period, the women's movement, the anti-racist movement, the environmental movement, might develop a counter-hegemony, forging progressive alliances on the left that might come to constitute a new 'common sense' in a society of the future (Laclau and Mouffe 1985).

Likewise, I would suggest it is appropriate to think of patriarchal ideology as successfully sustaining, through changing times, hegemonic control in our culture. One equality officer said of men, 'They're winning. Young women today do believe they're already equal.' Even the most surprising people – even the young, even women – believe in the biological essentialism that tells us women and men, being physically different, are also naturally destined for social inequality. I was told over and again in the course of this research that women's lower pay and lower status at work is no more than incidental to the economic class interests of employers and to the career-chances of male employees, that on the contrary it springs purely from the 'supply side' factor: women's inevitably domestic persona. These ideas are hegemonic in the sense that they appear as common sense truth to most men, and more significantly, to most women. It is exceedingly difficult to break away from hegemonic ideas and counter them with other thoughts because in doing so one is made to seem eccentric, extremist, flying in the face of reality. Feminism is represented as all these things.

Hegemony, we must finally add, is not an automatic attribute of rule. It is the achievement of political and cultural *work*. What I would suggest we can see in the gender relations of organizations such as High Street Retail and the Service is a struggle between hegemonic and subversive ideas. Women, feminists, equality activists are refuting patriarchal common sense, contradicting male power. Men are obliged therefore to do more cultural work to ensure the reproduction of male power. Now they use the verbal carrot, now the gestural stick, to talk and to 'relate' women into sharing the age-old masculist common sense. Ultimately, what is at stake, is the constitution of our identity as women. Without that active and continual cultural labour by men, to be a woman might be a very different thing. And women might be quicker to perceive their disadvantage, indeed their exploitation, and to form links with each other, not only to evade the power of men but more importantly to change the nature of organizations and the way power is used.

As it is, hegemony operates through the common sense tenet that we have little choice, that masculine and feminine are given by nature, that 'gender is not negotiable' and that the sexes are already equal (Brittan 1989:4). Women are not forced to accept such a belief. As Dorothy Smith says,

> At the interpersonal level it is not a conspiracy among men that they impose on women. It is a complementary social process between women and men. Women are complicit in the social practices of their silence (Smith 1987:34).

Everything in our culture, however, in childhood, in sexual partnerships, in employment, in the media is continually addressing women in the terms of patriarchal discourse. We produce each other as gendered creatures, women and men in complementarity, so that it is flying in the face of common sense to 'be a feminist', to suppose the world and the women and men who make it, could be other than they are.

Some such hegemonic process is needed to explain many things that we observe every day. Why else would women bring up their daughters to be compliant wives? Why would the secretary join in the men's sexual joking at her expense? Two women who had been sexually harassed at work said to me that they could not understand how it was that, despite their overwhelming feelings of anger and distress, they had not taken issue with the man who did it. 'I felt gagged. Mute. Why?' Women's oppression takes the form of an open secret that is continually exposed to view yet remains for ever unseeable and unsayable. Over and again we see the realities of male power. Over and again we say nothing and forget it. The king parades by with his retinue, naked as the day he was born – but his hegemonic sway appears to robe him so that we do not see his puny parts.

6

Of men and monsters

Equal opportunities policies in organizations are seldom limited to positive action for sex equality. Almost all include clauses on *race equality*. Most have brought their policies on employment of *disabled people* into the equality framework. A few employers, besides, include sexual orientation, guaranteeing equal treatment of *lesbians and gay men*. These activities within organizations are expressions of social movements without: the civil rights, black power and anti-racist movements which swept the USA and Western Europe in the 1960s and 1970s; Gay Pride and Lesbian Strength; and more recently a growth in self-organization among groups of people with different forms of disability.

The reasons for the growth of such 'identity' movements in the last thirty years have been widely discussed. It has been argued the emergence of new political 'subjects' is due to capitalism entering a new phase, marked by the growth of a world market, by decentralization, deregulation, a decline in the importance of the old industrial proletariat and a growth in numbers of white-collar service workers. 'As the working class, as conventionally conceived, appears to be more and more old-fashioned, rooted in a previous spatial and cultural fix, so newer forms of politics, which can provide also for the possibility of a reconstituted class politics, and newer forms of cultural experience have come to the fore' (Lash and Urry 1987:312). It also makes sense to suppose that the preconditions for the growth of equality and liberation movements can be found at an ideological level, in the undeniable failure of socialism and its working-class movements to deliver democracy in practice (Laclau and Mouffe 1985). Whether or not these various equality projects exist in a particular organization, the extent to which they are conceptually linked with each other and with positive action for sex equality, and finally the degree to which they are articulated with the class politics of trade unionism, can all be read as measures of the 'length' of the equal opportunities agenda.

The multi-faceted nature of the equality project has contradictory effects. In some ways it is damaging. Using one mind-set to deal with processes of exploitation and oppression that are very different tends to lessen both the analytical understanding of each specific process and the impact of any one corrective project. It can set up competition between the several groups for support and funding. Some people fall between stools. Black women, for example, are often overlooked in sex-equality projects run by white women, while 'race' equality units and roles are often staffed by black men who neglect gender politics. Women's units and race units are often reluctant to admit internal divisions and differences for fear of jeopardising the solidarity they need to face opposition from without. It was exasperation with this experience that inspired the title of a book by Gloria Hull and other women: 'All the Women are White, All the Blacks are Men – but Some of Us are Brave' (Hull *et al.* 1982; see also Allen 1982).

On the other hand, the necessary co-existence of at least four distinct projects helps prompt women to a greater consciousness of *differences* among and between women and the ways in which some women oppress, subordinate and exploit others. The heterosexism of straight women, the racism of white women and the neglect by non-disabled women of the experience of those who have disabilities have weakened the women's movement in the past. The organizational equality context today does offer us as women a series of new occasions to rethink our agenda with more sensitivity to each others' differences and needs.

Another advantage is that the real nature of systemic power becomes clearer. The upper reaches of the hierarchies in which class power is deployed are visibly peopled not just by men but by white men – primarily heterosexual and non-disabled men – a narrow, self-reproducing monoculture. More accurately (since there are always exceptions at the level of the individual), power can be distinguished as being not one but rather *a set of mutually-reinforcing dominance relations*. Different women relate in different ways on the one hand to the monoculture of the powerful, on the other to the diverse humanity that in one or more ways lives a subordinated and disadvantaged existence.

Third, while it remains the case that the processes of subordination and exploitation differ, it can be shown that there are cumulative advantages in being variously a man, white, non-disabled and heterosexual, which enable the individual to attain and hold economic and political power. A member of these groups can mobilize group resources, cooperating with like people in acceding to class power: large earned incomes, the ownership of wealth, possession and control of the means of production and positions of authority in the organizations through which capital, state and civil society carry out business. Looking simultaneously at the inequalities inherent in relations of gender, sexual orientation, ethnicity and disability reveals a pattern. Similarities exist in the ideological processes in which male identity is constructed as white, heterosexual and physically 'normal', an active subject formed in opposition to various non-selves.

Ethnicity, whiteness and the man

We saw in the last chapter how our bodies are positioned in a power-play within organizations. Sexuality, however, is only one of the fields in which our bodies are politicised. Another is 'race'. Scientific research in the past purported to demonstrate identifiable races on the basis of physiological characteristics and to assign them superiority and inferiority. Such theories are now discredited. 'It was generally concluded after the Second World War that the scientific concept of 'race' grounded in the idea of fixed typologies and based upon certain phenotypical features such as skin colour and skull shape does not have any significant scientific meaning or utility' (Miles 1989:37). Or, as a UNESCO document put it, 'for all practical social purposes 'race' is not so much a biological phenomenon as a social myth' (cited in Miles and Phizacklea 1984:14. See also Montague 1974 and Cohen 1988). The appeal to 'racial difference', therefore, the invocation of racial stereotypes and the valorisation of some 'races' over others, is ideological: it is *racism*.

Racism operates systematically in labour markets. Carole Pateman says 'the buyer is never indifferent to the sex of the owner of property in the person. He contracts for jurisdiction over a masculine or feminine body' (Pateman 1988:231). Likewise the buyer of labour power is never indifferent to ethnicity or skin colour. The purchase of labour power is not only a contract for the use of mental and manual skills at the lowest possible wage. It is also, as we have seen, a contract for the deployment of sexual identity and emotional capabilities. More than this, it is also a purchase of the services of a certain *kind of person*, someone with a perceived social status (it may be high or low), certain cultural attachments and certain looks, to all of which ethnicity and skin colour are germane. The system of male power that operates in and through major employing organizations in Britain is specifically *white* male power and the culture of management is almost solidly a white monoculture, identifying and excluding other groups.

We have seen some of the assumptions made about women and men, the different qualities attributed to each sex when allocating them to work. Such stereotypes also attach to ethnicity. Research on the recruitment behaviour of managers and institutions carried out at the Centre for Research in Ethnic Relations found recruiters defining West Indians as slow, lazy and happy-go-lucky, but as 'good mixers'. Some employers characterized them as aggressive and excitable. Asians, on the other hand were stereotyped, as hard workers, ambitious and more academic than West Indians. They were also seen as stand-offish (Jenkins 1986:114.) However, while sex-stereotyping involves an active preference for women in certain jobs, the black stereotype in the white employer's mind is almost always negative. A white person is preferred for most if not all jobs, even unskilled manual jobs. A person of ethnic minority origin will be employed only *faute de mieux*.

The study cited above found such stereotypes to be bound up with the notion of what is 'acceptable' in an employee. Most recruitment procedures were informal, with a good deal of 'word of mouth' recommendation, producing highly discriminatory effects. The selection criterion of acceptability derived its importance from the manager's quest for control of production. 'Given that workers are fully competent social actors, routinely likely, in a variety of ways, to resist passively or actively the impositions and disciplines of bureaucratic order and the capitalist labour process, it is important to managers that they should recruit those workers who will create the fewest possible problems for them in this respect'. And here we see the interaction between individual intentionality and institutional practice. For an 'acceptable' worker is a trouble-free worker and one kind of trouble never far from the employer's mind is any racist reaction on the part of the existing white workforce (Jenkins 1986:235).

Such exclusionary practices by the interactive efforts of employers, trade unions and groups of white workers have created in Britain an ethnically-stratified workforce, with a particular distinction between white and black. A rigorous quantitative survey of Asians, West Indians and white men in the mid-seventies demonstrated beyond any doubt that black workers were concentrated within the lower job levels in a way that could not be explained by lower academic or job qualifications. Even in broadly comparable jobs they had lower earnings than whites. They often did shiftwork, yet their shiftwork premiums did not succeed in raising their earnings above those of whites. As with women, black men were concentrated in certain firms, industries and occupations. They had to make twice as many job applications as whites before being accepted for a job. And they were much more vulnerable to unemployment (Smith 1977). A recent review of research and statistics shows racism continuing to disadvantage black workers today (Iles and Auluck forthcoming).

The position in labour markets of black women is, of course, doubly subordinated. They suffer the manifold disadvantages of the woman at work plus the discrimination and stereotyping accorded to black groups. They are disproportionately found in manual work (Phizacklea 1983). There are differences between groups of non-white women. West Indian women, as we saw in Chapter 3, are more frequently self-supporting and are more likely to work full-time (74% are economically active and of these 75% work full-time). They consequently experience more severe and exploitative childcare problems (Stone 1983:35). Personal accounts bear witness to a damaging interaction between patriarchal relations of control in the family and women's exploitation in waged work, particularly in Asian and especially in Moslem families (Wilson 1978). Often immigrant women work for little or no pay for ethnic minority business entrepreneurs to whom they are related (Anthias 1983, Phizacklea 1988, Westwood and Bhachu 1988). As mentioned previously, women whose cultural and religious traditions confine them to the home are among the most exploited of all categories of labour: homeworkers.

The disadvantage of black women is not, however, due mainly to their ethnic culture but to institutional and individual white racism. In a study of more than 300 young second-generation West Indian women Shirley Dex found it took black women longer than whites with the same qualifications to secure their first job, even though they spent more time searching. They were less often successful in obtaining the occupation they wanted and ended up more often with less-skilled jobs. They had a very much higher rate of involuntary redundancy or dismissal. Dex concluded, 'if there is a queue for hiring and for firing, West Indians seem to be behind whites for hiring but in front for firing' (Dex 1983:64). Many black women have written personal accounts of disadvantage in training and the job market (see for instance Bryan *et al.*, 1985.) Annie Phizacklea finds sufficient evidence to consider migrant women as a specific class fraction, a new and bottom-most layer in the segmented labour markets of Britain and continental Europe (Phizacklea 1983:109). Black women told me in interview how exclusion, not just as women but as blacks, from the white male monoculture affected them. As one put it 'I have to prove myself one hundred per cent to get anywhere. If someone's middle-class, white, male, tall, good-looking, blond, you know, he doesn't have to do much. He comes from the right "class".'

Race equality measures

Policies to overcome race inequality have often been introduced by employers alongside positive action for sex equality at work. As we saw in Chapter 1 they derive from the Race Relations Acts passed between 1968 and 1976 and the Local Government Act of 1966 which responded to what both Conservative and Labour governments of the seventies and eighties saw as a threat to social order arising from the open-door Commonwealth immigration policies of the postwar period.

Black people are not, in fact, the strangers to Britain they are often represented as being. African soldiers came here with the Roman legions several hundred years before either Angles or Saxons landed on British shores (Fryer 1984). Some came as a result of the slave trade; some came as merchant sailors. There were many living here before the Second World War. These black British populations were, however, considerably increased by West Indian and Asian immigration after 1945. British employers experiencing a labour shortage in the postwar boom advertised for labour in the West Indies and the Indian sub-continent. By the sixties the exploitation of immigrant labour had become a significant strategy of capital accumulation in West European countries (Castles and Kosack 1973). Substantial migrant communities clustered in the major cities where they rapidly became the target of white racism (Miles and Phizacklea 1984).

Racism was not limited to street and housing estate. It was also deployed in the workplace. Until the mid-seventies the Trades Union Congress did not put its weight behind measures against discrimination and it failed to oppose the racist bias of the Immigration Act 1971 (Miles and Phizacklea 1981). Though the TUC took a more positive position after 1975 many unions have been slow to put an end to the exclusionary practices of some of their branches and members. Despite the fact that proportionately more black workers than white joined unions, white workers continued to see blacks as cheap labour here to undercut their bargaining position (Wrench 1987).

The rising cost of British-based labour power, however, together with growing worker militancy in which migrant groups joined, brought about a gradual change in the strategies of international capital. In place of stimulating the movement of labour from one country to another, multinationals increasingly began to find it more profitable to shift capital, relocating investment in the export-processing zones of Third World countries, where they were able to take advantage of cheap, often female, workers whose discipline was guaranteed by repressive governments (Mitter 1986).

When black labour was no longer wanted in Britain both Labour and Conservative Parties shifted to a policy of immigration control. A series of Acts of Parliament effectively arrested primary (i.e. male breadwinner) immigration from the black commonwealth. The legislative process began with the Commonwealth Immigration Act 1962 restraining free entry from the Commonwealth and culminated in the Immigration Act 1971 which redefined citizenship in a way that discriminated indirectly against black people. In Britain and other West European countries official policy was thenceforward one of 'stabilisation'. A regime of harassment and threat of deportation subdued black populations and though the laws permitted women and children to join male immigrants with right of residence, they were vetted with intimidatory severity. The effect of the new laws was clearly to tag West Indian and Asian immigrants and their British-born offspring as 'unwanted' in Britain (Miles and Phizacklea 1979).

Such institutional racism fostered individual racism – some spontaneous, some orchestrated by extreme right-wing groups. The ensuing disruption was widely represented in the media as a problem caused *by* black people, especially black youth (Hartmann and Husbands 1974). Many black people were by now indeed angry at their treatment and fearful for the safety of their communities. By the mid-seventies there were signs of a degree of solidarity emerging between different black groups that alarmed the authorities (Sivanandan 1985). It was feared that high levels of joblessness among black workers, whom surveys (e.g. Smith 1981) certainly showed to be particularly vulnerable to rising unemployment, constituted a threat to social order. The upsurge of violence in some inner-city areas in the late seventies and early eighties was interpreted as being fired by a combination of enforced idleness and racial intolerance – though the relative guilt of young blacks, young whites and the police was widely disputed (Hall *et al.* 1978, Scarman 1982)

This was the context in which many local authorities developed race relations strategies for their communities and race equality policies for their employment. Some private sector employers too began to feel a sense of guilt or of responsibility to defuse the growing resentment of black people against racial discrimination in job recruitment and promotion. It is not surprising that, given the circumstances, the new measures met with scepticism. While gentler critics saw action on race inequality as 'less of a clear political commitment than a series of knee-jerk reactions to real or imagined dangers' (Solomos 1987), many black activists wrote off the new integrationist policies as frankly manipulative. They were seen as aiming to create a compliant black middle class of executives and bureaucrats. Race relations and race equality officers were no more than collaborators delivering to the authorities a docile black populace (Sivanandan 1985). The new language of 'multiculturalism' was seen as deflecting attention from the real problem: white racism (Anthias and Yuval-Davis 1983). The weakness of the legal provisions and plentiful evidence of attempts by the courts, as well as employers and trade unions, to evade the spirit and letter of the law could only foster scepticism (Gregory 1987:39).

Conformity as the price of access

The four organizations in my study had all introduced race equality policies by the mid-1980s. We have seen something of the strategies of High Street Retail and the Service. The adoption of a principle of non-discrimination had, however, been slow to produce measurable improvement. In High Street Retail between 1986 and 1988, despite a positive effort, the percentage of ethnic minority employees shifted only from 3.5% to 3.8%. It was also clear that they continued to be more common in low-status manual jobs (4%) than in the white-collar jobs with higher pay and more career potential (2.3%). In the Service 'non-whites' were 4.4% of total employment in 1989. They were clustered particularly in London, where the labour shortage and the fact that white people had better-paid possibilities in the private sector had forced the hand of selection boards. They were, besides, packed in the lower grades, being 5.2% of clerical grades, only 1.4% of the professional hierarchy.

One factor clearly distinguishing between the ethnic policies of the four organizations, however, was on the one hand a hostility towards autonomous black organization and activism, on the other support for it. While High Street Retail and the Service underlined integration and assimilation, the equality policies of the Local Authority and the Trade Union were much bolder in, formally at least, acknowledging the distinct group interests of their ethnic minorities. Albeit with much ambivalence, they did allow institutional space for black people to identify themselves, to meet together, challenge white racism and make their own demands on the organization.

The Local Authority had set up a race committee and funded many black community groups. It had invested a good deal of money into staffing central and departmental race units in the council. With 19% of its employees now black (albeit with few in higher grades) the council was on target, matching the proportion of black people in the local community. Support had been given to an active black council workers' group.

These policies had resulted in a bumpy ride for whites. The encouragement of self-organization and a positive anti-racist

approach to ethnic equality created a charged atmosphere, intensified by some highly publicised enquiries into racial discrimination
both in employment and services. Meanwhile black people had
witnessed a disappointing failure of institutional equality-measures
substantially to change the ethnic profile of the non-manual
workforce, particularly its upper reaches. This explosive combination led to open strife between black and white in many areas of the
council's activities.

The same issues of difference versus similarity, autonomy versus
assimilation, and self-organization versus integration were thrown
into salience by the race policy in the Trade Union. The white
leadership had for some time been concerned about the surprisingly
small proportion comprised by black people (possibly little more
than 2%) of this predominantly manual working-class membership.
They were also aware that too few black members were being
elected to union posts and that the paid officers were almost all
white. Following the report of a working group set up in 1983, a
series of decisions of national conference instituted positive action.
Racism was made a disciplinary offence in the union rule book.
National and divisional race advisory committees were established
and an equal rights officer was appointed. Branches were urged to
take steps to recruit and involve more black people. Educational
resources were committed to black members and to ethnic issues.
Ethnic equality was to become a demand in collective bargaining,
so that the Union would play a part in bringing change to the
workplace as well as within its own structure. A higher public
profile was adopted by the Union nationally in opposition to
immigration and nationality laws, deportations and lack of
accountability of the police. The Union also took the controversial
stand of support for Black Sections in the Labour Party.

In spite of all such steps to overcome institutional racism,
however, in 1989 lay representatives and full-time officers I
interviewed were emphatic that at an individual level racial
prejudice among the members was still widespread and was
damaging the interests of black people. 'The racism in my branch
is appalling', said one white branch secretary. 'There's a lot of it in
the membership', confirmed a white officer, 'it's terrible, spiteful.'
The new policies had shamed some racists into concealing their
views. Even so, racism was often shockingly open, they said. When
nominations were invited for branch secretary a member might say,

'we don't want no nig-nogs here', or at the workplace members would threaten, 'if they bring blacks in, I'm leaving'. There was a continual background noise of antagonism to the equality policy. I was told white members would complain of black people, 'They're always expecting more to be done for them' or (with reference to ethnic diversity in canteen menus) 'Why can't they eat bangers and mash like any Anglo-Saxon?.' Evidence certainly seemed to point to the continuation at an informal level of the old exclusionary practices. The unmistakable 'whiteness' of some branches and occupational categories could be explained only by white collusion in defining 'no-go areas' for blacks. Deals would be struck with employers with the implicit threat: you introduce blacks here and we withdraw cooperation.

A survey made by head office of branches' responses to the recommendations of the working party produced written evidence of the negative views of many branch secretaries. One branch had crossed out the whole questionnaire and returned it saying, without apology or explanation, 'none of the members in our service is black or ethnic minority'. One branch secretary complained that the equality code was being operated to 'penalise our white members unfairly' and was producing 'an intolerable state of affairs'. Several branch secretaries complained that the questionnaire was unnecessarily 'making an issue' of race. One said 'it's racial in itself . . . the reason we do not have any black, blue, pink or redskins here is probably due to the fact that there are not many in this area. We do not practice or preach racial hatred. The only ones that do that I know of are in the Race Relations Board (*sic*).' Another deplored positive discrimination and was 'heartily sick of people who denigrate the English way of life and Christian values in England whilst advancing foreign cultures'. A woman race activist, however, put the racism in a wider context.

> It's not only the union. The members are drawn from the greater society . . . . The people inside are only reflecting what they see around them. They read *The Sun*. They hear Mrs Thatcher talking about black people 'swamping the country'. Racism exists all around.

The provision of the compensatory structure of race advisory committees was acknowledgment by decision-makers in the Union that black people needed a forum to debate their problems and mobilize pressure on the organization as a whole. There was, however, no black membership organization in the Union nationally. Many whites would have been vigorously opposed. Their annoyance at the idea echoed men's dislike of women's separate activities.

> Black members hold a separate meeting? Why? How are they going to come into us, and us into them, if they're going to have separate black meetings? Some of the people on the outside, on the extremes, will say right away I'm racist [for that view]. But I'm not.

Individual racism fed back to conserve institutional racism. Some full-time officers told me the reason they stalled on anti-racist work was their nervousness concerning racism in the white membership. 'It's not number-one priority in the member's mind. And the union that forgets its members' priorities is soon going to lose members. Put it like that,' said one quite senior regional officer. Some officers opposed black self-organization for the same reason. 'You'd never get away with it at branch.'

One division, however, with head office support, had shown what could be done. They had created an energetic race advisory committee and were publishing a regular broadsheet on racial issues and actively offering schools and seminars to increase understanding. They planned the Union's first black members' conference. The aim here had been to help black people gain a sense of identity and then get them involved at all levels of the Union. What made these things possible was the presence of energetic local black activists and committed white divisional officers who were not afraid to afford scope to a black officer.

Different ways of doing things

What appeared to be occurring in all four organizations was a split in white intentions. Some, characteristically the equal opportunity officers and a few enlightened senior managers, wanted to encourage black recruitment and promotion. Other white people did not want to see any dilution of the white workforce by black incomers. The deal that was struck between the two white positions and between whites and incoming blacks cohered around the issue of cultural *assimilation*. Non-white ethnic groups would be 'acceptable' if as nearly as possible indistinguishable from the host group. '*If you want equality you must forego difference.*' It is the same theme we saw invoked in resistance to sex equality and will see again in the case of homosexuals and people with disabilities. It is of course a condition impossible for most members of out-groups to fulfil, even if a minority of individuals is able and willing to adopt protective colouring.

There were particularly clear expressions of this ideology in the Service. Here West Indian people, where they were to be found at all, were mainly in the base-line occupations of porter, cleaner, typist. On the other hand Indian and Pakistani men and women were beginning to find their way up the steps of clerical and professional grades. The whites they joined were more middle-class, better-educated and perhaps more shrewd than the manual work-ing-class host group of the Local Authority or the Union. White racism here was expressed in an indirect discourse in which the key terms were 'language' and 'style'. A minority, the anti-racists among the whites, expressed unqualified pleasure in seeing black people coming through at last into the professional ranks. A substantial proportion of both women and men, however, identi-fied in Asian people a particular shortcoming that made them inappropriate professional material: they had, they said, a 'language deficiency'. One white man, for instance, referred to 'members of whatever they're called, ethnic minority groups, who can't make themselves understood'. Others said they frequently came across Asian colleagues who simply 'aren't intelligible', had 'their own way of writing and talking English'.

> If you don't have the ability to speak, on a one-to-one basis or across a crowded room at a [meeting], there is a problem that will detract from the officer's [appraisal and reporting] performance . . . . It could be the same for a Caucasian person with a speech impediment.

The Service could not afford to compromise. 'If they've a language problem that affects their work, they're out. It's a tough world.'

The Great Language Problem merged imperceptibly with a second theme in the popular discourse about Asians among white officers of the Service. It was the issue of 'style'. Because of their 'lesser knowledge of our culture than is possessed by indigenous

Anglo-Saxons . . . one does on occasion have to lean over back-wards', explained a very senior officer. Asians were said to be 'good at clerical work but they want to do it *their* way'. They did not make suitable manager material, 'we have *problems* with them'. They had 'difficulty understanding the office set up, what is expected of them'. So these men and women who 'haven't had the education and don't know the English way of life' were doomed to remain in the lower clerical grades where they were not 'let loose on the public'.

There are several levels of truth here. The problem as cited by whites is exaggerated. Many Asians speak not with Asian but with Oxford, Bradford and Birmingham accents. Asian clericals, profes-sionals and members of the elite corps have passed through exactly the same Service training and qualifying system as whites. On the other hand, it is true that some Asians living in Britain do speak with identifiable Asian accents. It is often overlooked, however, that English has been a *lingua franca* in the Asian sub-continent for centuries and Asian people have developed a specific set of usages that are as valid for them as our own are for us. Britons no longer *own* English, a fact that it is difficult for many to accept. It is now a world language with regional variations. As imperialism spread Western languages round the world, so it spread bureaucracy. Asians have participated in the practice of public administration in its very proving grounds in the course of centuries of colonial and post-colonial bureacracy.

We return here to the theme of 'acceptability' in recruitment and promotion (Jenkins 1986). White men in the lower ranks of the Service have only recently begun to succeed in their bid to diversify its monolithic upper-class English culture. Until recently – and still today in the upper ranks – a working-class or regional accent was 'unacceptable' and could hold you back. Now white officers seem to be closing ranks against a new sound – defining native forms of English as the only acceptable accents, silencing Asian voices. Francesca Klug (1989) wrote:

In Britain there has been an attempt to construct the nation around the myth of a continuous line of Anglo-Saxon people with unique rights to claim Britain as their 'homeland'. In reality the British Isles have for centuries been inhabited by a variety of peoples with different cultural, linguistic, racial and even national identities.

The discourse of the Great Language Problem in the Service seems an attempt of this kind to create a cultural island within an island.

The Service is not alone in this thrust to impose cultural uniformity. It is part of the creation of national hegemony by a white ruling group.

> Ethnic hegemony involves a . . . distinct set of strategies whereby a particular power elite lays claim to represent an ethnic majority in such a way as to impose their own norms of language and culture on the rest of society as ideals or models to which all should aspire (Cohen 1988:26).

White people make cultural integration, on someone else's terms, the price of acceptability for other ethnic groups. The minority must assimilate to a 'host' society represented as monocultural. Gloria Watkins, the black American educationist who writes under the pen-name bell hooks, has said

> while assimilation is seen as an approach that ensures the successful entry of black people into the mainstream, at its very core it is dehumanizing. Embedded in the logic of assimilation is the white supremacist assumption that blackness must be eradicated so that a new self, in this case a 'white' self, can come into being (hooks 1989:67).

Of course, since 'we who are black can never be white', the process is a charade doomed in most cases to failure. Should the disguise succeed the result is a kind of suicide.

The fact that white women share the racism of white men does not mean that there is no gender dimension to the race issue. There is a particularly intense relation of domination and resistance binding white men to black men. In fact, when black individuals were problematised in the discourse of either sex I found it was almost always a black *man* that was referred to. Black women were largely invisible (a mixed blessing, of course). It seemed that if a black woman was problematized it was more likely to be because she was a woman than because she was black. The reason race issues invoke in white men more anger and fear than do gender issues is because a *male* protagonist is involved. Black men are menacing in the eyes of white men in a way that women, white or black, can never be. For one thing they are seen as threatening physical violence. They partake not a little in male power, sharing some of the social weaponry of white men.

This dominance/resistance relation between white and black men has a long history. Imperialism was a masculine project in which a white male ruling class imposed its will on the black male power systems of pre-colonial cultures (Mies 1986, Miles 1989). The black independence movements, like the European class revolutions, were a kind of parricide – black bastards taking arms against white fathers. Now, in the tension-ridden patriarchal class structures of British organizations the white brotherhood are continuing to hold at bay a challenge from alien men on their own territory. The 'difference' of the latter must be represented as constituting 'inferiority' and as incompatible with 'acceptability' in employment.

The sexual contract, however, gives white and black men some common ground. Black men in my study shared with white men a resistance to the women's movement and a distaste for positive action for sex equality. Black men have stepped from a colonial condition of actual or near-slavery, a condition in which they were obliged to submit to white male control of black women, into citizen status, as yet only formal and unsubstantiated, within the framework of the social and sexual contract of Western liberal political philosophy. Though white men ban black incursions into the white man's sexual territory, men of all ethnic groups in Britain are the beneficiaries today of male sex-right, the notional right to control of their *own* woman's labour in the home, her sexuality and her reproductive power. Even if the group that rules organizations is white men, and though white women participate in white power, the group that rules women is men, black and white.

Homosexuals: the other 'Other'

We saw that gender relations in organizations are profoundly sex-ualized. To be more precise, they are profoundly *hetero*sexualised. All the assumptions in everyday relationship and discourse are heterosexual. The costs to a lesbian woman or gay man of being 'out' about her or his sexual orientation at work are such as to keep most 'in the closet'. This has to be recognized as of itself constituting disadvantage and subordination. There is also, how-ever, a more tangible disadvantage: discrimination in recruitment

and victimisation, leading to dismissal or failure to promote. The
law was liberalized in 1967 to decriminalize homosexuality between
consenting adult men. (Lesbianism was never proscribed, another
instance of invisibility that is a mixed blessing.) There is, however,
no law comparable to the sex and race discrimination laws to
protect homosexuals from discrimination in employment. It often
occurs that employees, school teachers and youth workers in
particular, lose their jobs when it becomes known they are gay.
With the creation of a gay liberation movement in the 1960s and
1970s the question of equal treatment at work and in organizations
was put on the agenda.

The Labour-led London councils in the mid-eighties pioneered
policies on lesbian and gay rights. The Greater London Council
came under the control of a left-wing Labour Party in 1981. Under
pressure from local groups both of feminists, including lesbians,
and of gay men, who found a handful of supporters among the
Labour councillors, it set up a working party and subsequently
began to develop policy for lesbians and gay men in the council and
the community. Some Labour-led inner London boroughs followed
suit. Soon the Labour Party was being lampooned for 'loony
leftism' – which was the tabloid-press term for an 'equalities'-
conscious socialism. It was later claimed that the Labour Party paid
dearly in votes for its support of 'the equalities'. Yet the support
had been far from wholehearted and seldom went beyond a concern
with 'civil liberties'. Ann Tobin, who worked in the GLC Women's
Committee Support Unit in 1985 concluded from this experience

Labour politicians often had no greater justification for adding gay
rights to their pantheon of causes beyond the simple statement that since
many gays were working-class, it was a class issue. This approach was
central to the Party's support of gay rights, indeed to the Party's
espousal of all the politics of identity that led to the creation of the
new equalities strategies and equalities units. There had been no real
organic growth of feminist, Black or gay politics within the Labour
movement. The new politics were forced upon an often unwilling and
certainly unenthusiastic Labour Party by socialists who were also
feminist, by socialists who were also Black and by socialists who were
also gay. New Left politicians who started to adopt the equalities
strategies often had . . . happily opened a Pandora's box without having
a clue as to what was inside (Tobin 1990:58,59).

Tensions in male sexuality

The Other in opposition to whom men build their masculine identities has a curious duality. At one moment it is woman, at the next it is the homosexual. Strategically, it seems, the project is one. When men develop and deploy a discourse that dissociates them from homosexuals (limp-wrist mockery, poufter jokes) they are bidding for solidarity with each other on an implicit basis of cooperative domination of females. Likewise the sexual banter about women and women's bodies that affirms, man to man, their sexual authority over women, serves to push deep into the unconscious the latent homosexuality of 'normal' men.

The relationship of male homosexual liberation to women's liberation has been ambiguous. On the one hand, homosexuals were viewed with some hope by feminists because they were seen to contradict the accepted characteristics of men and women and the complementarity of the sexes (Carrigan *et al.* 1987:171). Lynne Segal points out, however, that while gay liberationists in the 1970s declared one of their goals to be ridding society of the gender-role system, in practice this hope was disappointed and 'the huge growth in self-confidence and assertion did not seem to lead to the general blurring of sexual and gender boundaries, the transition to androgyny, or the triumph of more 'feminine' values . . .' (Segal 1990:148).

There are undeniably aspects of contemporary male gay culture that reinforce misogyny and the subordination of women. Male homosexual discourse often represents women and women's bodies as loathsome – 'fish' is the coded term. The practices of drag, transsexualism and transvestism literally 'travesty' femininity. Historically, it is clear that male homosexuality is not of itself intolerable to some forms of patriarchy. In classical Athens institutionalized homosexuality among ruling-class males co-existed with the subordination of women.

Male homosexuality does, however, create a bitter division in male ranks. Perhaps its most subversive effect is in undermining the universality and normalcy of the family, with male head of household and subordinate, if not dependent, wife with children, which has historically been the keystone of patriarchy. Secondly, by converting the male body to an object, as opposed to the universal subject, of desire, it threatens to contradict the ideology of

heterosexuality. In contemporary Western society women are
subordinated by the very structuring of heterosexual sexuality.
'The sexual act' is represented as only one thing: intercourse
between men and women in which the erect male penis enters the
female vagina and ejaculates. Simultaneously the phallus is
represented as source and symbol of power, a weapon. Men wield
it, women are subject to it. When men, in homosexual sex, submit
to penetration this, in heterosexist ideology, feminizes and diminishes all men. A third source of anxiety for heterosexual men in the
open acknowledgment of homosexuality in employment policy is
the knowledge that for many heterosexual people, homosexuality
lies latent not far beneath the surface of their conscious being.
'Homoeroticism binds straight men to gay men with a mixture of
fascination and loathing' writes Jonathan Rutherford. 'We cannot
be freed because homoeroticism is part of us . . . homosexuality
and homophobia are historically constructed partners' (Rutherford
1988:60).

Men are not in a position therefore to marginalize homosexuality
by ignoring it. The daily business of organizations, their operation
as male power bases, depends on men generating a closeness
between men. Clubbing and socializing, as we have seen, helps
men control information. The transmission of power from one
generation of men to another, for example, calls for the sponsorship
of younger men by older men. Homo*sociality* is thus the dominant
cultural form in male-dominated organizations. Yet homosociality
is always in danger of tipping over – in appearance or in reality –
into homoeroticism. Many of the gestures and forms of speech men
use with each other – the slap on the shoulder, the jocular punch,
the noisy ebullience – are nicely calculated to establish sociability
without sexuality, friendship without intimacy.

Michael Roper, in an analysis of male managers' career histories,
demonstrates the 'single man's intensely fraternal and competitive
culture' in early career days. He notes that career advance
characteristically depends on the help of an older 'mentor',
involving a 'highly charged relationship' with 'an extra intensity
of affection' between older and younger man. Roper clearly
identifies a homoerotic content to these relationships, an element
of same-sex desire. He suggests that 'promotion is not dependent
upon business skills alone but . . . also pivots on the display and
arousal of male desires'. The managerial discourse itself 'is under-

laid with male sexual definitions. Much of the socialization for management consists of learning homoerotic play. For the postwar generation it was perhaps the public school, or the services, which provided the schooling in such values. Today the schooling might have changed, but the play itself remains the same' (Roper 1988:57) The modern school of business management might reward study from this perspective.

Defence of lesbian and gay rights at work

When organizations in their new equality policies include a guarantee of equal treatment for homosexuals therefore, not only is it an action unsupported by law, it is an intervention in a highly contentious area of social relations. Equality for homosexuals is even more conflictual than equality for women, ethnic minorities or disabled people. Yet of the organizations I studied only High Street Retail had ducked out of any mention of homosexuality in their policy.

By far the most far-reaching policy was that of the Local Authority. Here in 1984 a lesbian councillor had obtained agreement to setting up a working party on lesbian and gay issues, with members drawn from council departments, the community and trade unions. The unions had been particularly supportive, making space for self-organization among lesbians and gay men in the council workforce. Because of the up-front approach of gays and their supporters in this borough council the backlash from conservative straight councillors and staff was fierce and outspoken. Even some feminists and others on the left, were wary of the homosexuality issue. Nonetheless in the years immediately following the 1982 election the balance of power in the council lay with the progressives. In response to the working party's recommendations a permanent committee of the council was set up, a centre was funded in the locality and four posts were made available to staff a lesbian and gay unit in the council, reporting, like the women's unit and race unit, directly to the chief executive.

The unit's workers began research into the needs of lesbians and gays in the borough and the council to guide council provision. New policies were developed. In housing, for instance, it was agreed that a lesbian or gay tenant could have her or his partner added to the tenancy agreement 'with an open mind and without questions being asked, no prying'. The legal position of such a couple should be exactly the same as that of a common-law husband and wife. The authority did not make the mistake of some boroughs of tackling head-on the thorny issue of heterosexism in school education. Yet the local media were destructive. One meeting, called for cleaning staff to discuss heterosexism and the new policy on homosexuality, attracted a good attendance. Several participants found the courage to speak out honestly about painful experiences. The local newspaper, however, had infiltrated an undercover reporter who later ridiculed the event in the paper and caused distress and embarrassment to those who had attended. Such mishaps apart, however, even those who disliked the idea of the council's support for homosexuals had to admit that the committee and unit worked effectively and, mostly, with tact.

The aim of the councillor who had put so much energy into the new policy had been to 'create an atmosphere in which people could feel safe about their sexuality and could come out if they wanted to, secure against discrimination, not just in the workforce but in the community'. She felt the policy should be an affirmation of the existence of homosexuals, a statement that it was 'not an aberration to be lesbian or gay'. This policy did have a noticeable impact on the organization. In contrast to High Street Retail, for instance, where it was difficult to use the word homosexual without raising a blush, staff in the Local Authority talked in a matter of fact way about homosexuals and council policy for them. There were few senior officers expressing open or outright hostility to the policy. Personnel department was behaving professionally on the issue. The equality policy had made it easier to be 'out' and maintain a tolerable existence in at least some areas of council employment. These gains, however, need placing in a wider context. As a council employee pointed out, 'we've got women, blacks and gays in the [equality] units, but it's still white straight men where it counts – at the top of the hierarchy.'

Soon in any case the tide turned against homosexuals even in this supportive corner of the world. As we saw, in 1987 drastic expenditure cuts brought a retrenchment in all equality policies. The AIDS panic which peaked in Britain around 1987 was allowed, indeed exploited, everywhere to create animosity towards gays. Then the Conservative government joined the witch-hunt, acting directly against local authorities such as this with the introduction of a clause in the Local Government Act 1988 to prohibit councils from 'intentionally promoting homosexuality' or publishing material with that intention. A conviction that the Tory law was an attack on local democracy brought some council officers who would otherwise have been critics of lesbian and gay policy to the defence of the council against 'Clause 28'. But the events drove others in the opposite direction. Prejudices emerged more freely. The more conservative councillors felt justified in resisting expenditure on the policy.

It is interesting to compare feelings about homosexuality in male-dominated organizations with contrasted cultures. In the Local Authority I was able to identify and meet with active lesbians and gays and their heterosexual supporters. In the Service this needed more research. In High Street Retail I failed. The 'homophobia' that in the Local Authority had been driven underground by the positive policy of active gays and feminists was still rampant in High Street Retail where no such campaign had yet been waged. I asked men there if they felt it would be appropriate to add protection of the employment rights of homosexuals to their equality policy. Few had any inhibitions about voicing a resounding 'no'. 'It's wrong to foster these bent attitudes', 'they are spreading disease – it's not good for the nation or the company' were views widely echoed. Others said, 'I'm not into these bloody weirdos, I just don't want to know', 'it's disgusting, turns my stomach', 'if you want to be "out", it's out *you* go as far as I'm concerned'.

In popular discourse in this firm, then, homosexuality is pathologised. It is associated unthinkingly with drug and alcohol abuse. The category 'homosexual' is said to differ fundamentally from 'women' or 'ethnic minority' because the latter 'do not *choose* to be what they are'. The implication is that homosexuality is elective, political, a 'proclivity', a 'persuasion'. It is equated with religion: homosexuals want to 'convert' everyone else to homosexuality. It is also assumed that homosexuals are obsessed with sex and more likely than heterosexuals to molest the objects of their desire. There were men in High Street Retail who said without compunction that, far from having an equality policy on homosexuality, they frankly did not want to share a workplace with 'queers'. In such a climate of opinion it is not surprising that top management and personnel managers were alarmed by their responsibilities concerning AIDS. Already one of their employees had died of the disease. How best to defend the employment rights of AIDS sufferers, yet avoid an outbreak of hysterical homophobia? It was not only in High Street Retail that this policy matter was being discussed behind anxiously closed doors.

In the Service, by contrast, a greater sophistication ruled. Homophobia here was muted by a civil service tradition of tolerance. I was told repeatedly of male officers at 'very senior levels' who are quietly accepted as gay. These 'extremely charming' people were 'widely respected'. I found relatively few professional men condemning homosexuality out of hand. The form taken by prejudice here was, rather, a criticism of 'openness'. Anything was acceptable so long as a person was discreet, did not 'flaunt it', kept his relationship to himself, didn't want to 'talk about his lifestyle' or (an unfortunate expression that is widely used in this context) to 'ram it down your throat'. Provided a person conducted himself with dignity, his career progression need not be affected. A very senior member of the elite corps told me about men in the Service of whom 'the fact that they were of a homosexual disposition was widely known and it in no way held them back from very important work and very significant advancement'.

The jokes in this fraternity were less at the expense of gay men than of the naive homophobe. There were wry jibes at the expense of senior men caught out in 'uncool' postures on the issue of homosexuality. Where prejudice against homosexuals was openly expressed here it was characteristically by younger or less-educated men of the clerical grades including black men, who were less aware of the political expediency of disguising one's prejudice. Thus a young black clerical said that he would have hesitated to apply for a job had he known the organization had a non-discriminatory policy for homosexuals. 'You'd think "what sort of a place am I going to work for!"' What would it tell him about the organization? 'Well, that you'd need to watch out for yourself there.' Such a view would be considered unsophisticated by many of the higher-class men of the white male professional fraternity.

What we see here is different ways in which men negotiate male solidarity around a heterosexual principle. In High Street Retail any homosexual that may have inhabited the power structure was obliged to remain tightly closeted. It was still possible here for heterosexual men to close ranks against all gays. In the Service, by contrast, where gay men had acceded to the upper reaches of the hierarchy, the strategy was an affirmation of a select white male brotherhood. 'I think the fraternity of [the Service] would protect the gay person' as one man put it. The terms of acceptance were strict, however: gays must play the fraternal game, and maintain the male hierarchical culture. Above all, gayness must not be 'out'. It must depend upon heterosexual men's tolerance, remaining the 'open secret' of the Service.

Women are not exempt from anti-gay views and several expressed distaste for both homosexuality and a policy protecting homosexuals' rights at work. In all the organizations, however, I found women on the whole less outspokenly intolerant, gentler in their exploration of the problem. It was, for instance, a woman who responded happily 'my son's gay and I adore him'. A somewhat less frenzied prejudice against male homosexuality among women than among men would be explainable by the fact that women have less at stake in the defence of male solidarity and a male-dominant heterosexual principle. It is not *their* power that is threatened.

Lesbians at work

Lesbianism has very different political implications for both sexes from those of male homosexuality. Lesbianism does worry many heterosexual women and they associate it, as we saw in Chapter 5, with a political choice and with feminist 'extremism'. Again in High Street Retail's head office women's prejudices were more outspoken than in the Service where 'out' and 'open secret' lesbians were not unknown to most women. The relatively tolerant environment here meant that careful lesbians in senior posts were accorded a similar tacit loyalty as that given senior gay men.

A young lesbian I spoke with, 'out' in her district office where there were also a couple of 'open secret' gay men, found her life tolerable and relationships relaxed. It was, she confirmed, a much less macho atmosphere than that of the business world. After two years working in her district office she had decided to 'come out' because, she said,

> I found it incredibly frustrating at work because, of course, there are discussions of what you've been doing at the weekend and I was having

to make up stories of what I did. I found it difficult to socialize. I felt I was being dishonest about my private life.

She waited for an occasion when she was about to transfer to another office.

It was mostly married women in the office and on that evening I decided since I wouldn't be seeing any of these people again I would come out to them. I made a deliberate point of going round saying, 'It's been nice knowing you, and by the way I don't know if you realize but I'm in fact gay.' I wanted to do that. To tell them that we'd been working together for two years. And I was thought quite highly of. I wanted them to know that you could be gay and likeable.

Necessarily this young woman was then 'out' in subsequent posts in the Service. She was harassed only by one person, however – an older Asian man whose aggression she learned to deflect by teasing. In general she felt accepted. She welcomed the existence of a policy of non-discrimination. She did, however, doubt her career chances were as good as they might have been had she kept her lesbian identity secret. There is, of course, certainly no lack of evidence of discrimination against lesbians in the workplace (Hall 1989) and even the existence of an equality policy does not guarantee an end to covert exclusionary practices.

In the more typical working environment of High Street Retail and the lower ranks of the Service, however, heterosexual men often mock lesbianism viciously ('What do they *do*, for god's sake?'). They also, however, feel threatened by it. As a GLC Women's Committee publication put it

lesbians arouse anger for challenging the assumption that women need a man emotionally, sexually and financially. They are accused of trying to be 'like men' by rejecting what are regarded as essential feminine mannerisms or ambitions – in fact, any woman who refuses to acquire and display these is threatened with being labelled lesbian, whether or not she is (Greater London Council 1986:7).

In contrast to the case of gay men, many of whom want to maintain their place among the brothers in the hierarchies of a patriarchal society, lesbianism, when it takes on political conscious-ness, tends to align women with women and to problematise the male hierarchy. Men do not have bargaining power, either individually or collectively, over lesbians in the way they have over heterosexual women. They only have the power to punish. Lesbians cannot be dealt with conceptually in the way men deal with the male gay 'Other'. Marny Hall makes the point that the lesbian is simply unavailable to the masculist project because she steps outside the 'self and other' narrative and presents a reality that opposes it. 'The penalty for this mutiny is, within the organization, at the very least, a forfeiture of good will; at the most retaliation, harassment and the loss of one's job' (Hall 1989:127).

The inclusion of positive support for self-identified and self-organized lesbians in an organization is an important extension of the agenda of equal opportunities for women. As we saw in the last chapter, the oppressive culture of heterosexism is damaging, not just to lesbians, but to heterosexual women too. And lesbianism is used as a category with which to control heterosexual women. 'If you show there's even a little bit of your life in which you don't need a man, you're written off as lesbian.' A strong politics for heterosexual women would be to recognize this common ground. Few do so, however, and the problem of creating alliances is acute.

Disability: work fit for people

In the past, if an organization gave any consideration at all to the special employment needs of disabled people, they were usually held to be the concern of the welfare officer. Today some organizations are making disability an equality issue. Equal treatment for people with disabilities may be found in an equal opportunities statement alongside reference to women and members of ethnic minorities (Doyle 1987). In the Service, for example, disability had been removed from the remit of the welfare committee and given to the equal opportunities committee. The responsible officers were now those personnel officers who had acquired the equality job. In the Local Authority disabled people's interests were represented by an adviser, a unit and a council sub-committee, comparable to the structures for women, black people and homosexuals. Such acknowledgement, however, does not yet compensate the decades of neglect. Disability is still Cinderella, even among the equalities.

There is some irony in this, since people with disabilities are the only group for which the law actually permits positive discrimination in direct access to jobs. The Disabled Persons (Employment) Acts 1944 and 1958 are the basis of today's organizational policies. They provide for disabled people who wish to do so to register their condition. They require employers with more than twenty workers to ensure that a minimum of 3% of their workforce is drawn from among the registered disabled. Register and quota, however, are little observed. Few people with disabilities see any purpose in registering, and the numbers on the register fell by 60% between 1950 and 1986. Employers find exemptions easy to obtain. The percentage of exempted employers rose from 28% to 56% between 1965 and 1986. Despite the fact that 17% of employers in 1986 were below quota without exemption, prosecutions have been rare. There were precisely ten in the forty years to 1986 (National Audit Office 1987:3).

An interesting and highly disputed attempt was made by Lambeth Borough Council in 1986 to take the law at face value. It announced a decision that only disabled candidates would be considered for its job vacancies until its quota was met. The media predictably slammed this 'crackpot scheme', said the council was taking equal opportunities to 'absurd extremes' and predicted a disastrous collapse of public service. Recruitment did inevitably slow up. After three months' trial period the policy was modified. Despite criticism, however, the council's strategy succeeded in recruiting many talented newcomers and within eighteen months Lambeth had become one of the largest mainstream employers in Britain of people with disabilities (London Boroughs 1988).

Two international initiatives have signalled an awakening to the needs of disabled people in recent years. In 1975 the United Nations agreed a Declaration of Rights of Disabled People; and in 1981 a world programme of action was launched. Despite these prompts from the world community, British official statistics of disability are inadequate and their basis disputed (Abberley 1989). However, surveys commissioned by the Department of Health and Social Services from the Office of Population and Censuses, carried out between 1985 and 1988, do indicate the existence of over 6 million people with disabilities in Great Britain – a startling 14% of the population (Martin *et al.* 1988; see also Walker and Townsend 1981). Research undertaken for the Institute of Personnel Management suggests that 27% of people in Britain have a disabled person in their family; and 62% of people have a personal contact with disability (Birkett and Worman 1988). The disabled themselves then are no small minority; and disability as an issue is something close to most of us.

Quite apart from the difficulties of daily life experienced by many disabled people, their relationship to work is particularly problematic. Their level of unemployment fluctuates between two and four times that in the workforce as a whole and people with disabilities are three times more likely to be longterm unemployed (Walker 1984:24). This is partly due to a failure in rehabilitation services, partly the recalcitrance of employers (Cornes 1982). Peter Townsend's comprehensive study of poverty in the UK found clear evidence of disabled people's work disadvantage. 'Fewer are employed; fewer have high earnings and more have low earnings; more hours tend to be worked to secure the same earnings; and slightly fewer have good conditions at work' (Townsend 1979:715). Disabled people as a consequence are often poor people. They own fewer assets than the average, they live in worse housing and have a less adequate diet than non-disabled people (Townsend 1979).

Women, of course, are also on average poorer than men. To be female and disabled is a double disadvantage. Women are also more deeply involved than men in paying the social costs of disability since they are more frequently the ones who care for disabled relatives or tend the disabled in institutional jobs. It is beginning to be acknowledged that women among disabled people have special needs (Lonsdale 1990). Mary John, in a recent report to the European Economic Community, advised on the vocational needs of disabled women. She pointed to the double inequality of disabled women in employment. She also made the point that, just as women at large always have to juggle job and domestic responsibilities, so do disabled women. To focus only on rehabilitating women for paid employment 'represents very much a male view of the major problem'. It failed to acknowledge the complex lives women actually lead, in which a family, relationships and caring for others are often important factors (John 1988:49).

Official statistics on disability in Britain do not adequately specify ethnicity. The OPCS survey cited above did not treat the ethnic variable systematically. Some groups have begun to develop their own analysis (Confederation of Indian Organizations 1987), but more detailed attention to the special needs of black people with disabilities in a racist society is still called for.

The making of handicap

It is not so long since the disabled were known as 'the handicapped', a term seen as referring to a purely physical or mental condition. For some years now a different terminology has been coming into use that distinguishes between the somatic and the social. Today loss or abnormality of a psychological, physical or anatomical structure is normally termed *impairment*. The word *disability* relates to total or partial loss of a functional ability. *Handicap* is now taken to mean 'any disadvantage arising from a flawed interaction between an individual and their environment' (World Health Organization cited in Birkett and Worman 1988:5). Handicap, then, is socially constructed. It is the many impediments the non-disabled, wittingly or unwittingly, put in the way of the full functioning of the disabled (Finkelstein 1980, Brechin *et al.* 1981, Shearer 1981, Hahn 1984, Oliver 1990). 'It's not the lack of a limb, it's the lack of a lift that's the problem.'

The social construction thesis goes further, however. Impairment itself can be seen to be as much a social as a physical phenomenon. Disability can result, for instance, from the administering or withholding of medicinal drugs. Advances in medicine have increased the survival rate of previously 'non-viable' human beings. Dangerous and damaging work creates many impairments. 'Germs, genes and trauma' therefore may be significant, but 'their effects are only ever apparent in a real social and historical context, whose nature is determined by a complex interaction of material and non-material factors' (Abberley 1987:12).

Though poor educational facilities and inadequate benefits hold disabled people back, *employers* are a significant source of handicap. They erect, or fail to remove, many of the social barriers to disabled people's careers. When disabled people apply for jobs they seldom get shortlisted or interviewed. When they do they often encounter recruiting managers who underestimate their potential, who set up interviews in ways that limit their ability to demonstrate their full capacities and are ignorant about both disability and the resources available to employers to ease the employment of disabled people. Often employers are too mean to make the adaptations they could to the environment or too narrow-minded to restructure jobs to enable people with abilities and disabilities that differ from the norm. There are many positive steps it is within the powers of an employer to take with regard to employment of disabled people. (Helpful guides are Kettle and Massie 1982, Confederation of British Industry 1983, Hill 1985 and Smith *et al.* 1989.) Trade unions, it must be said, have been slow to represent the needs of disabled members. The Trades Union Congress, however, published a guide for use in bargaining (Trades Union Congress 1985) and individual unions have developed policies on disability in recent years. NALGO encourages self-organizing groups of disabled members.

The experience of disability

As I went around interviewing people for this research I had in mind that a certain proportion of the interviews should be with men, a certain proportion with women; that a particular proportion of both sexes would be black. But I quickly realized that in the case of disability all I could do was set a minimum. Many of the people I had sampled for other reasons turned out in fact to be disabled, to have long-term debilitating illnesses or to have had accidents from which they had recovered. This is a significant feature of disability. Much of it is hidden and, rather like ethnicity, it is infinitely graduated.

Disabled people have much to say about their experience of employment and employers. One woman felt management was deeply *afraid* of disability. People applying for work, she said, are driven to hide any disability if they can. If you say you are epileptic (as she is) you don't get the job. But if you don't tell the employer and later have an attack at work you will be blamed for withholding the information, even fired. Employers who overcome this fear and recruit a disabled person sometimes exploit the 'success story' for publicity purposes. One computer specialist who was blind felt he was just such a token to his employer. He felt they had been prepared to give him a job but had been much slower to recognize his capability for a career in computing. And he felt he had done most of the adapting while the employer took the credit.

Colleagues can make life hard for disabled people. A woman pointed out, 'the British sense of humour is organized around "difference": jokes about women, about Irish people and about "spastics".' This was illustrated by Peter Ferryman, a young amputee:

> I get verbal sort of things thrown at me. Like one guy, my mate. It doesn't bother me, but, seriously, it's like being a black person. Having comments thrown at you. Like, he says 'you know what they do to horses. They shoot 'em. That's what they should have done to you.' I'm not bothered by it. But it worries me that they say those things. Do they mean it when they say it? Do they not understand what disability is about? It seems to be part of society that you take the mickey out of anyone who's a little bit different to you.

Listening to disabled people speaking, it is striking that they for their part do not always or necessarily see their impairment in a totally negative light. People with certain kinds of disability can rely on other abilities. They learn, for instance, to be good organizers, to be productive against all odds. They may become more sensitive to the needs of others. Indeed for Peter Ferryman his impairment had not only made him more effective in his role as a union representative, it had redirected his life for the better.

> In all honesty I feel – and you'll probably laugh at this – but I feel it's the best thing that ever happened to me. I came off a motorbike. It was a fantastic experience, losing a leg. If I had the choice I wouldn't have lost it. I'd like to have kept it. But I got over it and . . . it's been beneficial. For me personally, it's made me a different person, it's made me a person who can think now. I've got the ability to sit and listen to other people, as opposed to saying people are just wrong. It's made me a better person from a lot of angles, really.

Disabled people feel their positive qualities are too seldom recognized by employers and colleagues.

Rather few of the non-disabled people I spoke with spontaneously raised the issue of equal opportunity for people with disabilities. It is the forgotten corner of personnel policy. When people cast around to recall 'Do we have any disabled people here?' they are often oddly narrow in their image of disability. Usually it is someone in a wheelchair they are thinking of.

Many employees raised management difficulties in the way of employing disabled people, even when they themselves did not have management responsibilities. They would say 'if they've got the brain, yes, but . . .', 'you have to consider the cost equation', 'managers have enough problems as it is'. People project their prejudice on colleagues: 'if you go too far you get antagonism from others'. They purvey mythical horror stories. There is the one about the 'blind secretary' imposed on a manager by an idealistic welfare officer when 'everyone could have told him she couldn't possibly do the job'. There is the one about the physically disabled person integrated into an office at the expense of 'an awful lot of trouble' only to prove 'a difficult kind of person'. There is the 'fully qualified deaf typist' who is also a 'fully qualified lunatic'.

The most chilling encounters I had on disability, however, were in the upper reaches of management, because here the link between individual insensitivity and organizational discrimination was so clear and direct. Thus very senior professionals in the Service admitted, 'We are not taking positive action . . . We wouldn't adopt the positive view and say "here is a job a disabled person could do, let's go out and find one".' On the contrary, 'These things are not the foremost things . . . . This doesn't appear at the top of the list'. One such officer did have a wish (expressed with mild irritation) to 'hit the damn target' of 3%. And he wistfully mused on the possibility of broadening the definition of disability to enable the Service to proclaim itself on quota.

Not everyone's views on employment of disabled people, however, were negative. Many found it the easiest aspect of equal opportunities to be positive about. People with disabilities seemed somehow more 'deserving' than women and ethnic minorities. I found, perhaps not surprisingly, that people who have disabled children, parents, partners or friends are those who are most likely to be aware of and sensitive to the needs of people with disabilities.

Work can damage your health

The fear I sensed in non-disabled people talking about the disabled seems to spring from the knowledge that at any moment you yourself may join that group. All it takes is the kind of accident that can happen to anyone any day: a fall from a ladder, a car crash. 'The disabled are the minority group anyone can join at the drop of a hat.' Alternatively, disability can be lying in wait there inside you in the form of some degenerative illness, or just old age. The anxiety is intensified by the knowledge that a great deal of disablement is produced by work itself. All inflexible work organization is damaging. There is increasing anxiety, for instance, about the repetitive strain injuries generated by women's routine manual jobs.

The much-publicised stress of the business executive's life with its high risk of coronaries and other illnesses was evident in High Street Retail. The most damaging job I encountered, however, was, perhaps surprisingly, that of full-time officer in the Trade Union. It was described by one such officer as 'a time bomb waiting to go off'. We saw in Chapter 4 how the union officer is likely to be out at meetings two or three nights a week and will have union-related commitments on many weekends of the year. The job involves coping with disputes, strikes, crisis. 'People are battle-weary. We only ever talk to people who have problems. They only phone us to complain, either about the employer or the union.' Taking on other people's problems, often without the needed counselling and support for oneself, leads to stress and illness, said another officer. The job is associated with heavy drinking and smoking. In one divisional office alone I heard of local officers who were afflicted by strokes, physical accidents, long-term diseases and heart conditions. Some had had nervous breakdowns: 'thrown a wobbly' as this informant put it. The ethic of service to the union fosters the pressure. 'You don't let on if you're less than a hundred per cent fit.' 'If you're ill you feel you're letting people down'. A woman officer said,

> there's something wrong with the whole style of trade unions. [This union] has a reputation for having able and committed full-time officers, so there are high expectations. But this means a macho image. 'I've worked 99 hours this week and driven a thousand miles. What have you done?'

We saw in Chapter 4 that some women in the union were arguing that the job should be restructured to make it more possible for the average woman to tackle. It was recognized too that such adaptations would make the job a healthier one for the average man to do (and less demanding on partners). Many male officers of the old school, however, felt that doing the job differently would mean doing the job worse. Yet they cannot altogether suppress the worry that their hard-driving, alcohol-abusing, tobacco-ridden lifestyles threaten their health. Three deaths from heart attacks among the senior officers of a sister union had recently made them pause for thought about the cost of labour movement heroics.

There is thus an undeniable but seldom recognised link between the issue of employment of disabled people and the issue of *health and safety at work*. 'The disabled' may be new job applicants. They may equally be existing employees who have recently acquired some impairment to their health and functioning. In some cases that impairment may be work-related. Yet the two issues are seldom if ever linked in policy.

The Health and Safety at Work etc. Act 1974 is the principal piece of legislation governing occupational health and safety. The Act imposes a duty on employers to ensure the wellbeing of their employees, and that includes providing a safe working environment that offers no risks to health. The Health and Safety Executive which was set up consequent to the Act has an Employment Medical Advisory Service working with employers. There are also Disablement Rehabilitation Officers approaching employers from a different direction. Yet within organisations it is unusual for the personnel or welfare officer dealing with disabled employees to be the same person or even in the same team as the health and safety officer. The roles are seen as entirely distinct. Indeed I was told by a trainer in this field that

> health and safety at work people, far from individually reaching out [to the disabled] are often very, very obstructive. They see disabled people as risks. Wheelchairs are obstacles. The deaf are a hazard because they can't hear the fire alarm. The blind are a danger because they can't find their way out of the building. Emotional, mobility and sensory problems are re-interpreted as safety problems.

She had, she said, found health and safety officers all too often 'ignorant, prejudiced and obstructive about disability, worried mainly about their own liability'.

Mechanisms of subordination

'Policing cripples' (in Paul Abberley's disturbing phrase) has been a lasting concern of the state. How to ensure the ablebodied do not evade the discipline of low-paid exhausting toil by swelling the bands of vagrants and beggars? Sixteenth-century laws distinguished between real and fake disability, legitimate and illegitimate idleness. The philosophy entered the nineteenth century in the Poor Laws and their concern with sorting the deserving from the undeserving poor. It lives on in the twentieth in the Thatcherite preoccupation with 'scroungers' and 'dependency culture'. And if cripples are literally policed in these ways, they are subject to a 'soft' or ideological policing too. Medical rehabilitation of the disabled has prepared them to enter the job market, psychology has aimed for emotional 'adjustment' to the impaired condition, suppressing disabled people's very reasonable anger at their social handicap. Sociology too, overlooking society's involvement in the production and reproduction of impairment, has contributed to an ideology in which 'acts of God' cause disability while society merely picks up the insurance tab (Abberley 1985).

Disability, however, is at last being politicised. It is edging its way into discourses of power and powerlessness, supremacy and subordination, where it is finding a place along with class and ethnicity, gender and sexual orientation. With the increasing self-organization of disabled people, the oppression factor in disability is being recognized and contested. In 1981 a breakaway group from the official Rehabilitation International, calling itself the Disabled People's International, held its first world conference, 'A Voice of Our Own'. There was a call for more consultation of disabled people, more involvement by the disabled in 'finding and providing their own solutions' (Disabled People's International 1983). In Britain Vic Finkelstein has argued, as a disabled person, 'real integration . . . can [only] be achieved on the basis of a full recognition of our differences and this in turn will depend a great deal on us making the free choice to identify ourselves as a social group' (Finkelstein 1987).

Disabled women are emerging as a specific interest group and feminists are now organising within groups of disabled people. In the Spinal Injuries Association, for instance, women have recently carried out a survey and published a book on women's experience of paralysis. In it they say,

The message is neither how awful life is for a disabled woman, nor how wonderful we are. If we have a message it is anger at how our concerns as spinally injured women are isolated within each individual's private world and so very rarely made part of the public world. When we 'appear' as a public issue it is usually in the way the non-disabled world defines us and our concerns, and not in the way we would wish to appear ourselves (Morris 1989:7; see also Saxton and Howe 1987, Lonsdale 1990).

Meanwhile, employers, with the 'main aim' of capital accumulation or public sector cost-efficiency in mind, take a blinkered view of their responsibility for disabled people. At best they wonder, 'Could this disabled person possibly do the job we are offering?' It is a rare employer that thinks 'Which jobs could we restructure – by team working, maybe – to make it feasible for a person with this or that disability to do them?' They do not calculate 'A person with this disability will have these abilities and capacities. How can we best enable them?' Even less do employers evaluate the organisation and its jobs by criteria of health. 'Are we a health-promoting organisation? Do we threaten the health of our employees?' We shall discuss further in the final chapter just what our expectations of employing organizations with different purposes might realistically be.

An equal opportunities policy for disabled people, then, potentially generates a remarkably long agenda. Begin by talking about people's fitness for work and you can end by questioning the fitness of work for people. People with disabilities can place demands on our perceptions of jobs, workplaces and employers that, if responded to, could transform organizational life for everyone. As a woman said to me in interview 'It could be an even more revolutionary re-evaluative process than doing the same thing for women or for black people.'

Present and speaking: a politics of the body

This chapter has added to the category 'woman', the subject of previous chapters, three more categories of subordinated person that have in recent years become the subjects of autonomous social movements, have pressed to be identified as disadvantaged groups and have consequently become the subject of equal opportunities policies in organizations. They are 'ethnic minorities', 'homosexuals' and 'disabled people'. Woven through all the accounts has been a fifth strand in the web of power relations that some would say was the fundamental expression of power: class domination. What will by now be clear is that women do not come in one kind. Nor are women, by virtue of being oppressed, innocent of the oppression of others. Feminists have found their theory has to tangle with 'difference' – and not just women's difference from men but the things that differentiate them from one another.

The accounts of four kinds of oppression, over and beyond class oppression, have shown the specificity of each set of mechanisms of subordination. What I want to do here is consider some of the similarities and explore the conditions for a progressive politics of alliances. This is not a search for some ambitious 'unified field' theory, like that of the physicists. It is more a matter of bringing together excerpts from a series of dialogues to create a 'round table' between people in different subject positions. The dialogue necessarily takes place around the themes of *identity*, *bodies* and *knowledge*.

We are seeing today an awakening of a new scepticism about what have been termed 'grand narratives', systems of thought that have purported to represent total accounts or universal renderings of reality. We are refusing anyone's claim to represent the one and only truth. The first such narrative to tumble has been the classical liberal humanism of the Enlightenment, already challenged by Marxism. We have seen something of Carole Pateman's feminist critique of a key theme in Enlightenment discourse: the social contract. In classical humanism, 'rational consciousness' exists in only one invariant form. It is (without even acknowledging it) the consciousness of the ruling class of Western Europe. Marx and subsequent thinkers in the Marxist tradition have chiselled away at this world-view, asserting an alternative rationality and proposing a different, though still unique, conscious subject of history: the working class.

New-wave feminism has entered this field of theory, contributing to post-Enlightenment and post-Marxist ways of thinking. Feminists have pointed out (e.g. Lloyd 1984) that not only the rational consciousness of classical humanism but also the working-class subject of Marxist theory (e.g. Barrett 1980) are *male*. Women quite simply do not exist as knowers, as agents of history. As Mary O'Brien puts it, Marxism, no less than the philosophies it challenges, is 'male-stream thought'. For Marx, human oppression arises in the material necessity of individual survival that drives men to production. Women, the necessity of species survival and the labour of reproduction, are absent from the Marxist account of human history. Now feminism asserts that, rather than one, there are two poles of human necessity and 'the common ground of both liberalism and socialism . . . shrinks and trembles at the logical implications of woman's humanity' (O'Brien 1981:162).

Women, the subordinate half of humankind, have now turned attention back on the author of 'civilization', the ruling class of Western Europe, now visibly white and male. We can see that masculine hegemony has operated through the power of men to define woman as not-man. 'She is defined and differentiated with reference to man and not he with reference to her; she is the incidental, the inessential as opposed to the essential. He is the Subject, he is the Absolute – she is the Other' (De Beauvoir 1949). Examples of this self- and other-representation have been visible in the discourse of the ordinary women and men, black and white, homosexual and heterosexual, disabled and non-disabled, who have spoken in this and earlier chapters. We can see all subjects with the power to do so defining another as excluded, different and inferior, someone over whom dominion is legitimate.

Self and the alien other

It can be shown historically how European identity has been created in differentiation from those of other geographical areas, people defined as physically different and culturally inferior. Robert Miles recounts how Greco-Roman cartographers mapped on to the unexplored margins of their world mythical tribes of one-footed or dog-headed creatures (Miles 1989). They were an imagined 'Other' in opposition to which humans were constituted as fully human. Migrations, trade and warfare inevitably brought populations in contact with each other and their interaction gave rise to comparisons and evaluations of strangers. The Chinese had their 'barbarians', Islam its 'non-believers', Christianity its 'infidels'. The nation-states of Western Europe in the period of imperialist expansion had their benighted savages awaiting the civilizing mission of the Europeans.

It is interesting to note how the concept of monstrosity links the two discourses of 'race' and disability. The word 'monster' has the same root as 'demonstrate' or 'admonition'.

Within the Greco-Roman world, natural events considered to be indicators of God's intentions towards human beings were defined as *portenta* or *monstra*. Initially *monstra* defined unusual individual or anomalous births, but its meaning was extended through the Middle Ages to include whole populations of people supposedly characterised by anomalous phenotypical characteristics, although the sense of divine warning remained (Miles 1989:16, citing Friedman 1981).

Even today we are accustomed to measure ourselves against a model of physical perfection (never, of course, attained or even closely defined) in contrast to which an impairment is perceived variously as a curse, an omen and a source of shame. The model is male. Women's bodies are characterised as less strong, less effective. Menstruation is 'the curse', pregnancy and menopause are disabilities. The model is also white. White Europeans have equated blackness – the blackness of the Moor, African or Jew – with ugliness. Many black people have felt compelled to attempt to whiten their skin or straighten their hair to achieve this norm. Finally the model is physical 'fitness'. There are many resonances between these processes of valorisation and depreciation. Skin colour has been represented as a 'visual impairment', equivalent to pockmarks, birthmarks or man-made stigmata – the slave's brand. Robert Miles has said it is as though 'monstrousness, sin and blackness' are the obverse of the Christian trinity (Miles 1989:16/17). Any visible or even cultural difference is stigmatized, designated non-normal and inferior (Goffman 1968).

One of the dimensions of differentiation and inferiorization lies along the axis *nature/culture*. Women have throughout the ages been represented as 'nature' to men's 'culture'. The process has two steps. First human nature is itself represented as a dualism, as combining 'sensory, impulsive organic *nature* and rational, regulated *culture*' (Sydie 1987:38). There is the beast in man and the angel. This dichotomy is then mapped on to sex difference so that man, the subject of history, projects on to woman the natural aspect of the human face, and depreciates it. (Some feminists have accepted this gender stereotyping and endorsed women's closeness to nature, celebrating women's 'difference' from men in this respect (e.g. Griffin 1984, Merchant 1982). They have achieved a powerful and inspiring reaffirmation of women's strengths but at the cost of leaving the positive qualities of reason and culture as the properties of men.)

In a similar process of dichotomising, splitting and inferiorizing, black people too have been 'naturalized' in the course of white self-differentiation. The colonized peoples in the eighteenth and nineteenth centuries were made the object of the emerging science of biology. While white men of the ruling class, and to a lesser extent white working-class men, remained the legatees of culture, black people were made the object of science.

> Here they were characterized in one of two ways: as akin to apes or wild men, driven by more or less brutal instincts which had to be subjugated by special disciplinary techniques, or as noble savages or children of nature, who were uncorrupted by civilization and should as far as possible be preserved in their separate and primitive estate (Cohen 1988:19).

A further curiosity of supremacist ideologies is the way in which 'nature' having been contrasted to 'culture' and given lower status is once again split, this time into the 'natural' (good) and the 'unnatural' (bad). In this formulation un-natural is not non-natural – rather it is perverted naturalness. The process is powerfully operated to distance black from white, woman from man, ablebodied from disabled and homosexual from heterosexual. Cohen points out that Africans were sometimes portrayed as a 'missing link between the animal and human estates'. They were 'held to be the descendants of matings between Europeans and apes; conversely, apes themselves were the product of illicit intercourse between Europeans and Africans' (Cohen 1988:20). Women who aspire to success in the public sphere, to acquiring the powers or freedoms of men, are castigated as 'unnatural', 'flying in the face of their true nature'. Homosexuals and their 'perversions' are relegated to the realm of the unnatural. Disabled people too are first 'naturalized' and then inferiorized as 'freaks of nature'. Paul Abberley draws an interesting parallel between the naturalization of disabled people and women. Impairment is represented as a product of genetics, disease or unavoidable accident; women are inescapably governed by their biology. Second the social being of disabled people is devalued. People with disabilities become invisible, unproductive and useless; women become the second sex whose place is in the home (Abberley 1985:61).

Within the notion of the natural, of course, is comprised the sexual. Robert Miles notes the association of the colonized 'Other' with 'excessive and unrestrained sexuality'. African women, for instance, were portrayed as sexually voracious, African men as having an unusually large penis and fearful sexual potency (Miles 1989:27). There are direct parallels with white women in European culture, who have been seen as the embodiment of sexuality, introducing sexuality with their very presence. Homosexuality receives similar treatment. We saw in the responses of women and men to the issue of homosexuality in the workplace that homosexuals were commonly supposed to be more obsessed with sex than heterosexuals and to be more likely to foist their attentions on unwilling victims. One aspect of the prejudice against disabled people, it should be added, is the fear, embarrassment and distaste evoked by any suggestion that people who have disabilities, no less than people who do not, are entitled to sexual self-expression and to procreation.

Men's fear, not only of women's supposed sexual nature but of their control of reproduction has generated in men an obsession with the idea of 'breeding'. We saw how men have felt the necessity to appropriate women partly in order to know and control their own children (O'Brien 1981). This appropriation is not only an individual project; it is a strategy of group power. Cohen points to women's importance in 'breeding true' both in class and 'race' terms. He refers to 'the great divide between those with breeding and those who merely breed', the working class (Cohen 1988:36). White men also greatly fear black men's sexual access to white women. In becoming the repositories of 'breeding' women become in some sense comparable to animal stock. This was starkly true of black women slaves. For white European women too, cherished and protected though they might be, the implication was less than full human identity.

The patrimony of the free-born Englishman was from the outset something from which women and children were excluded. In the very act of being coupled together as representing the 'future of the race' they are pushed to the margins of the body politic . . . (Cohen 1987:36).

Embodiment and knowledge

An important part of our many projects of liberation, then, is the reclaiming of our bodies. We have to assert our bodily reality, make our bodies visible, invest them with new value. For black power in the sixties, 'black is beautiful' was an important statement of identity. In new-wave feminism women have reclaimed our beauty for ourselves, both in lesbian desire and in a greater autonomy among heterosexual women in choosing clothing and adornment. We began to see menstruation, pregnancy and menopause as bodily processes with which we could feel comfortable, unashamed, of which we could even be proud. In gay liberation, gay men represented the male body in an unaccustomed way, as the object as well as the bestower of regard. And today with no less determination people with disabilities are coming out of the closet into which they have been shut, accepting their own differences and making it clear they expect non-disabled people not to avert their gaze but to support them in their project of being bodily present, acknowledged, accommodated and enabled on the street, in the workplace and in organizational life. It is hazardous of course, because our bodies are a key site of our stigmatization and exploitation. There are understandable reasons why so many of us try to 'pass' for something we are not. But this new sense we have, as subordinated groups, of fully inhabiting bodies of which we are no longer ashamed can be the source of both new knowledge and new politics.

Science, philosophy and sociology have purported to be knowledge of 'mankind', equally valid for man and woman, black and white. In reality they have been the world-view of an author whose own identity has remained unstated, unremarked. It is white men of the ruling class who have been the unique source of authoritative knowledge about the world. It has been this relatively small group that have had the power to see and categorize all other groups while themselves remaining unseen and unspecified. Beneath, silenced and marginalized, have been many alternative representations of reality as it is lived by many subordinated groups. There is a black reality. But there is also a woman's black reality. We are contesting the old arrogant positivistic certainties. But can we simply substitute a feminist for a male-stream story about the world, or an account by colonized peoples for an imperialist world-view, and expect it to be more valid? If not, are we adrift in a sea of relativity? Who is to say, today, 'I am right and you are wrong'?

In a remarkable essay Donna Haraway has gone some way to transcend the dichotomy between discredited knowledge-claims and mere relativity. She uses the metaphor of 'vision' to fashion a more workable theory of knowledge for a world in which we recognize and value each other's difference. None of the individual subordinated viewpoints gives a similar account of reality. Nor is 'reality' itself standing still, waiting to be discovered. Yet every vision from below is more likely to produce valid usable knowledge than the universalizing view from above; from, as she puts it, the brilliant space platforms of the powerful. 'The only position from which objectivity could not possibly be practiced and honored is the standpoint of the master, the Man, the One God, whose Eye produces, appropriates and orders all difference' (Haraway 1988:587). Partial viewpoints promise more, not less, adequate representations of the world because each is the perception of an *embodied* eye, producing local, situated knowledge.

> I am arguing for politics and epistemologies of location, positioning, and situating, where partiality and not universality is the condition of being heard to make rational knowledge claims. These are claims on people's lives. I am arguing for the view from a body, always a complex, contradictory, structuring and structured body, versus the view from above, from nowhere, from simplicity. Only the god trick is forbidden (Haraway 1988:589).

Such a way of understanding our differences can be productive for our politics. It becomes clear that the one who *sees* has the power to render the Other now visible and stigmatized, now invisible and marginalized. We can understand and resist the dual strategy of rejection or assimilation to which (as we have seen) white male ruling groups try to subject those women, black people, homosexuals and disabled people that seek access to their organizations. It gives us a potentially politicized concept of multiculturalism, one that is not an excuse for abandoning an anti-racist project, that indeed reaches far beyond culture as ethnicity. We can speak of women's culture, of lesbian culture. Some disabled people are beginning to speak positively of a disability culture. It provides us, besides, with a language in which to begin talking about the necessary conditions for political alliances between subordinated but very different groups, alliances which are necessary if we are to dismantle the white male monoculture of power.

7

Towards parity

Activists for sex equality in all kinds of organization today are standing back and evaluating the results of the efforts of the 1980s. Those with whom I spoke in the course of the research reported in this book were coherent and united in their disappointment with the achievements of 'equal opportunities'. The law, they say, is too weak and difficult to use. Organizations taking positive action are too few and their goals and methods too limited. Organizations choose high profile, cost-free measures and neglect the more expensive changes that would improve things for a greater number of women. Policies adopted are seldom implemented. Implementation is not monitored. Non-compliance is not penalized, nor is cooperation rewarded. There is, besides, a widely-shared belief among those working for sex equality in organizations that the problems are not only a legacy of history. There is active resistance by men. They generate *institutional* impediments to stall women's advance in organizations. At a *cultural* level they foster solidarity between men and sexualize, threaten, marginalize, control and divide women.

'Equal opportunities': the short and the long agenda

In the foregoing chapters we have followed the attempts in four organizations to equalize the position of women with that of men. The positive action involved was combined with equality measures for black people, homosexuals and people with disabilities. Taking the purpose and content of the action issue by issue, it has been possible to see in each case contrasted agendas for change. There was always a 'short' agenda, the minimum position supported by top management, without which no equality policy would get started. There was, however, also a 'long' agenda involving more substantial kinds of change, the aim of equality activists, official and unofficial. Others – women trade unionists, women managers – lent their support to some items on the longer agenda while remaining unconvinced or negative about others. The majority of men, however, were unmistakably engaged in a damage-limitation exercise, holding 'equal opps' to its shortest possible agenda.

In the case of the recruitment, training and promotion of women (Chapter 2) we saw that management today may be willing for both pragmatic and moral reasons to try to remove sex-bias from their human resource management practices, to open up to women careers in managerial, professional and technical fields. There are, however, conflicting interests among men in organizations. Relatively powerful men, in supporting equality activism, are often obliged to sell out the gender interests of less powerful men. Less powerful men are finding it increasingly difficult, after twenty years of anti-racist and anti-sexist movements, to find convincing arguments for continued discrimination. They nonetheless manoeuvre, usually successfully, to defend the masculinity of the hierarchy. They use the organizational levers available to them. They do their best by cultural means to deter women (especially black women) from aspiring to top jobs, or succeeding once in them. They strive to retain women's loyalty to men and to the *status quo*, to prevent any organization or movement among women and particularly to discourage women who 'make it' from identifying with women at the bottom of the organization.

Many women, however, have different ideas. They do not want to be token women; they want full and fair representation of women in men's jobs. They hope women will play such roles differently from men. They do not want to be the ones who do all the adapting, but to be active subjects in transforming the organization itself. Paradoxically there are women who dislike aspects of the short agenda yet are nonetheless in favour of aspects of a longer agenda. Positive discrimination in favour of individual women is unpopular with women, who feel obscurely that it adds one more unfairness to an unfair organization. Yet they welcome the idea of transformative change that could improve things, they believe, for both women and men. For their part, however, most men, even those in top management who are the sponsors of positive action for women, put energy into limiting any extension of the agenda beyond bias-removal, an opening of doors and, at most, some remedial training for women.

A second aspect of sex-equality policy was the improvement of provisions to enable women to combine work with domestic responsibility (Chapter 3). Here we saw how some men at the top, either because they were generally supportive of equality for women or because they were increasingly aware of the imperative of competing for women's labour power in a tightening labour market, were willing to extend paid and unpaid maternity leave, to provide child care and to make women's terms of employment more flexible. Such 'mothers' privileges' are contradictory for managers. They secure women's services but involve expense and new administrative difficulties. They are also, however, a mixed blessing for women. They enable women to sustain careers, of a kind, but confirm them as the domestic sex. The longer agenda of some women therefore is to see men make use of these benefits to the same extent as women, to see men sacrifice some of their time and their career priorities to share child care and other domestic tasks with women. Very few men follow women thus far. They resist simply by refusing to change their practices. Personnel managers do nothing to encourage men to relate to work and home in the manner of women.

Giving full value to women's traditional skills and labour (Chapter 4) rarely makes it on to the management equality agenda. Re-evaluating women's low-paid jobs (which are those in which black women are disproportionately found), regrading them, affording them a value comparable to that of traditional male jobs, these demands on the part of women run headlong up against the 'main aim' of most organizations and their top managements. Profit has primacy in the case of business; cost efficiency in the case of public bodies. The demand of 'equal value' is in contradiction with the functioning of labour markets, in which the weak bargaining power of women with domestic ties is an important advantage to employers. They also run into opposition from men of lower grades who see both their social status and their sense of identity as men as dependent on having women mainly beneath them, seldom equals, never above.

There are, however, yet more far-reaching equality-aims in this connection: the restructuring of the organization to reduce status distinctions for everyone, and the democratising of the organization to afford greater participation by all, particularly those in the lower grades where women and black people are clustered. Some working men who are disadvantaged in the hierarchy, and the trade unions that represent them, support such an interpretation of 'equality': 'it is equality for men too'. Getting better status or representation for lower grades does not necessarily mean more power for women, however. Working-class men can ensure that it is men who mainly gain. In most organizations, besides, the structuring of the hierarchy and the decision-making process is kept well out of reach of ordinary employees. It rests in the hands of very senior managers, mainly men and mainly white.

Equal opportunities policies usually broach, at some point, the matter of sexist language and terms of address, and offensive pin-ups on the wall (Chapter 5). Women often go further and raise the question of sexual harassment. The equality agenda, however, seldom extends to include awareness-training to help men learn the required behaviours, nor to strict enforcement of rules. Manage-ment are seldom willing, when it comes to the test, to discipline offenders against either sex or race codes. Men (and white people of both sexes) too often, in the last resort, protect each other. Among individuals, those men who dislike sexist behaviour in men seldom, if ever, stand up against their male colleagues when they encounter it. (The same can be said of white people in the case of racist behaviour.)

The long agenda of equality involves more than this, however. Organizations, as we have seen, routinely exploit women's (and men's) emotions and their sexuality. An organization's regime involves both officially sanctioned, indeed enforced, gendered behaviours (sexually-stereotyped occupations and recruitment, dress requirements) and unofficial heterosexual cultures. Men reward women for sexual difference when they are in their proper place; penalize them for it once they step into men's place. These are means whereby men control women. They exert a masculine cultural hegemony that makes it unlikely that women will willingly forfeit men's approval, will identify with each other or with feminism. Official equality policies seldom if ever tackle these deeper aspects of organizational culture.

Finally, in Chapter 6, we drew together the strands of the narrative on ethnicity and racism that had been present in the preceding account and discussed the fact that positive action in organizations is often simultaneously for both sex and race equality. While recognizing the specificity of racism, it was possible to see similarities in the process whereby a ruling group defines itself in contrast to an alien and inferior 'Other'. White people create a black other in a discourse easily recognizable to women: the Other is biologically different; closer to nature; more sexual; distant from culture; threatening to civilization and order. A parallel discourse defines 'real men' in opposition to homosexuals. People with disabilities are stigmatized in a similar process.

Through these processes, in interaction with class relations, a dominant group is forged of those who have the power to define all other groups as inferior. It is a white male heterosexual and largely ablebodied ruling monoculture. It retains control of material and ideological resources and is thus mapped on to class power. It exacts 'norm'alisation and assimilation of other categories as the price of acceptance: you may find a place as long as you simulate the norm and hide your difference. We will know you are different and continue ultimately to treat you as different, but if you yourself specify your difference your claim to equality will be nul. The long agenda of equality policy is, then, combating sexism, racism, heterosexism and discrimination against people with disabilities, acknowledging and according high value to different kinds of bodies and different kinds of cultures – all perceived as equivalent, all afforded parity. Often, by contrast, white men in powerful positions play off the 'equalities' against each other in a process of divide and rule.

Equality activists, both paid officers and interested individual women, conclude that women's bid for visibility, recognition and parity is being actively and passively obstructed by men. Of course, the world is not open to immediate transformation in the interest of any disadvantaged group. We inherit from history complex structures – the power of the state, the legal system, the pattern of ownership, the mode of production, the operation of labour markets – all of which sustain class, sex and race inequalities. Feminists, however, make a critique of these structures, analyse their adverse effect on women, speak out against them and organize in opposition. The test of men is whether they do the same: they rarely do so. Equality activists are not so naive as to suppose a capitalist firm can operate for long at a net loss. They may, however, suggest that some additional costs, either above or below the famous 'bottom line' – extra costs of production or a diversion of net profits – may be justified in the name of social responsibility. Few men do. Within organizations there are long-lived structuring practices that disadvantage women, patterns of relationship, rules and regulations, that are difficult to turn around. Women challenge them; men on the whole do not. On the contrary, where they have the power to do so, they routinely manipulate organizational rules, regulations and processes in men's favour.

Why do men so determinedly resist the changes women say they need for their liberation? The answer is that they do it very often in spite of themselves. For men are caught up in the compulsion of patriarchal relations as much as women are. Male power is not occasional, incidental or accidental. It is *systemic*. To say that it is systemic is to say it is longlived – though not timeless, for woman-centred societies have existed in the past and sex equal societies will exist in the future. It is also to say it is adaptive, with a tendency to self-reproduction. To interrupt that reproductive process calls for active and conscious contradiction. But patriarchy, after all, is a system of domination. Women do win some advantages from their position in patriarchy. For example, they are not called on to be prepared to kill other people to prove their femininity, as men are their masculinity. Men, however, gain hugely from patriarchy.

For men to oppose women's liberation is, therefore, on the face of it, nothing if not logical. In the short run, men do not gain by a situation in which quantities of women as individuals and as a sex compete with them for money and status. In addition, however, men have always understood that when women take power as a sex, it threatens a more qualitative, revolutionary change. With women trundle along the principles of reproduction, domesticity and care, infesting the public sphere, upsetting the fundamental tenets of male political and civil life. In Aristophanes' play, *The Congresswomen*, the comedy hinges on women and household organization taking over the *polis*. For Aristophanes, 'to put women in charge of the city is to transform it. The plays make it clear that a public role for women would inevitably involve the destruction of the *polis* itself' (Hartsock 1985:204).

Men will resist, therefore, because they (rightly, in their own terms) equate male power with 'civilization'. While women have in reality always created the society and economy of nurture that sustains men's civilization, yet to men, as Carole Pateman says, 'women represent all that men must master to bring civil society into being' (Pateman 1988:102). Mary O'Brien has suggested that men, alienated from their seed in the procreative act, negated in reproduction, have sought to dominate women to win control of their offspring. Further, they have turned to production, to organization-building, the institutionalization of life in a kind of mimicry of reproduction, creating their own historical continuity independently of women. Men beget their own 'immortal children of the mind' (Hartsock 1985:253).

Organization is the essential process of effecting power. No individual, however, wealthy, however, armed, can impose his will for long without organizing others to act in his interest. Without organization he is a King Kong or a Rambo, reduced to mortal muscle. Organizations, then, are not just of casual interest to men as a sex. They are crucial to the production and reproduction of power. Men will not readily let women in. As O'Brien puts it, 'women are competing with men not only in the workplace but in making history' (O'Brien 1981:166).

Power, however, is complex. Patriarchy is not the only relational system governing western societies. Gender relations are lived as class relations. Class relations are gendered. Patriarchy today is capitalist, as capitalism has always been patriarchal. In some respects, as we saw in Chapter 2, the imperatives of capitalist production are in contradiction with those of patriarchy. Shifts in the class relations of capitalist societies today – for instance, in changing both the nature of work and the balance of women and men in the labour force – are creating disturbances in gender relations. New feminism is a product of new political and economic conditions.

Men and masculinity: continuity and change

Gender, furthermore, is a relation, and we must suppose that, since masculinity and feminity only make sense in some kind of complementarity to each other, masculinity is under pressure from its other half. Either women must accept their place in society or men must find new ways of being men. Some men, a small minority, are prepared to take this step. They have recognized that not only does systemic male dominance oppress women, it deforms men. They are saying that the masculine identity required of men causes most boys to be brought up to hide their kinder nature, to be unnecessarily competitive, to be controlling and to be violent. They point out that men are more likely than women to spend time in prison, that they have a shorter life-expectancy, and die more frequently of stress-related illnesses and from violence (Tolson 1977, Metcalf and Humphries 1985, Seidler 1989). In the 1970s some men's consciousness-raising groups formed to explore creative ways men might respond to feminism both by finding a more comfortable and socially desirable identity for themselves but also by supporting women's demands. But such groups were few and most were shortlived. What about the majority of men, who probably never heard of them? Are they showing signs of changing, either in their attitudes or in their gender identity, in response to women's wish for parity?

The responses men were making to feminism and ideas about women's equality in the four organizations represented here are not dissimilar to those observed by other researchers. Mary Ingham interviewed a hundred men, mainly white-collar employees and professionals, apparently white. It was the early eighties. She found 'the majority of men felt that the women's movement was very much alive . . . "I'm fed up with women's lib." They were almost unanimous in feeling that feminism made women unfeminine and although its ideals were right it was going completely the wrong way about realizing them.' What had to many women become a new world in the seventies, men seemed quite unmoved by. 'It was rare for a man to admit that his own life had been touched.' Most of these men agreed with equal pay and equal rights 'but . . . almost unanimously, believed that the sexes are different; equal but different; and in defining these differences they ended up by defending conventional roles'. Ingham's conclusions were not optimistic for the outcome of organizational equality struggles. 'The rules by which men are brought up, especially in relation to work, do not include responding to the *needs* of others. So why should the rules be bent to accommodate the needs of women to be treated as equals?' (Ingham 1985:204–6). Yvonne Roberts in in-depth interviews with 45 men was told again and again 'that feminism was about women who want to be men; women who burn bras; women who hate men. Not once was I told it was about a freedom from stereotyping for women *and* men; the right of choice for females *and* males; the end of an abuse of power by the strong over the weak' (Roberts 1984:13).

Men's negative response to feminism is partly anger, partly distress. Men subordinate women but are dependent on this subject woman they have created. When we slip the silken leashes of hegemony we create a new woman's presence far less comfortable to men than the old. As one man puts it, feminism

> subverts the femininities that have brought men sexual stability and the ordering of our internal worlds. What happens when women no longer belong to men, when female identities and practice begin to refuse the patterns of male heterosexual desire? Men are bereft. We have fashioned [woman] as the source of our solace, she fills an inner void, the wordless room that we occupy and neglect, she speaks that language, without her we are nothing. And yet, sometimes her presence threatens us with the same fate (Rutherford 1988:52).

It is not only feminism that challenges men and disrupts current notions of masculinity and femininity. Transformations in the economy and in political structures are doing this too. The masculine identity of working-class men has been threatened by new technology, by the decline of heavy industry in Britain and a shift to a service economy, and by widespread unemployment. Middle-class men have been affected too. Andrew Tolson writes:

> the postwar reconstruction of British society has stripped away all the idealistic cloak surrounding middle-class work and has revealed, for the first time, its naked insecurity. More and more men have begun to see the career-structure as futile and impossible to sustain . . . with no ethical commitment to the institution he serves, the middle-class man comes face to face with his motivation to work at all . . . in an increasingly bureaucratic society his experience of work slowly compromises a man's heroic vision (Tolson 1977:86–90).

There is no shortage now of research and analysis problematising masculinity, exploring the mechanisms in which it is generated, searching for indicators of stress and change. 'Men's studies' is a burgeoning literature (Brod 1987, Kaufmann 1987, Kimmel 1987a, Hearn and Morgan 1990). One of its popular themes is a supposed 'crisis' in masculinity. Michael Kimmel has compared today's confusion about what it is to be a 'real man' with similar periods of crisis in Restoration England and in the United States two centuries later, times when structural changes were transforming the institutions of personal life, particularly marriage and the family, important sources of gender identity (Kimmel 1987b). Another theme of men's studies literature is the need for men to shed their 'character armour', to 'get in touch with their feelings'. As Vic Seidler puts it, 'as men we are only publicly assured of dignity if we identify with our reason. We learn to despise our softer feelings as 'feminine'. We put these at a distance from ourselves . . .' (Seidler 1989:195).

Men are beginning to point out that becoming a man in the conventional mould is a long hard journey. Sometimes the individual is lost *en route*. As R.W. Connell puts it, 'masculinity does not fall from the heavens: it is constructed by masculinizing practices, which are liable to provoke resistance, can go wrong, and are always uncertain in their outcome. That, after all, is why so much effort has to be put into them' (Connell 1983:58).

This relatively new perception of gender-in-process has led to the theme of 'multiple' masculinities and femininities.

> Femininity and masculinity as character structures have to be seen as historically mutable. There is nothing to prevent several forms of sexual character emerging in the same society at the same time. Multiple femininities and masculinities are, I would suggest, a central fact about gender and the way its structures are lived (Connell 1987:63).

There is increasing recognition that the gender identity of a working-class man is not the same as that of a middle-class man; there are gay masculinities (Carrigan *et al.* 1987), black masculinities (Mercer and Julien 1988). Which brings us to that latest addition to the family of man, The New Man. Even the media have caught on to the idea that today a man is visible who shows marked differences from the classics of the age of the British Empire or the Vietnam war. Whether he is, in fact, an artefact of the media itself is a disputed question. Certainly the white man we see in contemporary fashion and other kinds of advertising (the black man gets different treatment, often as athlete) is a softer, more sensuous fellow, somewhat narcissistic. He is someone who loves the good things of life. On the other hand he has no doubt that he is one of them. He is still god's gift to women, but a male viewer too could be forgiven for falling in love with him.

Women have grasped at the idea that this man, who is not afraid to wear glasses, look coy, snuggle up to a woman rather than sweeping her off her feet, is likewise disposed (in a carefully controlled context) to wear an apron or wheel a pushchair. Some are optimistic that signs of this kind herald a substantial change in Western European men today under pressure from women's bid for freedom. Lynne Segal, for instance, reads such shifts as signs that 'men can and do change'. She points out, very reasonably, that 'not all men have found it possible, and not all men have found it desirable, to participate in the social relations which generate dominance' (Segal 1990:130).

Others are more cautious about taking this new Face at face value. Rowena Chapman indeed sees him as an adaptive hybrid, 'better able and more suited to retain control' (Chapman 1988:235). Some pro-feminist men are among the sceptics. John Rutherford, for instance, does not feel New Man has the whole field to himself. Just as prevalent today is Retributive Man. Struggling to reassert a traditional masculinity, 'he confronts a world gone soft, pacified by traitors and cowards, dishonourable feminized men'. It is not that men are not changing. 'The disruption of our sexual identity has produced a new flexibility in masculinity. But what hasn't happened is any attempt to address this potential for change.' Radical politics, Rutherford points out, has made little attempt to address men as a sex and to offer alternatives (Rutherford 1988:39; see also Cockburn 1988a). And indeed the pressures on men are producing some odd mutations. Robert Bly, for one, is uneasy with the new 'soft' man and harks after a recovery of the old 'wild man', the 'deep male' that lurks in modern man (Thompson 1987). It is doubtful if feminists are going to welcome him as a bedfellow.

While it it is helpful that we can see gender and its relations as changing over time and differing in different classes and cultures, there is a danger that the idea of 'multiple masculinities' at the level of culture is allowed to deflect attention from the consistency in men's domination of women at systemic and organizational levels, from the continuation of material, structured inequalities and power imbalances between the sexes. Arthur Brittan points out that '"classical man" is still in charge of the state, the economy and reproduction' (Brittan 1989:184). 'Troubled' masculinity may be, but male power is defending itself systematically and ferociously. 'It is in this context that the proliferation of new local masculinities must be evaluated' he says (Brittan 1989:18).

What then of men whom we have seen in this study helping women introduce and implement equality strategies? Some of course were never more than nominally involved. A few, however, had put their heart into it. They had been important both in winning the acceptance of such policies by other men at the top of their organizations and defending women activists when they had come under attack. One woman equality officer said to me, 'I've worked for the first time with a man I respect. My life's not been full of them.' Without male allies such as this, equality projects would be non-starters. We should not underestimate the contribution a few men have been making, and many more could yet make, to the movement for change in organizations. Likewise, however, we have to hear what these men tell us: that their good efforts, like ours, are continually deflected, ridiculed and made impotent by the majority.

My study besides points up not only a difference between pro-equality and anti-equality men, but a difference within the former between those who are willing to be active for 'equality of opportunity' and those, much rarer, who are supportive of women's autonomy and a women's movement. Men, even the activists, tended to have a shorter agenda for the equality project than the women with whom they were working. There was often a simple condition attached to their participation: 'so long as you drop the feminism'.

The anti-feminism of men, which is such a heavy sanction against separate identity for women, needs to be challenged by supportive men as well as feminists. Men have to be prepared to take risks with other men's regard, just as feminist women have had to be willing to forfeit it. An unusual example of positive response by men comes from one London local authority. Here a white male departmental director decided to take 'equality' seriously. He recognized a need for men to go beyond support for women's activism to exploring the ways in which men must *shed* power in order for women to be empowered. In his department he called a series of meetings with all men managers on 'men's attitude to women'. Together they planned the changes they could make to departmental practice. Learning to listen to women; ensuring a visible and structured agenda for business so that women would not be excluded by men's informal networking; valuing equally the contribution of all staff regardless of their grade; giving more responsibility and credit to those at the bottom. Every policy proposal in this department now has to state not only how the issues it deals with bear on women and ethnic minorities but more precisely, 'if we implement this policy these would be the direct benefits to women. It would leave the following problems unresolved.' Many people, this director said, argue that such practices are too political. 'The way I answer is to say that the really political act is to do nothing in a situation where discrimination exists. There is no neutral position. There is no way of being unpolitical.' Hard as it may be for men, those of them that are not part of the solution are part of the problem.

Potentials for transformative change

It could be that positive action for sex equality in organizations is a passing fad. The 1980s may be remembered as the period in which the new-wave feminism of the seventies drained away into the sands of institutionalization. If this is so it will be because the movement was sanitised, immobilised and defeated in its encounter with men in places of power. My guess, however, is that some such efforts will persist for many years to come, fostered on the one hand by employers' need in the 1990s to court women in the labour market and on the other by a return to a social-democratic political climate. As more organizations declare themselves 'equal opportunity employers', the first wave will shift emphasis from policy-making to implementation and monitoring. They will be put to the test of really changing organizational practices, management procedures and workplace cultures. It is relevant to ask what is needed for further advances towards parity for women in organizations. (I will not write here of parallel steps needed to tackle other forms of disadvantage.)

There are certain necessary conditions that are external to individual organizations, developments that would make it both easier for women to engage in work and public life more generally and easier for equality activists to pursue their goals inside organizations. First, developments are needed in social policy, redistributing resources towards women as a sex and towards support for those caring for human health and reproduction. Extension and improvement of the welfare state is crucial for women if the burden of their caring responsibilities is not to diminish their chances at work and their presence in the public sphere. Community nursery care should be available for every child under school age as well as holiday provision for older children. It is a matter of quality as well as quantity, however. Nurseries and other services, if they are to be acceptable to women, must be to a standard as high as that currently provided by women unpaid. They should be under the popular, local control of women (and men) carers.

Second, an economic policy is needed, backed by trade unions, that would move us eventually towards a 30-hour standard week for both sexes, restrictions on overtime, a fair statutory minimum wage and the implementation throughout the economy (through action not only in the courts but through government incentives to employers and through collective bargaining) of equal pay for work of equal value. Part-time workers should have the same protection in law and the same right to benefits (*pro rata*) as full-time workers.

Third, we need a strengthening of the law. Positive discrimination for women, so long as they remain demonstrably disadvantaged or represented in any particular field, should be not only legal but (as in the United Nations Convention of 1979) mandatory. The government should end its veto on the European initiatives to restrict overtime and give part-time workers full rights. Employers in Britain should be required to monitor the composition of their workforce and where women and black people are under-represented in any grade or type of work they should be obliged to adopt equality targets, submit proposals for positive action and demonstrate improvement within a fixed time scale. The burden of proof in law should be on the employer to prove his or her innocence of discrimination, rather than on the employee to prove she has been wronged. Penalties against employers found guilty of sex discrimination should be increased. The law of equal value should be amended to allow for group actions so that substantial numbers of women might benefit from any one case. Government should withhold subsidies and grants from employers that are found guilty of discrimination or that take no steps to end disadvantage. Contract compliance should be legalized once more, so that public bodies may purchase goods and services only from companies that comply with equality policy. The Equal Opportunities Commission should be rendered more accountable to feminist organizations and have a stronger feminist presence in its leadership.

These are only some of the changes that law centres and women's groups dealing with equality issues have been calling for. Jeanne Gregory has pointed out that 'if the tribunals and courts remain out of step with the fundamental aims of the equality laws, new loopholes and escape routes will open up as fast as the old ones are closed. At the end of the day the understanding and attitudes of the people who adjudicate is more important than devising a new form of words.' She believes 'It will require nothing less than a vigorously enforced and carefully monitored programme of positive action throughout the legal profession before the monopoly of elderly, white men from privileged backgrounds can be broken and confidence in the integrity and representativeness of the judicial system be assured' (Gregory 1987:151–3).

Such developments would create a climate in which positive action for women and other disadvantaged groups within organizations could be effective. Currently, there are few grounds for optimism that these things will occur in the near future. And it goes without saying that even a successful struggle in this direction depends on the existence of an active feminist movement, which is not now in a moment of growth. We might, however, begin to foresee a strategy at organizational level that distinguishes the different possibilities for transformative change afforded by different types of organization.

Given their membership nature, political parties and trade unions are of all organizations those most open to organized pressure by large numbers of active women members: direct access to power by seeking majority or near-majority positions on decision-making bodies, if necessary by 'quota' arrangements, for which the law does allow. In theory there is considerable, as yet scarcely tested, scope for trade unions to transform themselves in the interests of their female, black and lowest-paid members. Once transformed, their influence for sex and race equality in employing organizations could be great, not least because they are more likely than employers to introduce a class dimension into the strategy.

Voluntary organizations are usually not governed by profit motives. They are usually relatively small and have social aims that are clearly defined. They are normally controlled by some form of representative management committee within the terms of a written constitution. Unfortunately, voluntary organizations are often the site of conflicts and disappointments. Those who work in them find that an ethical 'main aim' does not necessary translate into ethical personnel management. Nonetheless such bodies offer the most scope for an approach that uses ethical arguments, where combined action for women's parity by the committee, senior managers and clients, as well as employees, may not be unrealistic in some cases. The best of voluntary organizations could be pioneers of transformative change, models to hold up against both public and private sector organizations.

Public sector organizations are in theory subject to transformation from above, below and outside. That is to say, a government department is subject to instruction from the Government, political direction from the majority party in Parliament and pressure from employees. The Whitley Council industrial relations structure gives civil service unions a degree of input into management. Government departments are, however, cumbersome bureaucracies and their internal practice is rather autonomous of political pressure. Free of pressure to be profitable, they are nonetheless subject to budgetary constraints. So far equality achievements in major services have been disappointing. The National Health Service, for instance, has not been the leader it might have been. Since they are large, however, and usually have branches all over the country, there is potential scope in government services for far-reaching changes imposed centrally, backed up with active pressure from women's organizations and their trade unions.

Local authorities are in theory yet more responsive to internal and external pressure. Local constituency political parties can mobilise for change through elected councillors; trade unions have considerable influence; and so do community groups. Yet the number of local authorities with genuine positive action achievements is small. Led by the Greater London Council, a few inner-city local councils have made impressive efforts in the past and could do so again in more favourable political circumstances. Many mistakes were made, precisely because councils pushed equality action further than other organizations. They are mistakes, however, that could be learned from. The most compelling argument for transformative change in local government is that its officers are gatekeepers. Without proper representation of both sexes, all ethnic groups, homosexual and heterosexual people and people who experience various kinds of disability, the services they offer to the community will be inappropriate, inadequate or delivered in a discriminatory way. Though the same could be said of any organization, the argument has special cogency in the case of local elected bodies.

No mention has been made in this study of the lost opportunities in the education sector. Schools, colleges, polytechnics and universities with their influence on both the content and the social relations of learning are potentially at the heart of social change. Few have emerged as leaders in sex equality, however, and where energetic positive action has been attempted it has met with equally energetic resistance (Cockburn 1988b, Lees and Scott forthcoming).

Perhaps the biggest question-mark hangs over the possibilities for positive action in the private sector, where 'equal opportunities' to date has tended to be more cosmetic or instrumental than real. We have seen that some employers, perhaps a growing number, now see some advantage to their business interests in a short-agenda equality policy for women. The longer agenda, however, costs more money, seriously threatens class relations of exploitation, flattens the hierarchy and runs up against the resistance of male employees. On the face of it, it is difficult to argue against the profit imperative. Yet a careful examination of what business does with its gross or net profits would show that money is often spent on social and political aims that have nothing to do with the business. If a company can sponsor community development or the Conservative Party there is no reason why it should not spend money on putting its own house in order. The private sector may be more vulnerable to public image than the public sector; and in some industries unions are not without effect, even now. The influence for sex-equality of the Banking, Insurance and Finance Union, for instance, where feminists share in leadership, has been impressive (Personnel Management 1987).

The world has moved on from the days in which the only alternative to capitalist ownership was state ownership, when the cry had to be 'seize the means of production in the name of the working class'. We have seen the people of the Eastern bloc use their new freedom by voting with their feet in a flight from public ownership. The disappointments of social democracy and state socialism have long since disabused the British voter of the idea that to nationalize the coal mines or the banks will be enough to ensure transformative change in social relations and in the content of work and policy. We now guess that organizations, whether under private or public control, will have to change, if they change at all, from a combination of government controls and incentives and pressure from employees and their unions, together with clients or share-holders and their organizations. The peril of ecological catastrophe may well impel business corporations to become generally more socially responsible entities. In 1968 rebellious students talked of 'the long march through the institutions'. Equal opportunities activism, with its perspective on multi-faceted power, may well be a better starting point than class struggle ever was for that transformative march. Doing things women's way, however, it will probably be something less mannish and military than a march – a subversive burrowing, perhaps.

For a feminist practice in organizations

Within the organization, then, what should feminists aim to do? The following eight strategies emerge from the experience of equality activists in this research as important in carrying 'equal opps' beyond the minimum intended by most male managements. None of them are easy to effect, which is why they are missing from most equality projects. They could, however, at least be used as criteria to evaluate aims and outcomes.

First, the evidence seems to show, we need to seek to get *the equality initiative placed in a high and secure position* in relation to the male hierarchy, so that the policy is delivered from the start with authority. Of course, this means facing the dangers that the equality unit or officer/s may be out of touch with women at the base and subject to co-optative pressure from management. Yet top management alone has the power to change organizational structures and, more modestly, to set the operating rules that influence behaviour and build constituencies for further change. It has, for instance, the power to make certain kinds of behaviour simply unacceptable. In the new Northern Ireland fair employment practice it is prohibited to display religious and political flags and emblems in the workplace. Equality activists report the cultural impact of this rule to be impressive. It could become as unthinkable to pin up a 'nudie' calendar on the wall as it is to fart or spit in public. Such changes may seem trivial but without them an environment will persist in which bigger changes will continually be contested.

If the equality activists are not to become isolated or co-opted, the policy must *commit energy and resources to building a women's movement within the organization* (and in the neighbouring environment). Equality activists say this is the hardest thing to achieve. It means developing consciousness, creating networks and building constituencies among women for equality work. Only this can generate the pressure from below that gives legitimacy to demands made on the management by the equality officer or unit. Besides, it is particularly important that women who are lifted into exposed senior positions through positive action should not be left isolated, prey to the male resentment and revenge they usually encounter. Networks are needed therefore to support women managers and women entering non-traditional jobs. It is helpful to have women's groups within trade union branches and groups campaigning for particular demands such as a workplace nursery or a rest room. Wherever possible, therefore, some of the resources made available to the equality process should be directed towards building a women's culture in the organization, enabling women's activities, events, films.

All of this means working from the start to establish *the legitimacy of separate activity and a discourse of 'difference on our terms'*. Women must feel free to be fully present as women, whether this identity is expressed in terms of bodies, emotions or values, without being marginalized, stereotyped or put down for this. This seems to be the key step in shifting from an ideology of 'equality', individual women joining a male culture, to an ideology of 'parity', women as a sex having full representation in the organization.

Fourth, it has proved important *to develop practical alliances with supportive men*. This means to differentiate between men, to work consistently with those who show themselves willing to engage creatively with the equality project, to help them to understand what they can do. We need to help men to take responsibility for working to change the consciousness and culture of other men. Men will listen to other men more readily than they will listen to women, but too few men are ready to speak.

A fifth important strategy is to *ensure the equality project has a class dimension*, which in many organizations has been lacking in the past. It should be acknowledged from the outset that this is not positive action for the few aspiring and educated women whom managements perceive as a potential asset to themselves. The 'unskilled', part-time and temporary women workers who usually exist in large numbers at the base of the organization must be seen as within the scope of the project from the start. This means working with the trade union or unions – both insisting to management that the trade union should participate in the process, and to union officers that they should seek involvement.

Sixth, *the transformative aims for the equality project should be conscious*, and actively discussed among activists, if not always with management in the early days. The aim should always extend the meaning of equality. It should be a question not only of 'women into power' but of 'what kind of power?'; not only 'women up the ladder' but 'how might women want to restructure this ladder?' Some women (like some men) will always remain at the bottom. How could their worth and voice be amplified?

The two final points require more elaboration. The first of these is the need for *a strategic approach to the role of equality officer or women's officer*. Equality officers are often isolated. If they are lifted into the organization from outside they come as strangers, lack friendship and support, and are subject to widespread suspicion. If they are appointed from within they are often uneasily aware of having chosen a job, or been chosen for it, that is like no other in the organization, that some will suspect of being a non-job, with no guidelines for doing it. If they do it well they may become alienated from some former colleagues and jeopardise their careers. The equality officer is little different from any other token woman manager in one respect. The common pattern is for competent women, and particularly black women, to be lifted into an exposed position, to be deprived of support, become demoralised and leave. Some feel they have been set up to fail. Generating a women's movement around the equality officer is necessary, if only for her own survival and that of the equality process.

Equality officers are in many ways comparable to the local authority community workers whose numbers increased so greatly in the 1970s. As they were, equality officers are a relatively new kind of employee, inserted to be an interface between a particular constituency of interests and the management system. Where the community worker continually had to juggle her loyalties to the community in which she was situated and the authority that employed her, so the equality officer has to tread the thin line between being a resource for women and being a manager answerable to more senior managers. Both community workers and equality officers are subject to stresses that can threaten personal survival. If they do the job to the benefit of their constituency they incur the wrath of their employers. If they satisfy their managers they will certainly be blamed for treachery by those they hoped to assist. Both jobs attract progressive people and both jobs destroy them.

It is interesting, however, that for all its similarity to community work, equality work is not so far generating a comparable political theory and practice. By the late seventies community work and community action had an extensive literature discussing tactics, legitimacy, loyalties. Equality work is still comparatively untheorised. There is no training comparable to the community worker's training in group work and advocacy. Each woman starts anew to learn for herself. There is no escaping the fact that, as with community work, sustained equality work does depend on identifying who one's constituency is, which side one is ultimately on, and being ready to lose or resign the job if the contradictions become too great. Equality work is unlikely, if done well, to lead to a further career in the organization. Unless, that is, the equality process is succeeding and the organization is changing fast. There are increasing numbers of equality officers today, in the different countries of Europe, in all the regions and cities of Britain, and in various types of organization. They face similar problems and could provide each other with counselling and a supportive environment, a feminist reality to oppose to organizational reality. Contradicting male power is hazardous work and should not be undertaken without a safety net.

Finally, the eighth point, a feminist strategy for transformational change in organizations, women are widely acknowledging, needs to *address the question of forming alliances between the disadvan-*

taged groups that are the subjects of equality policies. This merits a longer discussion.

Alliances for change

Identity politics only takes us so far, and if we are not careful it diverts us into the trap of mutual recriminations over our positioning in a hierarchy of oppressions. There is, besides, always the knotty problem of who feels able to share in what identity, and when.

In the heady days of new-wave feminism the women who awoke to a new sense of women's oppression and the possibilities of women's liberation believed that 'sisterhood' was indivisible. The trouble was that most of the women active in that movement were white, middle-class, educated and living mainly in Western Europe and North America. The movement was racist – because it was blind to ethnic difference and racism. It was naive – because it thought it could speak for all women about an oppression all women could be assumed to experience in a similar way.

Black women later told white feminists: listen to what we have to say. They pointed out that white women had shared with white men the benefits of colonialism and slave society. When white women spoke of the oppressiveness of confinement to the home and a preoccupation with housewifery and feminine trivia, black women – labouring as hard as any man from dawn to dusk – could not recognize themselves in this discourse (Carby 1982). They showed how white feminists' critique of the family ignored the fact that harassment and racist attacks from white women and men made the family for some black women a place of refuge and solidarity (Bhavnani and Coulson 1986). White women's campaigns against male violence seemed to black women to ignore the violence visited on black men by the white police. 'What's the point of talking about male violence if you haven't dealt with state violence?' (Organization of Women of Asian and African Descent, cited in Bryan *et al.* 1985:174). Between black and ethnic minority women, too, differences surfaced. Moslem women, Hindu women, women of Caribbean origin, wrote and spoke about specific oppressions, unique ways in which a woman's life could be structured by interlocking hierarchies of class, sex and race (Wilson 1978, Anthias 1983, Bryan *et al.* 1985).

Comparable divisions appeared between heterosexual and lesbian women. Too often women's discussions of sexuality assumed that all women were involved with men, that heterosexuality *was* sexuality. Lesbians felt as invisible to some feminists as to the straight world (Lesbian History Group 1987). But some black women complained that lesbians' appeal to the idea of lesbian sisterhood was ill-founded. 'The notion of lesbian nation or lesbian tribalism is a white woman's dream . . . an effective lesbian politics will have to be based on diversity and multiplicity' (Bonnie Zimmerman in Ramazanoglu 1989:163). Somewhat later, as we have seen, women with disabilities began to speak out from within both the women's movement and the movement of disabled people, complaining of their invisibility (Morris 1989, Lonsdale 1990). Why were women's meetings, like those of the male world, so often organized without wheelchair access, without interpreters for the deaf?

Briefly, then, by the mid-eighties a coach and horses could have been driven through the holes worn in the cherished web of sisterhood. In local councils, where equality activity was in full swing, race units, women's units, lesbian and gay groups and disablement officers were coming into existence. The tensions, as we have seen, were painful. The advocates for one oppressed group would claim for it a greater legitimacy than its rivals. Each unit blamed the other (often with justification) for ignoring the problems arising from any form of oppression other than the one to which it was established to respond. Women's units were blamed for making too few appointments of black women, of spending too much of their grant aid on white women's groups. Race units were condemned for being as masculine and as masculist as any white patriarchal outfit. Those responsible for promoting the interests of the disabled complained of being the poor cousin of the equalities. Lesbians often split from gay men because the latter could prove as oppressive as straight men. On some issues, such as paedophilia, women's and minority men's interests seemed bitterly opposed. Some lesbians felt councillors, including feminist councillors, had allowed the government's attack on homosexuals through the Local Government Act 1988 to be an excuse for withdrawing support.

These dissensions were often fomented, to their own advantage, by the white men in power.

To raise the question of feminist alliances, then, let alone progressive alliances for transformative change involving supportive men, is to tread on broken glass among which lie many hurt feelings. Yet if a movement in organizations is to progress at all, some attempt has to be made to learn from past errors and form workable and enduring links between groups of women who may see their interests very differently.

If we are to move beyond identity politics and a hierarchy of oppressions we need first to know how to celebrate each others' differences. The most detrimental pressure that women, black and white, black and other ethnic minority men, lesbians and gays and disabled people suffer in organizations is the pressure to 'pass' as something they are not. Women are expected to mimic men as they climb the hierarchy. Domesticity, reproduction, our bodily reality we have to keep tactfully at home. We have to hide the plastic shopping bags in the cloakroom, avoid phone calls to the children's school, eschew colourful clothes, never mention PMT or menstruation.

We have seen how lesbians and gay men are acceptable only if they never speak of their difference, respect the embarrassment of their heterosexual colleagues, listen endlessly to sexual chat that makes them feel like freaks and outsiders with never a word about their own life and loves. A similar pressure to be invisible bears on disabled people. Harlan Hahn writes,

> in the past, many persons, deprived of positive references which would enable them to identify their physical differences as beautiful or as sources of dignity and pride, have attempted to disguise or ignore their disabilities in the hope of gaining greater acceptance by the non-disabled majority. But disabilities do not have the qualities of a chameleon, and 'passing' is a luxury which can be indulged in only at great psychological peril (Hahn 1984:11).

We have seen, finally, how people of ethnic minorities are expected to shed their difference and join what is represented as a singular, identifiable 'British' culture as the price of acceptance in white organizations. The history of colonialism has been one of the annihilation of cultures, as colonised peoples have been educated for assimilation.

A liberatory practice in organizations, then, whether feminist or anti-racist, a practice of gay liberation or the newly-developing liberation movement of people with disabilities, is bound to assert, not hide, physical and cultural difference. This, perhaps more than anything else, contradicts patriarchal power. For as Nancy Hartsock says, 'virility, or the masculine gender carried by power, requires the denial of the body and its importance'. In patriarchy creation is an act of the intellect and the spirit. The flesh is irrelevant (Hartsock 1985:176). We have seen how masculine discourse emanates as if from a disembodied invisible man. That way it can appear to speak with universal authority, for every-*body*. Dorothy Smith has reflected that men, to participate fully in their abstract mode of action and ruling, are liberated (by women's labour) from having to attend to their own physical needs. To begin from the standpoint of women is to begin from a subject who stands, fully embodied, in a material, local world (Smith 1987:83). If all our many standpoints, including those of men, are to have an equal validity we must bring men back to their bodies. In an equal, democratic world, truth can only be a negotiation between clearly 'situated and embodied knowledges' (Haraway 1988).

Once our differences are acknowledged and affirmed we can begin to look for common ground and negotiate our needs. We will be clearer by now, as June Jordan put it, that 'partnership in misery does not necessarily provide for partnership in change: when we get the monsters off our backs all of us may want to run in very different directions . . . . The ultimate connection cannot be the enemy. The ultimate connection must be the need that we find between us. It is not only who you are, in other words but what we can do for each other that will determine the connection.'

To be concrete about this, we might consider as an example the prerequisites for an effective alliance of disabled and non-disabled women. What would be involved? First, as a non-disabled woman I would have to recognize my own prejudice and misperception of people with disabilities. (In writing this book I have encountered mine again and again. Indeed it is others, people with disabilities, who have pushed and pulled at my understanding until this material is halfway acceptable. Even now, in spite of this help, disabled women will find flaws in it.) Recognizing our own prejudice and relearning our relationship to people with disabilities means a lot of delving in our own half-hidden feelings. It seems that disablement in others restimulates the feelings of helplessness and pain we experienced as children. To become politically effective on the issue of disability we may need to deal creatively with those past emotions and face up to our present fears about our bodies, accident, illness and death. This is not to say, of course, that non-disabled people are the only ones who need to work on their prejudices. As women have internalized misogyny, so disabled people have internalized disrespect for impairment. And disabled women are no less inclined to be racist and homophobic than non-disabled women.

Secondly, non-disabled women need to listen to what disabled women tell us are their priorities and rethink our own liberation agenda to include them. Some of our needs will be found to coincide. If the interests of women pushing pushchairs are met, so may be those of people in wheelchairs. If places are made safer for women they will be safer for disabled people.

Third, non-disabled women have to listen to disability groups and lend support to their activities. We should be as expert in the practice of improving organizations to serve people with disabilities as we are in the practice of improving them for women as women. There is a problem here, of course. Many groups of women share an oppression with men and wish to work politically with 'their' men. This can be difficult for some other feminists who prefer autonomy. What is the alternative? If disabled women say they share interests with disabled men, non-disabled women must be prepared to work with such men – while negotiating reciprocal respect for women and women's interests. It may not be easy.

A final prerequisite of strategic alliance, however, is the development of political theories that can explain all our oppressions and prefigure liberation. We need a theory of power. Feminism has produced two useful insights into power. The first is that most of us are implicated in it. We may think at times we can identify a common 'enemy', but we really know that power does not begin and end with the white male monoculture of the very powerful. We can feel self-righteous about being powerless only if we think in one dimension. 'I am working-class', 'I am a woman'. When we recognize power as multidimensional we see that it is spread around and that almost all of us share in it a little, say on account of being heterosexual (in relation to gays), or physically and mentally fit (relative to someone who is disabled).

Secondly, however, we have learned that not all power is negative. Nancy Hartsock has said that theories of power speak for and about the interests of those who generate them. The conventional view of power in capitalist-patriarchal societies is that power means, and is bound to mean, domination. A ruling group is unlikely to visualize power in any other way. Yet, as Hartsock says, 'theories of power are implicitly theories of community' (Hartsock 1985:3). The way we understand power is the way we understand society, and to use power differently is to create a different world. Women and other subordinated groups are potentially able to recognize and use power not as domination but as *capacity*.

Our theories can be hegemonic, insofar as they have resonance with many different groups. But they can never be totalizing – never authoritative. We have exposed the white man's falsely universalizing viewpoint; we can scarcely want to replace it with another. As Donna Haraway puts it, there are 'only highly specific visual possibilities, each with a wonderfully detailed, active, partial way of organizing worlds'. She invites us to explore alliance from the basis of 'an elaborate specificity and difference and the loving care people might take to learn how to see faithfully from one another's point of view' (Haraway 1988:587).

Where the liberation movements lead us, even in their weak guise as equality projects, is towards a bigger conception of socialism and democracy. Socialism will be not a falsely unifying and enforced collectivism but an enabling of individual and group identity. Democracy will be not 'one man one vote' but '*démocratie paritaire*'; not the will of the majority but the enabling of many voices in negotiation.

References

Abberley, Paul (1989) *Handicapped by Numbers: a critique of the OPCS Disability Surveys*, Occasional Papers in Sociology, No. 9, Bristol Polytechnic.

Abberley, Paul (1985) 'Policing cripples: social theory and physical handicap', unpublished paper.

Abberley, Paul (1987) 'The concept of oppression and the development of a social theory of disability', *Disability, Handicap and Society*, Vol. 2, No. 1.

Abbott, Franklin (ed.) (1987) *New Men, New Minds: Breaking Male Tradition*, The Crossing Press (Freedom, CA).

Acker, Joan (1987) *Hierarchies, Jobs and Bodies: an outline for a theory of gendered organizations*, paper to the American Sociological Association Annual General Meeting, Chicago, August.

Acker, Joan (1989) 'The problem with patriarchy', *Sociology*, Vol. 23, No. 2, pp. 235–240.

Acker, Joan (1989) *Doing Comparable Worth: Gender, Class and Pay Equity*, Temple University Press (Philadelphia).

Adams, Carolyn Teich and Winston, Kathryn Teich (1980) *Mothers at Work: Public Policies in the United States, Sweden and China*, Longman (New York).

Allen, S., Purcell, K., Watton, A. and Wood, S. (eds) (1986) *The Experience of Unemployment*, Macmillan (London).

Allen, Sheila (1982) 'Gender, race and class in the 1980s' in Husband, Charles (ed.).

Allen, Sheila and Wolkowitz, Carol (1987) *Homeworking: Myths and Realities*, Macmillan (London).

Anderson, Gregory (ed.) (1988) *The White Blouse Revolution: Female Office Workers Since 1870*, Manchester University Press (Manchester).

Anthias, Floya (1983) 'Sexual divisions and ethnic adaptation: the case of Greek Cypriot women' in Phizacklea, Annie (ed.).

Anthias, Floya and Yuval-Davis, Nira (1983) 'Contextualising feminism: gender, ethnic and class divisions', *Feminist Review*, No. 15, Winter.

Apprill, Claudette (1990) *Aperçu du Conseil de l'Europe en faveur de l'égalité de la femme et de l'homme,* paper to the International Congress on Positive Action for Women, Vitoria-Gasteiz, Basque Country, Spain, June 27–29.

Bacchi, Carol (1990) *Same Difference: Feminism and Sexual Difference,* Allen and Unwin (Sydney).

Bain, G.S. (ed.) (1983) *Industrial Relations in Britain,* Basil Blackwell (Oxford).

Bain, G.S. and Price, R. (1983) 'Union growth: dimensions, determinants and destiny', in Bain, G.S. (ed.).

Bakker, Isabella (1988) 'Women's employment in comparative perspective' in Jenson, J. *et al.*

Barrett, Michele (1980) *Women's Oppression Today,* Verso (London).

Baude, Annike (1990) 'A dialogue that might yet take place' in Czarniawska, Barbara (ed.).

Beale, J. (1982) *Getting It Together: Women as Trade Unionists,* Pluto Press (London).

Beechey, Veronica (1987) *Unequal Work,* Verso (London).

Beechey, Veronica and Perkins, Tessa (1987) *A Matter of Hours: Women, Part-time Work and the Labour Market,* Polity Press (Oxford).

Bhavnani, Kum-Kum, and Coulson, Margaret (1986) 'Transforming socialist feminism: the challenge of racism', *Feminist Review,* No. 23, Summer.

Bindman, Geoffrey (1981) 'Positive Action' in Braham, Peter *et al.* (eds).

Birkett, Ken and Worman, Dianah (1988) *Getting on with Disabilities: an Employer's Guide,* Institute of Personnel Management (London).

Bisset, Liz and Huws, Ursula (1989) *Sweated Labour: Homeworking in Britain Today,* Pamphlet No. 33, Low Pay Unit (London).

Black, Clementina (1983) *Married Women's Work,* Virago Press (London), originally published 1915.

Blauner, Robert (1964) *Alienation and Freedom: The Factory Worker and His Industry,* University of Chicago Press (Chicago).

Bocock, Robert (1986) *Hegemony,* Ellis Horwood (Chichester) and Tavistock Publications (London).

Boston, S. (1987) *Women Workers and the Trade Unions,* Lawrence and Wishart (London).

Boyden, Tina and Paddison, Lorraine (1986) 'Banking on equal opportunities', *Personnel Management,* September.

Braham, Peter, Rhodes, Ed and Pearn, Michael (eds) (1981) *Discrimination and Disadvantage in Employment: The Experience of Black Workers,* Harper and Row (London).

Brechin, Ann, Liddiard, Penny and Swain, John (eds) (1981) *Handicap in a Social World,* Hodder and Stoughton and the Open University Press (Milton Keynes).

Brittan, Arthur (1989) *Masculinity and Power,* Basil Blackwell (Oxford).

Brod, Harry (ed.) (1987) *The Making of Masculinities: The New Men's Studies,* Allen and Unwin (Boston).

Bryan, Beverley, Dadzie, Stella and Scafe, Suzanne (1985) *The Heart of the Race: Black Women's Lives in Britain,* Virago (London).

Burrell, Gibson (1984) 'Sex and organizational analysis', *Organization Studies*, No. 5.

Burrell, Gibson and Hearn, Jeff (1989) 'The sexuality of organization' in Hearn, J. *et al.* (eds).

Cabinet Office (1987) *Working Patterns: A Study Document* (The Mueller Report), Management and Personnel Office (London).

Campbell, Beatrix (1989) 'Bargain women', *New Statesman*, 1 December.

Campbell, Beatrix (1990) 'Bottom of the heap', *New Statesman*, 5 January.

Carby, Hazel (1982) 'White Women Listen! Black feminism and the boundaries of sisterhood', in Centre for Contemporary Cultural Studies (ed.).

Carrigan, Tim, Connell, Bob and Lee, John (1987) 'Hard and heavy: toward a new sociology of masculinity', in Kaufman, Michael (ed.).

Carter, April (1988) *The Politics of Women's Rights*, Longman (London).

Castles, Stephen and Kosack, Godula (1973) *Immigrant Workers and Class Structure in Western Europe*, Oxford University Press (Oxford).

Cavendish, Ruth (1982) *Women on the Line*, Routledge and Kegan Paul (London).

Central London Community Law Centre (1987) *Organizing as Women Trade Unionists* (London).

Central Statistical Office (1990) *Social Trends*, No. 20, Government Statistical Service, HMSO (London).

Centre for Contemporary Cultural Studies (1982) *The Empire Strikes Back: Race and Racism in 70s Britain*, Hutchinson (London).

Chapman, Rowena (1988) 'The Great Pretender: variations on the New Man theme', in Chapman, Rowena and Rutherford, Jonathan (eds).

Chapman, Rowena and Rutherford, Jonathan (eds) (1988) *Male Order: Unwrapping Masculinity*, Lawrence and Wishart (London).

Clegg, Stewart and David Dunkerley (1980) *Organization, Class and Control, Routledge and Kegan Paul (London)*.

Cockburn, Cynthia (1983) *Brothers: Male Dominance and Technological Change*, Pluto Press (London).

Cockburn, Cynthia (1985) *Machinery of Dominance: Women, Men and Technical Knowhow*, Pluto Press (London).

Cockburn, Cynthia (1987a) *Two-track Training: Sex Inequalities and the Youth Training Scheme*, Macmillan (London).

Cockburn, Cynthia (1987b), *Women, Trade Unions and Political Parties*, Fabian Society Research Series No. 349 (London).

Cockburn, Cynthia (1988a) 'Masculinity, the Left and feminism' in Chapman, R. and Rutherford, J. (eds).

Cockburn, Cynthia (1988b) *Women's Progress: A Research Report*, Lancashire Polytechnic, Preston.

Cohen, Philip (1988) 'The perversions of inheritance: studies in the making of multi-racist Britain' in Cohen, Philip and Bains, Harwant S. (eds).

Cohen, Philip and Bains, Harwant S. (1988) *Multi-Racist Britain*, Macmillan (London).

Colling, Trevor and Dickens, Linda (1989) *Equality Bargaining – Why Not?*, HMSO (London).

Collinson, David L. and Collinson, Margaret (1989) 'Sexuality in the workplace: the domination of men's sexuality' in Hearn, J. *et al.*

Commission for Racial Equality (1983) *Code of Practice for the Elimination of Racial Discrimination and the Promotion of Equality of Opportunity in Employment*, July (London).

Confederation of British Industry (1983) *Employing Disabled People* (London).

Confederation of British Industry (1988) *Workforce 2000: An Agenda for Action* (London).

Confederation of Indian Organizations (1987) *Double Bind: To Be Disabled and Asian* (London).

Connell, R.W. (1983) *Which Way is Up? Essays on Class, Sex and Culture*, George Allen and Unwin (Sydney).

Connell, R.W. (1987) *Gender and Power*, Polity Press (Oxford).

Coontz, Stephanie and Henderson, Peta (eds) (1986) *Women's Work, Men's Property: The Origins of Gender and Class*, Verso (London).

Coote, Anna and Beatrix Campbell (1982) *Sweet Freedom*, Pan Books (London).

Coote, Anna and Hewitt, Patricia (1980) 'The stance of Britain's major parties and interest groups', in Moss, P. and Fonda, N. (eds).

Coote, Anna and Pattullo, Polly (1990) *Power and Prejudice: Women and Politics*, Weidenfeld and Nicolson (London).

Cornes, Paul (1982) *Employment Rehabilitation: The Aims and Achievements of a Service for Disabled People*, HMSO (London).

Corr, H. and Jamieson, L. (eds) (1990) *The Politics of Everyday Life: Continuity and Change in Work, Labour and the Family*, Macmillan (London).

Coulson, Margaret, Branca Magas and Hilary Wainwright (1975) 'The housewife and her labour under capitalism: a critique', *New Left Review*, No. 89, Jan–Feb.

Cowan, Ruth Schwartz (1989) *More Work for Mother*, Free Association Books (London).

Coyle, Angela (1988) 'Introduction: continuity and change: women in paid work', in Coyle, Angela and Skinner, Jane (eds).

Coyle, Angela (1989) 'Women in management: a suitable case for treatment?', *Feminist Review*, No. 31, Spring.

Coyle, Angela and Jane Skinner (eds) (1988) *Women and Work: Positive Action for Change*, Macmillan (London).

Crompton, Rosemary and Gareth Jones (1984) *White Collar Proletariat: Deskilling and Gender in the Clerical Labour Process*, Macmillan (London).

Czarniawska, Barbara (1989/90) (ed.) 'Anthropology of Complex Organizations – 2', *International Studies of Management and Organization*, Vol. 19, No. 4, M.E. Sharpe (Armonk, New York).

Dalla Costa, Mariarosa (1972) *The Power of Women and the Subversion of the Community*, Falling Wall Press (Bristol).

Daly, Mary (1979) *Gyn/Ecology: The Metaethics of Radical Feminism*, The Women's Press (London).

Daniel, W.W. (1980) *Maternity Rights: The Experience of Women*, Policy Studies Institute (London).

Davidoff, Leonore (1990) 'Adam spoke first and named the orders of the world: masculine and feminine domains in history and sociology', in Corr, H. and Jamieson, L. (eds).

Davidson, M.J. and Earnshaw, J. (forthcoming 1990) *Vulnerable Workers*, John Wiley and Sons (Chichester).

Davies, Celia (1988) 'Workplace action programmes for equality for women: an orthodoxy re-examined', paper presented to the conference *Equal Opportunities for Men and Women in Higher Education*, University College, Dublin, September.

De Beauvoir, Simone (1949) *The Second Sex*, Penguin (Harmondsworth).

Department of Economic Development (1989) *Fair Employment (Northern Ireland) Act 1989: Code of Practice*, HMSO (Belfast).

Department of Employment (1987) *New Earnings Survey 1980–87*, Part A, tables 10 and 11, HMSO (London).

Dex, Shirley (1983) 'The second generation: West Indian female school leavers' in Phizacklea, Annie (ed.).

Disabled Peoples' International (1983) *A Voice of Our Own*.

DiTomaso, Nancy (1989) 'Sexuality in the workplace: discrimination and harassment' in Hearn, J. *et al.* (eds).

Doyle, Brian (1987) 'Employing disabled workers: the framework for equal opportunities', *Equal Opportunities Review*, No. 12, March/April.

Eisenstein, Zillah R. (ed.) (1979) *Capitalist Patriarchy and the Case for Socialist Feminism*, Monthly Review Press (New York).

Ellis, Valerie (1981) *The Role of Trade Unions in the Promotion of Equal Opportunities*, Equal Opportunities Commission/Social Science Research Council (Manchester).

Ellis, Valerie (1988) 'Current trade union attempts to remove occupational segregation in the employment of women' in Walby, S.(ed.).

Epstein, Cynthia Fuchs (1988) *Deceptive Distinctions: Sex, Gender and the Social Order*, Yale University Press (New Haven).

Equal Opportunities Commission (1983) *Women and Trade Unions: A Survey* (Manchester).

Equal Opportunities Commission (1985) *Code of Practice for the Elimination of Discrimination on the Grounds of Sex and Marriage and the Promotion of Equal Opportunities in Employment*, March (Manchester).

Equal Opportunities Commission (1988) *Women and Men in Britain: a Statistical Profile*, HMSO (London).

Equal Opportunities Review (1985) No. 2, July–August.

Finkelstein, V. (1980) *Attitudes and Disabled People*, World Rehabilitation Fund, Monograph No. 5.

Finkelstein, Vic (1987) 'Disabled people and our culture development', *Disability Arts In London*, London Disability Arts Forum, 25 April.

Floyd, Michael and North, Klaus (eds) (1984) *Disability and Employment*, Report on an Anglo-German Conference, Anglo-German Foundation for the Study of Industrial Society (London).

Foucault, Michel (1973) *The Birth of the Clinic*, Tavistock Publications (London).

Foucault, Michel (1977) *Discipline and Punish*, Allen Lane (Harmondsworth).

Foucault, Michel (1981) *The History of Sexuality Vol. 1*, Penguin (Harmondsworth).

Friedman, J.B. (1981) *The Monstrous Races in Medieval Art and Thought*, Harvard University Press (Cambridge, MA).

Fryer, Peter (1984) *Staying Power: The History of Black People in Britain*, Pluto Press (London).

Game, Ann and Pringle, Rosemary (1983) *Gender at Work*, George Allen and Unwin (Sydney).

Gearhart, Sally Miller (1985) *The Wanderground*, The Women's Press (London).

Gilligan, Carol (1982) *In a Different Voice: Psychological Theory and Women's Development*, Harvard University Press (Cambridge, Mass).

Goffman, E. (1968) *Stigma: The Management of Spoilt Identity*, Penguin (Harmondsworth).

Gorz, Andre (ed.) (1976) *The Division of Labour*, Harvester Press (Brighton).

Gramsci, Antonio (1971) *Selections from the Prison Notebooks*, Lawrence and Wishart (London).

Greater London Council (1986) *Tackling Heterosexism: A Handbook of Lesbian Rights* (London).

Gregory, Jeanne (1987) *Sex, Race and the Law*, Sage Publications (London).

Griffin, Christine (1985) *Typical Girls? Young Women from School to the Labour Market*, Routledge and Kegan Paul (London).

Griffin, Susan (1984) *The Roaring Inside Her*, The Women's Press (London).

Gutek, Barbara A. (1989) 'Sexuality in the workplace: key issues in social research and organizational practice' in Hearn, J. *et al.* (eds).

Hacker, Sally (1989) *Pleasure, Power and Technology*, Unwin Hyman (Boston).

Hadjifoutiou, Natalie (1983) *Women and Harassment at Work*, Pluto Press (London).

Hagen, Elizabeth and Jenson, Jane (1988) 'Paradox and promise: work and politics in the post-war years' in Jenson, J. *et al.* (eds).

Hahn, Harlan (1984) *The Issue of Equality: European Perceptions of Employment for Disabled People*, World Rehabilitation Fund, Report No. 29.

Hakim, Catherine (1981) 'Job segregation: trends in the 1970s', *Employment Gazette*, December.

Hall, Marny (1989) 'Private experiences in the public domain: lesbians in organizations', in Hearn, J. *et al.* (eds).

Hall, Stuart, *et al.* (1978) *Policing the Crisis: Mugging, the State and Law and Order*, Macmillan (London).

Hammersley, M. (1989) *The Dilemma of Qualitative Method*, Routledge (London).

Hammond, Valerie (1988) *Women in Management*, Ashridge Management College (Kent).

Haraway, Donna (1988) 'Situated knowledges: the science question in feminism and the privilege of partial perspective', *Feminist Studies*, Vol. 14, No. 3, Fall.

Hartmann, Heidi (1979) 'Capitalism, patriarchy and job segregation by sex' in Eisenstein, Zillah (ed.).

Hartmann, P. and Husbands, C. (1974) *Racism and the Mass Media*, Davis-Poynter (London).

Hartsock, Nancy C.M. (1985) *Money, Sex and Power: Toward a Feminist Historical Materialism*, Northeastern University Press (Boston).

Hearn, Jeff (1985) 'Men's sexuality at work' in Metcalf, Andy and Humphries, Martin (eds).

Hearn, Jeff and Parkin, Wendy (1987) *'Sex' at 'Work': The Power and Paradox of Organization Sexuality*, Wheatsheaf Books (Brighton).

Hearn, Jeff *et al.* (1989) *The Sexuality of Organization*, Sage (London).

Heery, Edmund and Kelly, John (1988) *Union Women: A Study of Women Trade Union Officers*, Imperial College of Science and Technology and London School of Economics (London).

Hennig, M. and Jardim, A. (1978) *The Managerial Woman*, Marion Boyars (London).

Hey, Valerie (1986) *Patriarchy and Pub Culture*, Tavistock Publications (London).

Hill, D.J. (1985) 'Employment of the disabled', *Industrial Relations Journal*, Vol. 16, No. 1.

Hochschild, Arlie Russell (1983) *The Managed Heart*, University of California Press (Berkeley CA).

hooks, bell (1989) *Talking Back: Thinking Feminist, Thinking Black*, Sheba Feminist Publications, (London).

Horn, P.D. and Horn, J.C. (1982) *Sex in the Office . . . Power and Passion in the Workplace*, Addison-Wesley (Reading, MA).

Hull, Gloria T., Scott, Patricia Bell, and Smith, Barbara (eds) (1982) *All the Women are White, All the Blacks are Men – But Some of Us are Brave: Black Women's Studies*, The Feminist Press (New York).

Humphries, Jane and Rubery, Jill (1988) 'Recession and exploitation: British women in a changing workplace 1979–1985' in Jenson, J. *et al* (eds).

Hunt, Judith (1982) 'A woman's place is in her union', in West, J. (ed.).

Husband, Charles (ed.) (1982) *'Race' in Britain: Continuity and Change*, Hutchinson (London).

Iles, Paul and Auluck, Randhir (forthcoming 1990) 'The experience of black workers' in Davidson, M.J. and Earnshaw, J. (eds).

Ingham, Mary (1985) *Men*, Century Publishing (London).

Jenkins, Kate, Caines, Karen and Jackson, Andrews (1988) *Improving Management in Government: The Next Steps* (The Ibbs Report), HMSO (London).

Jenkins, Richard (1986) *Racism and Recruitment*, Cambridge University Press (Cambridge).

Jenkins, Richard and Solomos, John (eds) (1987) *Racism and Equal Opportunity Policies in the Eighties*, Cambridge University Press (Cambridge).

Jenson, Jane, Hagen, Elizabeth and Reddy, Ceallaigh (eds) (1988) *Feminization of the Labour Force: Paradoxes and Promises*, Polity Press (Oxford).

Jewson, Nick and David Mason (1986) 'The theory and practice of equal opportunities policies: liberal and radical approaches', *Sociological Review*, Vol. 34, No. 2, March.

John, Angela (1986) 'Introduction' in John, A.(ed.).

John, Angela (ed.) (1986) *Unequal Opportunities: Women's Employment in England 1800–1918*, Basil Blackwell (Oxford).

John, Mary Croxen (1988) *The Vocational Rehabilitation of Disabled Women in the European Community*, EEC Programme of Research and Actions for the Social Integration of Disabled People.

Jordan, June (1981) *Moving Towards Home: Political Essays*, Virago (London).

Kanter, Rosabeth Moss (1977) *Men and Women of the Corporation*, Basic Books (New York).

Kaufman, Michael (ed.) (1987) *Beyond Patriarchy: Essays by Men on Pleasure, Power and Change*, Oxford University Press (Oxford).

Kettle, Melvyn and Massie, Bert (1982) *Employers' Guide to Disabilities*, published in association with RADAR, Woodhead-Faulkner (Cambridge).

Kimmel, Michael S. (ed.) (1987a) *Changing Men*, Sage (Newbury Park).

Kimmel, Michael S. (1987b) 'The contemporary "crisis" of masculinity in historical perspective', in Brod, H. (ed.).

Klein, Viola (1965) *Britain's Married Women Workers*, Routledge and Kegan Paul (London).

Klug, Francesca (1989) '"Oh to be in England": the British case study' in Yuval-Davis, Nira and Anthias, Floya (eds).

Laclau, Ernesto and Mouffe, Chantal (1985) *Hegemony and Socialist Strategy*, Verso (London).

Lash, Scott and Urry, John (1987) *The End of Organized Capitalism*, Polity Press (Oxford).

Lees, Sue (1986) *Losing Out: Sexuality and Adolescent Girls*, Hutchinson (London).

Lees, Sue and Scott, Maria (1990 forthcoming) 'Equal opportunities: rhetoric or action?', *Gender and Education*, Vol. 2, No. 3, Autumn.

Legge, Karen (1987) 'Women in personnel management: uphill climb or downhill slide?', in Spencer, Anne and Podmore, David (eds).

Leonard, Alice (1987) *Judging Inequality: The Effectiveness of the Industrial Tribunal System in Sex Discrimination and Equal Pay Cases*, National Council for Civil Liberties (London).

Lerner, Gerda (1986) *The Creation of Patriarchy*, Oxford University Press (Oxford).

Lesbian History Group (1987) *Not a Passing Phase: Reclaiming Lesbians in History 1840–1985*, The Women's Press (London).

Lingsom, S. and Ellingsaeter, A.L. (1983) *Arbeid, Fritid og Samvaer*, Central Bureau of Statistics, SA 49 (Oslo).

Lloyd, Genevieve (1984) *Man of Reason: 'Male' and 'Female' in Western Philosophy*, Methuen (London).

Local Government Operational Research Unit (1982), *Women in Local Government: The Neglected Resource*, (London).

London Boroughs Disability Resource Team (1988) *Positive Action Towards Employing More People with Disabilities: Lambeth Council's Experience 1986–88* (London).

London Bridge (1987) *Equal Opportunities for Local Authority Workers: The Trade Union Experience in Seven London Labour Boroughs*, Empirica (London).

Lonsdale, Susan (1990) *Women and Disability* Macmillan (London).

Management and Personnel Office (1982) *Equal Opportunities for Women in the Civil Service*, HMSO (London).

Management and Personnel Office (1984) *Equal Opportunities for Women in the Civil Service: Programme of Action*, HMSO (London).

Marcuse, Herbert (1955) *Eros and Civilization*, Vintage Books (New York).

Marglin, Stephen A. (1976) 'What do bosses do?' in Gorz, A. (ed.).

Marshall, Catherine and Rossman, Gretchen B. (1989) *Designing Qualitative Research*, Sage Publications (Newbury Park).

Marshall, Judy (1984) *Women Managers: Travellers in a Male World*, Wiley (Chichester).

Martin, Jean and Roberts, Ceridwen (1984) *Women and Employment: a Lifetime Perspective*, Department of Employment and Office of Population Censuses and Surveys (London).

Martin, Jean, Meltzer, Howard and Elliot, David (eds) (1988) *The Prevalence of Disability Among Adults*, Office of Population Censuses and Surveys, HMSO (London).

Mayo, Elton (1933) *The Human Problems of an Industrial Civilization*, Macmillan (New York).

McClelland, Keith (1989) 'Some thoughts on masculinity and the "representative artisan" in Britain 1850–1880', *Gender and History*, Vol. 1, No. 2, Summer.

McKee, Lorna and Bell, Colin (1985) 'His unemployment, her problem: the domestic and marital consequences of male unemployment' in Allen, S. *et al* (eds).

Meehan, Elizabeth M. (1985) *Women's Rights at Work: Campaigns and Policy in Britain and the United States*, Macmillan (London).

Mercer, Kobena and Julien, Isaac (1988) 'Race, Sexual Politics and Black Masculinity: A Dossier' in Chapman R. and Rutherford J. (eds).

Merchant, Carolyn (1982) *The Death of Nature: Women, Ecology and the Scientific Revolution*, Wildwood House (London).

Metcalf, Andy and Humphries, Martin (eds) (1985) *The Sexuality of Men*, Pluto Press (London).

Michel, Andrée (1990) *Aspects juridiques des actions positives pour les femmes,* paper to the International Congress on Positive Action for Women, Vitoria-Gasteiz, Basque Country, Spain, 27–29 June.

Mies, Maria (1986) *Patriarchy and Accumulation on a World Scale,* Zed Books (London).

Miles, Robert (1989) *Racism,* Routledge (London).

Miles, Robert and Phizacklea, Annie (1981) 'The TUC and Black Workers: 1974–76' in Braham, Peter *et al.* (eds).

Miles, Robert and Phizacklea, Annie (1984) *White Man's Country: Racism in British Politics,* Pluto Press (London).

Miles, Robert and Phizacklea, Annie (eds) (1979) *Racism and Political Action in Britain,* Routledge and Kegan Paul (London).

Milkman, Ruth (1987) *Gender at Work,* University of Illinois Press (Urbana).

Mitter, Swasti (1986) *Common Fate, Common Bond: Women in the Global Economy,* Pluto Press (London).

Montague, A. (1974) *Man's Most Dangerous Myth: The Fallacy of Race,* Oxford University Press (Oxford).

Moore, Suzanne (1988) 'Getting a bit of the other: the pimps of post-modernism', in Chapman, R. and Rutherford, J. (eds).

Morris, Jenny (ed.) (1989) *Able Lives: Women's Experience of Paralysis,* The Women's Press (London).

Moss, Peter (1980) 'Parents at work' in Moss, P. and Fonda, N. (eds).

Moss, Peter and Fonda, Nickie (1980a) 'Introduction' in Moss, P. and Fonda, N. (eds).

Moss, Peter and Fonda, Nickie (eds) (1980b) *Work and the Family,* Temple Smith (London).

National Audit Office (1987) *Employment Assistance to Disabled Adults,* HMSO (London).

O'Brien, Mary (1981) *Politics of Reproduction,* Routledge and Kegan Paul (Boston).

Office of Population Censuses and Surveys (1987a) *General Household Survey,* HMSO (London).

Office of Population Censuses and Surveys (1987b) *Labour Force Survey,* HMSO (London).

Oliver, Michael (1990) *The Politics of Disablement,* Macmillan (London).

Pateman, Carole (1988) *The Sexual Contract,* Polity Press (Oxford).

Personnel Management (1987) 'Realising the dividends from positive action', October, pp. 62–67.

Peters, Thomas J. and Robert H. Waterman Jr (1982) *In Search of Excellence,* Harper and Row (New York).

Phillips, Anne (ed.) (1987) *Feminism and Equality,* Basil Blackwell (Oxford).

Phizacklea, Annie (1983) 'In the front line' in Phizacklea, Annie (ed.).

Phizacklea, Annie (1988) 'Entrepreneurship, ethnicity and gender' in Westwood, Sallie and Bhachu, Parminder (eds).

Phizacklea, Annie (ed.) (1983) *One-Way Ticket: Migration and Female Labour,* Routledge and Kegan Paul (London).

Piercy, Marge (1979) *Woman on the Edge of Time*, The Women's Press (London).

Policy Studies Institute (1984) *Black and White in Britain* (London).

Political Economy of Women Group (1976) *On the Political Economy of Women*, Conference of Socialist Economists, Pamphlet No. 2 (London).

Pollert, Anna (1981) *Girls, Wives, Factory Lives*, Macmillan (London).

Pringle, Rosemary (1988) *Secretaries Talk: Sexuality, Power and Work*, Verso (London).

Pringle, Rosemary (1989) 'Bureaucracy, rationality and sexuality: the case of secretaries' in Hearn, J. *et al.* (eds).

Ramazanoglu, Caroline (1989) *Feminism and the Contradictions of Oppression*, Routledge (London).

Reiter, Rayna (ed.) (1975) *Towards an Anthropology of Women*, Monthly Review Press (New York).

Robarts, Sadie (1981) *Positive Action for Women: The Next Step in Education, Training and Employment*, National Council for Civil Liberties (London).

Roberts, Yvonne (1984) *Man Enough: Men of 35 Speak Out*, Chatto and Windus, The Hogarth Press (London).

Robinson, Olive (1988) 'The changing labour market: growth of part-time employment and labour market segmentation in Britain' in Walby, S. (ed.).

Roper, Michael (1988) 'Fathers and lovers: images of the 'older man' in British managers' career narratives', *Life Stories/Récits de Vie*, No. 4, International Sociological Association.

Rosaldo, Michelle Zimbalist (1974) 'Woman, culture and society: a theoretical overview' in Rosaldo, Michelle Zimbalist and Lamphere, Louise (eds).

Rosaldo, Michelle Zimbalist and Lamphere, Louise (eds) (1974) *Woman, Culture and Society*, Stanford University (Stanford).

Rowbotham, Sheila (1973) *Hidden from History*, Pluto Press (London).

Rowbotham, Sheila (1980) 'The trouble with patriarchy', *New Statesman*, February 1.

Rowthorne, Bob (1976) 'Late capitalism', *New Left Review*, 98, pp. 59–83.

Rubin, Gayle (1975) 'The traffic in women' in Rayna Reiter (ed.).

Rutherford, Jonathan (1988) 'Who's that man?' in Chapman, R. and Rutherford, J. (eds).

Sanderson, Kay (1989) 'Women's lives: social class and the oral historians', *Life Stories/Récits de Vie*, No. 5.

Sargent, Alice (1983) *The Androgynous Manager*, AMACOM (New York).

Saxton, Marsha and Howe, Florence (1987) *With Wings: An Anthology of Literature by and about Women with Disabilities*, The Feminist Press (New York).

Scarman, Lord (1982) *The Scarman Report: The Brixton Disorders 10–12 April 1981*, Penguin Books (Harmondsworth).

Segal, Lynne (1990) *Slow Motion: Changing Masculinities, Changing Men*, Virago (London).

Seidler, Victor J. (1989) *Rediscovering Masculinity*, Routledge (London).

SERTUC (1989) *Still Moving Towards Equality: A Survey of Progress Towards Equality in Trade Unions*, Women's Committee (London).

Sharpe, Sue (1984) *Double Identity: The Lives of Working Mothers*, Penguin (Harmondsworth).

Shearer, Ann (1981) *Disability: Whose Handicap?*, Basil Blackwell (Oxford).

Sheppard, Deborah L. (1989) 'Organizations, power and sexuality: the image and self-image of woman managers', in Hearn, J. *et al.* (eds).

Silverman, D. (1985) *Qualitative Method and Sociology*, Gower (Aldershot).

Sivanandan, A. (1985) 'Race Awareness Training and the degradation of black struggle', *Race and Class*, Vol. xxvi, No. 4, Spring.

Smith, Brenda, Povall, Margery, and Floyd, Michael (1989) *Managing Disability at Work: Improving Practice in Organisations*, Rehabilitation Resource Centre, The City University (London).

Smith, D.J. (1977) *Racial Disadvantage in Britain*, Penguin (Harmondsworth).

Smith, David J. (1981) *Unemployment and Racial Minorities*, Report No. 594, Policy Studies Institute (London).

Smith, Dorothy E. (1987) *The Everyday World as Problematic*, Open University Press (Milton Keynes).

Snell, Mandy, P.Glucklich and M.Povall (1981), *Equal Pay and Opportunities: A Study of the Implications and Effects of the Equal Pay and Sex Discrimination Acts in 26 Organizations*, Research Paper No. 20, Department of Employment (London).

Solomos, John (1987) 'The politics of anti-discrimination legislation: planned social reform or symbolic politics?', in Jenkins, Richard and Solomos, John (eds).

Spencer, Anne and Podmore, David (eds) (1987) *In a Man's World: Essays on Women in Male-Dominated Professions*, Tavistock Publications (London).

Spender, Dale (1982) *Women of Ideas (and What Men Have Done to Them)* Routledge and Kegan Paul (London).

Stamp, Paddy and Sadie Robarts (1986) *Positive Action for Women: Changing the Workplace*, National Council for Civil Liberties (London).

Stone, Isabella (1988) *Equal Opportunities in Local Authorities*, Equal Opportunities Commission, HMSO (London).

Stone, Karen (1983) 'Motherhood and waged work: West Indian, Asian and white mothers compared' in Phizacklea, Annie (ed.).

Svenska Institutet (1987) *Fact Sheet on Sweden* (Stockholm).

Sydie, R.A. (1987) *Natural Women, Cultured Men*, Open University Press (Milton Keynes).

Taylor, Frederick W. (1947) *Scientific Management*, Harper and Row (New York).

Taylor, Steven J. and Bogdan, Robert (1984) *Introduction to Qualitative Research Methods: The Search for Meanings*, John Wiley and Sons (Chichester).

Thompson, Keith (1987) 'What men really want: an interview with Robert Bly', in Abbott, Franklin (ed.).

Tobin, Ann (1990) 'Lesbianism and the Labour Party: The GLC Experience', *Feminist Review*, No. 34, Spring.

Tolson, Andrew (1977) *The Limits of Masculinity*, Tavistock Publications (London).

Townsend, Peter (1979) *Poverty in the United Kingdom*, Penguin (Harmondsworth).

Trade Union Research Unit, (1986) *Women and Trade Unions: Trade Unions and Women*, Technical Note No. 100, Ruskin College (Oxford).

Trades Union Congress (1979) *Equality for Women in Trade Unions* (London).

Trades Union Congress (1985) *TUC Guide on the Employment of Disabled People* (London).

Vogel-Polsky, Eliane (1989), *Les actions positives et les contraintes constitutionnelles et législatives qui pèsent sur leur mise-en-oeuvre dans les états membres du Conseil de l'Europe*, Conseil de l'Europe (Strasbourg).

Wajcman, Judy (1983) *Women in Control: Dilemmas of a Workers Cooperative*, Open University Press (Milton Keynes).

Walby, Sylvia (1986) *Patriarchy at Work*, Polity Press (Oxford).

Walby, Sylvia (1989) 'Flexibility and the changing sexual division of labour', in Wood, Stephen (ed.).

Walby, Sylvia (1990) *Theorizing Patriarchy*, Basil Blackwell (Oxford).

Walby, Sylvia (ed.) (1988) *Gender Segregation at Work*, Open University Press (Milton Keynes).

Walker, Alan (1984) 'New policy directions', in Floyd, Michael and North, Klaus (eds).

Walker, Alan and Townsend, Peter (1981) *Disability in Britain*, Martin Robertson.

Wallace, Claire (1987) *For Richer For Poorer: Growing up In and Out of Work*, Tavistock Publications (London).

Walters, Patricia (1987) 'Servants of the Crown', in Spencer, Anne and Podmore, David (eds).

Webb, Janette and Sonia Liff (1988) 'Play the white man: the social construction of fairness and competition in equal opportunities policies', *Sociological Review*, Vol. 36, No. 3.

Weber, Max (1947) *The Theory of Social and Economic Organization*, Routledge and Kegan Paul (London).

Weedon, Chris (1987) *Feminist Practice and Poststructuralist Theory*, Basil Blackwell (Oxford).

West, Jackie (ed.) (1982) *Work, Women and the Labour Market*, Routledge and Kegan Paul (London).

Westwood, Sallie and Bhachu, Parminder (eds) (1988) *Enterprising Women: Ethnicity, Economy and Gender Relations*, Routledge (London).

Wilson, Amrit (1978) *Finding a Voice: Asian Women in Britain*, Virago (London).

Wood, Stephen (ed.) (1989) *The Transformation of Work?*, Unwin Hyman (London).

Wrench, John (1987) 'Unequal comrades: trade unions, equal opportunity and racism' in Jenkins, Richard and Solomos, John (eds).

Yuval-Davis, Nira and Anthias, Floya (eds) (1989) *Woman-Nation-State*, Macmillan (London).

Zaharova, N., Posadskaja, A. and Rimasevskaja, N. (1990) 'Comment nous résolvons la quéstion des femmes', *Sociétés Contemporaines*, No. 2, (Paris).

Zimmeck, Meta (1986) 'Jobs for the girls: the expansion of clerical work for women, 1850–1914' in John, A. (ed.).

Zimmeck, Meta (1988) 'Get out and get under: the impact of demobilization on the Civil Service, 1919–32', in Anderson, G. (ed.).

Index